Lovestrong

Lovestrong

A Woman Doctor's True Story of Marriage and Medicine

by
Dorothy Greenbaum, M.D.
and
Deidre S. Laiken

NYT
Times
BOOKS

Names of places and people as well as case histories of patients have been changed, where appropriate, to avoid identification and to protect privacy.

Published by TIMES BOOKS,
The New York Times Book Co., Inc.
130 Fifth Avenue, New York, N.Y. 10011

Published simultaneously in Canada by
Fitzhenry & Whiteside, Ltd., Toronto

Library of Congress Cataloging in Publication Data

Greenbaum, Dorothy.
  Lovestrong.

  1. Greenbaum, Dorothy.   2. Medical students—United
States—Biography.   3. Medical students—United States—
Family relationships.   4. Pediatricians—United States—
Biography.   I. Laiken, Deidre S.   II. Title.
R154.G7668A35   1984   610'.92'4 [B]   83-45923
ISBN 0-8129-1110-5

Designed by Doris Borowsky

Manufactured in the United States of America

84 85 86 87 88 5 4 3 2 1

To Eddie, my husband, my lover, my best friend.

You gave me courage to fly,
and I love you more now than ever before.

Acknowledgments

Eddie and I want to thank:

My beloved parents, Bernice and Sidney Fink, who stood by us and gave us their unselfish love and support. We are forever grateful, and we love you.

Our beautiful children, Evie and Matthew, who fill our lives with joy and love. We cherish you.

Thelma and Harry Greenbaum and Al and Helene for their loving support.

Dr. Joseph Pedulla, who set an example of caring that I hope someday to approach.

Dr. Jules Golubow, who had faith in me before there was reason to.

Alan Schneider and Deidre Laiken, our dear new friends.

All those beautiful children whose lives I was privileged to share, with special love to the families of L. R., L. G., and P. T.

All the dedicated doctors and nurses who taught me everything I know.

And very special homage to the memory of my grandma Eva.

Deidre and I are especially grateful to our agent and friend, Berenice Hoffman, whose constant support, sensitivity and savvy helped make this book possible. We wish to thank the staff at Times Books, especially Kathleen Moloney for her careful reading of the manuscript.

To Fredrica C. Freidman we owe a special debt. She was always encouraging and on target with her invaluable editorial guidance.

Contents

Lovestrong

Prologue

The long gray corridors of the hospital twist endlessly. Stretchers, wheelchairs and IV poles gleam in the dim fluorescent light. An orderly wheels a huge metal oxygen canister down a silent hallway. It is three o'clock in the morning. A temporary calm settles in on this steamy August night.

I am dressed in my surgical greens. My ankles swell over the tops of my sneakers, which are stained with purple dye, Betadine and blood. My hair is matted with heat and perspiration, and the scent of my body merges with the odor of alcohol, disinfectant and benzoin. The hospital smells have become a personal perfume I carry with me. Some nights they linger, following me as I make my way toward the darkened parking lot and home.

I have been on duty now for thirty hours, and I have six more hours to go. Fighting the fatigue, I ride up to the fifth floor. The elevator stops haltingly—pediatrics. In this city of wards, it is here that the children sleep. Painted faces of Lucy, Linus and Snoopy stare from behind glass partitions. Behind each cartoon

3

smile a sick child lies folded in a cagelike crib. High bars protect small bodies from accidental falls.

I walk quietly, checking each chart, arranging tiny limbs, making sure no IVs have been accidentally disconnected. One child stirs, fighting in her sleep against the cotton restraints that keep her securely attached to a cardiac monitor. The air is thick with dreams.

I approach the preemie ward. Here, miniature people—4 pounds, 3 pounds, 800 grams, 600 grams—tenaciously hold on to life. At three A.M. there are no anxious mothers tugging at my sleeve, no fathers searching my face for answers and consolation. I am alone in the pinkish glow. The sweet scent of benzoin permeates the air. As if hypnotized, I watch the chest of a 600-gram baby boy rise and fall in syncopation with the gentle beeping of the monitor. I could easily hold this child in my hands and not feel his weight; he seems almost too fragile to touch. An unwarmed stethoscope could put him into shock; one carelessly placed could crush his miniature chest. Just two days ago, after spending barely seven months *in utero,* he was unexpectedly thrust into this hospital world of whiteness and glass, catheters and monitors.

Exhausted, I stare at the numbers on the apnea monitor. Heart rate: 150; breaths per minute: 35; blood pressure: 60/40. Miraculously, he lives. I know if I stare long enough the numbers will appear double. For an instant I close my eyes and see my own baby, healthy and robust, sitting at the white Formica table. I envision him sleeping sweetly on his Mickey Mouse sheets, images of teddy bears, jack-in-the-boxes and choo-choo trains dancing on the wall over his head. I have not seen my family for almost two days. This world of miniature people, of restless children curled in tiny balls in narrow beds, has been my universe. At three A.M. on an August night I am standing on aching feet, watching the glowing numbers of the apnea monitor and waiting for blood.

I check my watch. I may have to wait two or three more hours until the clear plastic bags filled with fresh blood are delivered. One hundred and twenty ccs—about four ounces—will be enough to fill and refill all the veins and arteries in this tiny baby. Although four ounces is double the volume of blood pulsating through this entire body, it is less liquid than I heat to make my morning coffee, less detergent than I use to wash the family laundry. The exchange transfusion will be a long and arduous task involving almost two hours of counting and monitoring in the dim light of a sweltering ward.

Down the bleak corridor, not far from where I watch the numbers glow and listen to the reassuring hum of the respirators, there is a room with an oak door marked LAB. There is also a residents' lounge with a cot. Although I want to sleep, I can't help but think that in the room with the oak door there is also a telephone. With no one to listen, I can speak to Eddie and tell him that I'm sorry I ever made the decision, that I'm hot and tired and that being a doctor isn't nearly as romantic or heroic as I had imagined. I can tell Eddie that I'm lonely and I'm frightened and I want to go home.

My feet are transporting me instinctively to the lab. Exhaustion makes simple movements mechanical, decisions automatic, yet I know if a voice over the speaker should interrupt me with the words "Dr. Greenbaum: ninth floor—*stat!*" these aching feet will move instantly, responding automatically to a hospital code that means: "Come quickly. A child is dying."

The last time I called Eddie it had been daylight and I had just done a spinal tap on a six-year-old girl. Wheeling her from her bed to the treatment room, I tried not to notice how much she resembled my own daughter. Later, while waiting for the slide to dry, I dialed the familiar number. Eddie's voice assured me that Evie had done her homework and was safely tucked in bed. They had eaten cheeseburgers for dinner. They had missed me. Eddie's voice was soothing. His assurance that everything was normal at home helped me to remember that there was a world out there—a world where children did not cry in pain or lie motionless, barely breathing.

Tonight when I dial the number it rings only once. When I hear Eddie's voice, heavy with sleep, I fight back the tears.

"I don't think I can do this anymore. I don't think I'm curing anyone. It's so depressing here. I belong at home."

I tell him about the exchange transfusion. Eddie, a junior high school social studies teacher in the South Bronx, knows nothing about exchange transfusions on a 600-gram baby at three A.M. But he is my husband. He is also my best friend. He begins to talk me down.

"Dorothy, don't think about tomorrow," he says. "Just get through the next six hours. Tomorrow we'll have a quiet dinner together, I'll hold you in my arms, and you'll forget all about the hospital. Just put yourself on 'hold.'"

As he talks, I picture a solid black telephone switch. An invisible hand presses down on HOLD. Eddie has been helping me press this magic button through two years of residency, through internship, med school, premed and even before that. In fact, for years now he has put his own life on hold for me. In the years when I had to study through the night, he sat beside me and held me in his arms as I read my organic chemistry, physical chemistry and biology.

Eddie and I have known each other since we were children, and now, as the sweat streams from beneath my greens and my eyes burn from lack of sleep, Eddie says the words that work. He says the words that transform me from fat Dorothy, the girl from the Bronx, into Dr. Greenbaum, the pediatric resident.

At a little after four in the morning, the blood arrives: fresh new blood for a two-day-old life. I dread this transfusion procedure, but I know it is necessary. When a baby is born with an immature liver, it can't clear its own red blood cells quickly enough. One of the breakdown products of the red blood cells is hemoglobin, and one of the breakdown products of hemoglobin is a yellowish pigment called bilirubin. If it is not reduced quickly enough, a high concentration of bilirubin can combine with the brain cells and cause permanent brain damage—even death. Very often babies become slightly yellow or jaundiced. These children are placed under bilirubin lights, which convert the pigment so that it is no longer dangerous. But when there are exceptionally high levels of bilirubin in the blood, an exchange transfusion (replacing two times the baby's whole blood volume with fresh whole blood) is essential.

The transfusion is painless for the child—it's done through a portion of the umbilical cord that has been left untied—but it is tedious for the physician. First the blood must be warmed, then a thin catheter connected to a syringe with a stopcock is placed in the child's navel. The blood must go in and out slowly and in very small amounts; in this case, five ccs at a time—about a sixth of an ounce. First the syringe pulls in fresh blood through the stopcock; then the stopcock must be turned so that it is open to the baby. The fresh blood is injected slowly and carefully into the navel. The syringe then pulls back the bad blood from the baby, and the stopcock is turned a third time so that this blood can be expelled into a refuse container.

I have performed this procedure many times before, and I know I have to be alert, that a tiny mistake on a tiny infant can be lethal. Throughout the transfusion I must carefully monitor heart rate and blood pressure. Transfusing blood too quickly can put this 600-gram preemie into shock.

My medical training has been thorough and precise, and my actions are all automatic. I take Eddie's advice. I put myself on hold.

For a few minutes my mind wanders. I am back in my mother's kitchen in the Bronx. It is a sunny afternoon. Rays of orange light filter through the thin curtains. No one else is home. I reach for a drinking glass. Accidentally, my arm brushes against a delicate china cup, and it falls to the floor, shattering into hundreds of pieces. I stare down at the broken thing. Carefully and methodically, I glue the chips back together. It is a complex puzzle, but I find the answers. I make a broken thing whole again. When I am finished, the cup sits perfectly reassembled—healed—on the shelf. No one will ever notice.

The baby has been readied for the transfusion. He lies flat in the open warmer, a motionless pancake held down with thin gauze strips and safety pins and covered with a green handkerchief-size cloth. Only his navel is visible.

A coiled tube filled with blood is submerged in warm water. I test the temperature with my gloved hand. I am on hold. I am objective. I am Dr. Greenbaum.

As I begin to insert the narrow tube in the exposed umbilical stump, something stirs. From beneath the green drape, a tiny hand appears; without warning, instinctively, five perfectly formed fingers, the length of straight pins, curl around my pinkie. Tears mix with my perspiration. I am no longer on hold, no longer objective. I hear my own voice as it cuts through the mechanical hum.

"It's okay, sweetheart. Mommy is here."

The fingers continue to curl around my pinkie, and I let them stay there. It is four-thirty A.M. The procedure will take nearly two more hours, but I will not notice the time. This little boy— this tiny wrinkled peanut—is worth the trouble. He is my patient. And he will live.

PART I

1

Beginnings

My husband, Eddie, is sleeping in the next room, stretched out regally on our king-size bed. It was on this bed that our daughter smiled her first smile. She is in her crib now and I am alone, savoring the silence of night.

From here on the sixteenth floor, I can hear the murmur of the el train as it passes alongside the building. Sometimes I imagine I can see faces in the faraway windows: husbands and wives huddled over steaming coffee cups, lovers tentatively embracing, children folded in neat infant packages in wooden cribs. This is the Bronx. I have lived here all my life, but now, for the first time, I don't resent it.

When I look across the living room, I see the antique French provincial piano that had always seemed out of place in my parents' dark Bronx tenement. It is all I took with me from my childhood home. I have not moved far from Creston Avenue, from the park where my father and I fed pigeons, from the house where my grandmother greeted me at the top of the staircase whose oak banister coiled into a polished spiral, and where the hallways smelled of cooked cabbage and pot roast.

My memories of those times are rich with smells and sounds, but there are also blanks, pieces of a puzzle that never exactly fit. I remember that I wasn't an only child. I had a brother, a sickly boy my mother held on her lap and allowed to sit on the seat of the blue stroller while I balanced on the handrail. Albie was my twin. Born only minutes after me, he remained small and frail while I grew taller and stronger. He died of a congenital heart disease, a defect that might be hereditary.

Sometimes a long-forgotten image moves behind my eyes. I see a bed draped with an oxygen tent, my mother listening intently for breaths that become increasingly labored and rasping, my father dressed in a yarmulke and tallith, bent over, praying to a God who doesn't seem to be listening.

That was the summer my brother died and I was sent to various relatives. I slept on fold-out couches with my mother, whose reddened eyes and suffocating embraces told me that Albie was gone and that I was all that was left. Eventually I went to a house where there was laughter and joy, where drapes hung by cords over dusty windows, and where two brothers shared a room littered with comic books and monster posters. This was where the Greenbaums, my parents' closest friends, lived. I was not yet five; Eddie, their youngest son, was only a year older than I was. In his backyard, we played under a white table with a red oilcloth. Together with his older brother, Al, and assorted friends and cousins, we planned talent shows and plays. But at night, I walked through the cluttered rooms and closed every door. Eddie's mother, Thelma, followed me, opening them—patiently, silently. I needed to shut something out. I longed for an orderly universe where everything belonged in a place and had a meaning. Something had been taken from me: a brother, whose face even now I cannot recall—a twin who left nothing behind but a few toys. During this time I began collecting empty milk containers, small half-pints with red letters, whose hastily rinsed insides still smelled sour, stale—dead.

At the end of that summer we moved back to the apartment building on Creston Avenue. This apartment was smaller, and there was just one bedroom—mine. It was filled with twin furniture and two mirrors that reflected only one face. My parents slept on a foldout couch in the living room. They remained inconsolable in their grief.

In the autumn the comforting smells of Creston Avenue returned. Running up the broken steps, I felt warmed by the scent of raisins and cinnamon; my grandmother was cooking again. I imagined the delicious treats she was baking, and I smiled with anticipation. I sought to fill the emptiness I continued to feel with the solace of sweets. The weight I gained added to my unhappiness.

Yet when I visited the Greenbaums, everything was different. Unlike my family, whose constant squabbling and long, oppressive silences remained the legacy of Albie's death, the Greenbaums seemed to be full of life and laughter. Eddie and I became inseparable. The only happy memories of my childhood were the times I spent with him.

The best times were the summers, when both our families sought the cool peace of the Catskill Mountains. Crammed together in tiny cottages, we spent our days together. My father, still deeply in debt from Albie's medical expenses, always chose the cheapest cottage—the one closest to the baseball field. Eddie and I laughed as we watched the balls whiz by so closely we could almost touch them.

Other summers we spent in Rockaway, in rented gray-shingled bungalows by the beach. As the sun reflected off our foil-wrapped sandwiches, Eddie and I buried peach pits in the sand and splashed at each other in the waves. Sometimes we would sneak away—two teenagers, two friends—talking about our lives and our hopes, listening as the waves moved in salt-scented cadences against the ragged rocks.

Returning to Creston Avenue after Labor Day was always difficult. It meant leaving behind the beaches or the mountains and the air that was perfumed with wild flowers. It also meant returning to the room where traces of Albie still stubbornly remained and where Eddie was not there to make me laugh and force me to smile when he sang off-key or played old Al Jolson albums. I was never ready for summer's end. Nevertheless, I packed my suitcases and with my tan still peeling and my mosquito bites still itching, I wearily trudged back to the Bronx and up the endless tenement stairs.

In late September the sweltering Indian summer days crept back, a cruel reminder of the salt-bleached bungalows or cool mountain cottages I had left behind. On those steamy days I remember my grandmother wrapping fifteen cents in the corner of an envelope, tying it with a rubber band, and throwing it down from the third floor so I could buy rainbow-colored ices in paper cups from the man in the white truck.

At that time my grandmother lived two floors beneath us. I walked down to her apartment, sat beside her on the ancient sofa, and felt safe and loved. She'd touch my face, ruffle my hair, call me "Devorah," and speak to me in a gentle, lilting Yiddish that recalled a life and a time I could only imagine. Looking at the photographs she hung on the walls and propped against the breakfront, I saw that once she had been young and had had a husband, an engineer, whose books still filled the chipped bookcases that lined the walls of her living room. Later, when she grew older and came to America, her fingers swelled and knotted with arthritis. She developed a tic that made her right eye twitch and her right cheek wrinkle as if she were squinting. But to me her face remained soft and loving. After Albie's death, when my mother went to work as an office manager, it was to my grandmother's apartment I returned to eat stuffed cabbage and talk about my friends or my days at school.

It was all so long ago, and yet it is the same Bronx I live in today. But in this building there are no welcoming smells. The halls are sterile and antiseptic. Yet, that has never bothered me.

I smile when I remember the room Eddie shared with his brother. The ceiling was painted blue and pasted-on cotton clouds and aluminum-foil stars denied the peeling plaster, the poverty and desperation of immigrant lives. Now when I think of my daughter sleeping beneath the giant decals of dancing pink hippos and blue turtles, my husband resting securely beside the laminated photograph of the two of us kissing on our wedding day, I realize that Eddie has brought a buoyant and defiant optimism into my life. He refuses to believe that we can't find the strength and inner resources to enjoy what there is and to make life better. It is an attitude he learned as a child under that starry-night ceiling, and it is a quality I have come to count on.

2

Eddie

Sixteen years after the summer of Albie's death, Eddie and I were married. The nights beside the sea, in the mountains and on the streets of the Bronx slowly transformed a childhood companionship into a grown-up love. Our friendship grew into a passion that made the familiar more exciting and the unfamiliar less frightening.

Both families were surprised. We had always been inseparable, engrossed in our discussions, laughing at each other's jokes, reciting poetry, listening to music. At Passover Seders and anniversaries and birthday parties we were automatically seated together. No one expected that the friendship would deepen. In fact, I realized that our relationship was changing long before Eddie did. As we reached our teenage years, our families discreetly separated us. I remember Eddie sleeping on the *ufshtel* bed, a form of folding cot we kept downstairs in the bungalow colony we called "Eden." I remember how he bragged that he slept in "the raw," made out with girls and had wild times. I hid his photograph beneath my pillow and hoped none of it was true.

One morning when I was walking through the short passageway of the bungalow that separated my room from his, I saw his face: familiar, friendly, blurred with sleep. The early-morning sun danced along the metal frame of the *ufshtel* bed. Eddie laughed when he saw me—so hopeful and expectant, peeking around the corner. "What a night I had last night, Dorothy," he sighed, raising his eyebrows in mock exaggeration. "I was so exhausted I just stripped naked and fell fast asleep." I admired his worldliness, his daring. Then from beneath the covers I saw a foot still covered in a navy blue sock. I think at that moment I began to realize that Eddie's exploits were calculated, planned and—for the most part—imaginary. Years later he confessed that beneath the feather quilt he not only wore socks but underwear and pajamas as well.

While I collected snapshots of Eddie at the beach, Eddie in the mountains, Eddie on Flatbush Avenue or the Grand Concourse, he collected stamps, Al Jolson records and photographs of every president of the United States. I tried everything to get his attention. At thirteen, I was five feet two inches tall and weighed almost 155 pounds. My new pants were a size eighteen. Eddie laughed and called me "roly poly." That summer I went on a diet and lost twenty-five pounds in six weeks. But still he didn't notice.

In our teens we both began dating neighborhood boys and girls. At parties, I'd watch in helpless, hopeless desperation as Eddie would put his arm around another girl's shoulders or kiss her. When I was nineteen and a graduate student in English literature at a New England university, I began dating more seriously, first a law student from Chicago, then an accounting student from Vermont. But with them there was none of the familiarity and none of the excitement I felt with Eddie. I was hopelessly in love with him. His breezy, casual letters from home made me aware that to him I was still just a friend.

It was 1967, and around me, like a multicolored pinwheel, the sixties swirled in blurred and hazy circles. I went on protest marches. I demonstrated against the war. I began writing my master's thesis on the sea imagery in the poetry of Matthew Arnold as I prepared to become a high school English teacher. It was a secure occupation—safe, unthreatening. But in everything I did, something important seemed to be missing. I missed Eddie.

In the autumn of 1968 my cousin Fran was getting married, and I was to be her maid of honor. It was the beginning of a new life for her, and somehow I was sure it was the last chance for me. I had not seen Eddie for an entire semester, and I had to make him notice me. I had to erase the memories of the little fat girl in two-piece bathing suits—the platonic pal who watched silently as he slipped out the door with a date.

My mother sensed my feelings. She knew that the gold-framed photograph of Eddie was packed in my suitcase when I went away to school, and it was placed on my night table every time I returned. Maybe she had even read the inscription that I had written in Spanish, sure that no one would understand: *Algún día voy a casarse con Eddie* (Someday I'm going to marry Eddie). My mother became determined in her old-fashioned, knowing way that she could make him notice me. And she was right. "Dorothy," I remember her saying, "men don't get it that fast."

My mother had a plan that would speed up the process.

On a warm day in late October we boarded the express bus from the Bronx and took a long ride down to the Lower East Side—the magical place where twenty-one years earlier my mother had bought the white crepe dress with the gold beads she had worn on her own wedding day.

On Sunday, the day after the Jewish Sabbath, the Lower East Side teems with shoppers hunting for bargains, merchants selling their wares, and vendors hawking pickles and knishes. It had not changed much since 1909, the year my father had emigrated here from Eastern Europe. Although the stores now sold jeans and fringed jackets as well as dark suits and modest dresses, it was "still the place," as my mother said, "to get an outfit that will make you look like a dream walking."

Rounding the corner of Delancey Street, we found a small shop, The Special Place on Clinton Street. There in the window was a bridesmaid's gown in peach chiffon. "This is it," my mother said. "This is the place."

Once we were inside, the seamstress, a tiny woman with gray hair wrapped in a neat bun and harlequin glasses that hung from a chain around her neck, looked me over very carefully. She stood me on a small raised platform and draped a bolt of raspberry chiffon across my chest. "This is the color for a girl with your complexion," she announced. My mother nodded.

By the time the fittings were over, we had returned to Clinton Street three more times. The dress, a frilly, low-cut chiffon gown, was topped with rhinestone clips at the shoulders and a rhinestone belt. It cost two hundred dollars. "So it cost a lot to be a dream walking!" my mother said with a wink.

Swathed in two layers of blue plastic, the chiffon dress hung in my closet for weeks. I only hoped that the Clinton Street magic would work, that the rhinestone clips and the matching earrings and the dyed shoes would make Eddie notice me in a way he never had before.

Touching the dress tentatively, hopefully, I thought about my cousin Fran. In only a few days she would become a married woman. This was the special day we had talked about during our many sleep-over dates in her apartment on Featherbed Lane. Huddled together in Fran's pink room with the larger-than-life-size posters of Tab Hunter, Rick Nelson and Troy Donahue, we would whisper about the shadowy strangers who would come into our lives, bring us "true love" and walk beside us on our wedding day. Long after Aunt Gertie had turned off the lights and said good-night, Fran and I would plot and plan: What would *he* look like? What would *he* say? How would love *feel?*

While Fran and I talked, we rolled our hair in spongy pink curlers and polished our nails. We watched *American Bandstand* and played Monopoly. We were growing and changing.

Fran's wedding was going to be the fairy tale she had always dreamed about—a Thanksgiving event complete with pink and red flowers, a sculpted chopped-liver bird, crystal chandeliers and red velvet wallpaper. Fran wasn't going to just walk down the aisle. Instead, an entire wall was going to miraculously roll up, and then, from a stage-lit platform, the bride would descend down a ribbon-bedecked staircase to the velvet-covered platform with the traditional canopy. I loved the idea of such a dramatic entrance.

I remembered all the secrets Fran had whispered to me during our many sleepovers in her room. I knew that being married— being someone's wife—was what she wanted most. "But you, Dorothy, you're the intellectual," she always said. "You're going to do something different with your life."

I smiled as I reached past the plastic and touched the chiffon dress. It seemed nothing was more important to me now than having Eddie fall in love with me. And if it didn't happen at Fran's wedding, I was sure it never would.

When I think back to that day, I see it all through a haze of hair spray, shoe boxes, lacy gowns and hundreds of cheek-kissing *mazel tovs*. What I remember most vividly was the second when Eddie opened the door to the bridal suite. "You look beautiful," he told Fran as her mother fussed with her hair and makeup. Looking directly at me, he added, "Hi, Dorothy," and slammed the door. My heart sank. I exchanged a hopeless look with Fran. "I guess I just blew two hundred dollars," I whispered. Then, as if on cue, the door to the bridal suite opened a second time, and Eddie appeared once again. His whole face seemed changed. "Is that *you,* Dorothy?" he asked. Eddie had noticed me. My shadowy stranger had finally arrived.

Sometime between the fruit cup and the roast turkey, amidst strains of "More" and "Till There Was You," Eddie held me in his arms and said, "Dorothy, I think I'm in love with you. I think I've been in love with you all these years." As he spoke, the times we had spent together flashed by like the reel of an old and familiar movie. I remember pulling back from his embrace, looking at him carefully—trying to freeze the moment forever. "It's about time!" I shouted. We looked at each other and laughed as we danced across the polished floor.

In those few seconds, the music and the champagne disappeared, as did the red velvet wallpaper, the crystal chandeliers, my mother and father, even the bride and groom. And for the first time in nineteen years, so did the fat, unhappy little girl from the bungalow colony and the beach. With Eddie's declaration of love I began moving in a direction that was to change the course of both our lives.

Everything happened quickly over the next few months. The other girls disappeared from Eddie's life. I went back to school in Connecticut and Eddie continued college in New York, but we spent every spare minute talking, writing, visiting and planning for the future.

Just two months after Fran's wedding I invited Eddie to visit me for a college weekend. I envisioned a romantic day filled with walks in the woods, quiet dinners, a time to be together—alone— away from the watchful eyes of relatives and family friends. The Eddie I anticipated meeting at the bus station wasn't going to be the same Eddie I had played with as a child. The dinners in the Bronx, the games in his grandmother's backyard—those were behind us now, or so I thought.

On the day of Eddie's arrival I fussed with my hair and my clothes for so long that my roommate made fun of me, but I wanted to make an impression when I picked him up at the bus station. I wanted it to be like all the movies I had ever seen and all the books I had ever read.

I arrived just in time to catch him as he stood impatiently waiting for his luggage to be unloaded. Eddie didn't run toward me, gather me in his arms and whisper words of love. He didn't even kiss me. Instead I was greeted by a gesture of total exasperation and the words "Dorothy, just try to lift this suitcase—I dare you!" He pointed to a battered brown bag that I had seen years before. This was not at all what I had expected. Stunned and disappointed, I reached down and grasped the worn leather handle. I could barely lift the bag off the ground.

"What's *in* here?" I asked, now curious as well as confused.

"Food!" Eddie said, laughing. "Your mother wouldn't let me leave without this. She's convinced that we'll both starve to death up here. This entire suitcase is filled with rye bread, salami, bagels, lox, cream cheese, roast chicken, tuna fish—even a can opener!"

By the time we returned to my dorm, we were starving. Attacking the contents of the suitcase like two hungry refugees from the Bronx, we soon littered the small room with aluminum foil, waxed paper and chicken bones. My roommate, a French major from a small town in Maine, looked dazed and confused. "What are those red things?" she asked, pointing to our half-pound of lox. Rather than try to explain, we urged her to join us. "Okay," she said in total innocence, "I'll try a lock." The look on her face as the salty smoked salmon passed her taste buds broke the ice for all three of us. Eddie and I laughed until the tears rolled down our cheeks. My roommate, good-natured and curious, shook her head in disbelief. She must have thought that eating food out of a suitcase was a strange way to begin a romantic college weekend. But she couldn't know about the comfort Eddie and I found in sharing meals such as these, or about the love that had grown out of so many years of friendship and trust.

That weekend and the ones that followed brought Eddie and me closer than we had ever been before. In the spring of 1969 we began planning our wedding. We would both be finished with school soon, and we were expecting to establish secure careers as teachers. I would teach English in a high school, and Eddie would teach social studies on the junior high level. Everything seemed to be in its place and going along on schedule. During those weeks of planning, I didn't feel different from any other young woman in love. I was twenty years old, finished with school, getting married and looking forward to becoming a teacher, a wife and eventually a mother. My life seemed to be following a predictable—even ordinary—course.

The wedding itself did not seem important to me. I had even suggested eloping and avoiding all the unnecessary fuss, but Eddie objected. He understood my parents' need to dance and cry and celebrate the only wedding they would ever give their only child. Eddie also understood about beginnings, and he wanted ours to be perfect, filled with tradition, the blessings of our families and all the special moments that would mark our transition from the narrow world of Creston Avenue into a world filled with possibilities we had not yet begun to imagine.

The wedding my parents planned was to be an exact duplicate of my cousin Fran's. I was planning to wear Fran's gown and to descend from the same stairway she had walked down exactly one year earlier.

As the wedding approached, my days became a frenzy of caterers, musicians, flower arrangements, gifts and relatives. It seemed that there was always one more thing to buy, one more alteration

to make and one more well-wisher to thank. It was in this mood of
frenetic activity that something happened which made it clear that
my wedding day, like my life, would take an unpredictable turn.

Just five days before the wedding, I began packing for our hon-
eymoon in Bermuda. While I packed, I talked to a friend on the
phone, and I paced around the bed, unaware that the telephone
cord was coiling around my left ankle. Suddenly, I looked up from
my conversation, and there was Eddie waiting by the bedroom
door. I had completely forgotten that we were supposed to go
out—I was already twenty minutes late. Eager to make up for the
time we'd lost, I jumped up and shouted, "I'll show you how fast I
can get packed!" In an instant the telephone cord brought me
crashing down to the floor. Pain moved through my left leg, and I
knew that something was broken. In a haze of "Oh, my God,
we've got to cancel the wedding," I was rushed to the hospital.

My ankle was badly broken. Eddie stayed with me as the bone
was set. He stood at the head of the bed and held my hand, reassuring me in a soft, soothing voice, "You're doing just fine. It's
almost over," as tears of pain and disappointment rolled down my
cheeks.

I left the hospital in a wheelchair. A heavy cast with an artificial
heel reached from my broken ankle all the way up to my knee.
Only the tips of my bruised toes protruded from the white plaster.

"We can't possibly go ahead with the wedding now," said Eddie's parents. "How can she get down those stairs in that wheelchair? How can a bride not dance at her own wedding?" But I
knew better. And so did Eddie. For the next five days I did nothing but practice walking up and down in the cast, leaning on the
artificial heel, learning just how much pressure my broken ankle
could withstand. I would not sit in a wheelchair at my wedding. I
was determined to walk down the aisle, to stand beneath the canopy, even to dance. No one would know that beneath my full-
length lace gown was a knee-length plaster cast.

On November 22, 1969, surrounded by cascades of pink roses and pale green silk ribbons, Eddie and I were married. With my father's help I descended the white staircase wearing one shoe and one white silk sock, and although I was a bit more clumsy than usual, I even managed to dance the hora on my wedding day.

In the months that followed, Eddie and I settled into our married life. We bought our king-size bed and moved into the apartment on 216th Street. I became an English teacher in a modern suburban high school. While the horrifying aftermath of Kent State rippled in shock waves through the outside world, I sat serenely in my classroom, checking homework assignments and reading Shakespeare, Shelley and Arnold aloud. But when I paused long enough to listen, I could hear my own voice as it became an empty echo in a room filled with plastic desks, green chalkboards, and bleary-eyed students who drove expensive foreign cars and experimented with drugs.

The perfect plan I had made for my life began to seem small, ordinary and unimportant. Every night as I made my way back to the Bronx, carrying papers to grade and lesson plans to prepare, I began to think that what I was doing didn't really matter. More and more I'd find myself repeating a question Eddie had asked me only half-jokingly when I had been writing my master's thesis: "If no one ever heard of Matthew Arnold again, what difference would it make?" One year before I was sure I knew the answer to that question. But now, as the time passed slowly by, the answer seemed more and more elusive.

Those days of commuting, teaching, collecting and redistributing papers combined to create an endless stretch of bland and colorless months. Returning home to Eddie and our tiny apartment was all that mattered. It became the only part of my life that was rich and filled with meaning. Unlike me, Eddie was content in his teaching position in a junior high school in the South Bronx. He was pleased with his choice of profession, his record collection and his books. For the first time I felt separate from him. I felt a gnawing emptiness that nothing—not even our love—could fill.

In October of the next year I became pregnant, and my empty, colorless days were now filled with the magic of carrying our child. My pregnancy was a delicious secret Eddie and I could not keep to ourselves. When I told my father, a look of hope appeared on his face—a look that had disappeared that year so long ago when he swayed back and forth praying in desperation beside my brother's bed. My mother paused for an instant before she enveloped me with hugs of joy and congratulations. In that instant I thought I saw a darkness—a foreboding—pass behind her eyes. But it was a fear I pushed away and did not want to see.

For me, pregnancy was the unfolding of a story. I became obsessed with the secrets that were transforming my body. The dullness of my job slipped away and became a minor theme, an unimportant part of a life that was now filled with thousands of incredible mysteries. When I took a maternity leave midway through the school year, I was relieved to be rid of the lesson plans, the dreary faculty meetings, and the long and tiresome commute to the suburbs. Now I was free to concentrate on the real drama—the one taking place inside my body.

I remember sitting on the blue couch, looking out at the world from our windows high above the street and thinking of the tiny crepe-paper surprise balls my mother used to buy me. Inside the many layers of tightly wrapped paper I'd find a plastic animal, a whistle or a brightly colored decal. This adventure was like a grown-up version of the surprise ball.

But of course I knew there was more to pregnancy than magic and mystery. My books of poetry were soon replaced by paperbacks on childbirth, child care and parenthood. But the popular descriptions of pregnancy, the full-page photographs of fetuses in every stage of development didn't answer all my questions. I wanted to know more. I became consumed with a desire for learning, for understanding more about genetic codes, chromosomes and DNA.

I visited libraries and secondhand bookstores. The popular paperbacks on pregnancy were now replaced with heavy books in worn leather bindings—medical texts. I read about biology, embryology, cytology and perinatal medicine. I discovered that there was a poetry in this knowledge, a drama and an excitement I thought could exist only in literature. What I had always dismissed as technical and dull now filled my waking hours with challenge and exhilaration. I felt I could find answers here. Even my dreams contained shadowy images of cells, molecules and atoms.

One afternoon as I waited for Eddie to come home, I began to think about a favorite pastime I had had as a child. When there was nothing to do and no one to talk with, I'd carefully take apart a clock or a watch. I'd examine every tiny part, every spring, gear and bit of glass. Sometimes I reassembled the timepiece perfectly; other times my surgery was unsuccessful. This childhood pastime of combining my manual and mental dexterity provided me with a pleasure I had yet to reclaim as an adult.

In July of 1971 our daughter, Eve-Lynn, was born. Healthy and robust, she was nine-and-a-half pounds of blonde perfection. In the evenings when Eddie came home from work, we'd sit by her crib and marvel at her face, her eyes, her tiny fingers and toes. We were constantly astonished at this life we had both created. But my curiosity did not end with the birth of my daughter. The medical texts continued to pile up in the corners of the bedroom. I kept them opened beside the baby food and alongside the high chair. I tucked them into the stroller when I took Evie for her daily walks in the park.

While my daughter napped, I grew restless. I found myself

looking forward to leaving the house, if only to buy a carton of milk or a newspaper. I became obsessed with cleaning. I began to use cotton swabs to dust tiny crevices. I waxed the floors. I vacuumed twice a day.

Sitting in the park with my friend Suzie, while we rocked our infants in unison and talked about toilet training, recipes, our husbands and our lives, I found myself thinking about returning to work. But I knew that work could not be teaching. For the first time in my life I began to wonder if maybe I had moved too rapidly. I had skipped grades in school, received my master's degree at twenty and chosen a profession that was safe and secure. Perhaps I had missed something along the way. Now that Eddie and I were settled and we had our baby, I felt we were following an inevitable course—a house in the suburbs and another child. I wanted those things, but there was something else I wanted, too. I had a feeling that in the medical books I would find answers.

Back in the familiar surroundings of our apartment, I watch as the Bronx night slowly becomes morning. My daughter is now seven months old, and I must make a decision. But I know it is one that I cannot make alone. I know that I need my husband's help. I rub my hands in nervous anticipation up and down the arm of the couch. Suddenly I am back in another apartment—the one on Creston Avenue. I am sitting on a couch that is old and worn. I can almost see my grandmother smiling at me, laughing, rocking back and forth, squinting from her right eye. She is repeating an expression I had almost forgotten. *"Mit dem emis ken men gehen tsu Gut"* (With the truth, you can go to God). I know that tonight I must tell the truth.

I hear the soft sound of Eddie's bare feet move across the carpet. He is wearing flannel pajamas and rubbing his eyes with his fists like a small child.

"Dorothy, what's wrong? Why are you sitting there? Come back to bed."

I try to hold back the tears, but he knows me too well.

"Something's wrong. Tell me."

I move my mouth, but the words don't come out. They are impossible words. I am about to ask this man who has loved me since we were children, who has expected to live an ordinary, happy life, to turn his world upside down. I hear my grandmother's wisdom whisper to me from a dark corner of the apartment, and I turn to my husband. "Eddie, there is something I want very much, something I don't have, and I'm afraid to tell you."

Silently he cocks his head to one side. Maybe he thinks I am asking for a new car or a fur coat. Those, perhaps, are possible.

Now I am saying the words, and I listen as they fill the room with longing and hope.

"Eddie, I want to be a doctor."

For a moment he is silent. His mouth is open. I have never mentioned anything like this before. For years I have been a student, a wife and now a mother. I have no background in science. We have an infant daughter. We are both schoolteachers, and we have less than two hundred dollars in the bank. Suddenly I want to erase the words, to pick them, one by one, out of the air, to say it was all a joke, that I didn't really mean it. But the words have been said, and they hang heavily in the darkness between us. I am hardly breathing as I watch Eddie wrinkle his brow. He turns to me.

"Where did this come from? How long have you been thinking about it? Are you *that* unhappy?"

I look into his blue eyes. I consider each word carefully.

"I know how lucky I am. I love you and our baby. I'm sure most people would think I'm crazy to want anything else, but I find myself reading those medical books over and over again. I'm frustrated because I need to do more than just *read* medicine. I know becoming a doctor isn't easy, but if I don't at least try I'll always have regrets. I can't do it without you. Do you think it's possible, or do you think this is a nutty idea?"

He puts his arms around me.

"We're probably *both* nuts," he says. "But I think you'd make a terrific doctor. We're going to have to work this out as we go, but if you're serious, we can make it happen."

I grab Eddie's hand and promise him I'll get started the very next morning. I've wasted too much time already.

3

Making Up for Lost Time

February greets me as I walk down the cement steps of my apartment building. The sky is a flawless blue and the bright sun stings my eyes. This is the kind of day that is sharp and impenetrable, the kind of day that exposes last night's dreams to a harsh, piercing light, making them seem foolish and impossible.

It feels odd to be dressed up—to be wearing my teaching clothes again. For almost a year, mornings such as these have had no particular meaning for me. They have simply been a time to take Evie for her walk, to throw on a pair of jeans and a burp-stained T-shirt and sit with Suzie in her spotless kitchen, or huddle on a park bench discussing infant feeding problems with dozens of other new mothers. But this morning is different. For a moment I miss the cozy safety of Suzie's warm kitchen. I'm still not sure about leaving this insulated, secure world of cleaning, bathing and cooking. But my feet automatically transport me toward the platform of the el.

As the subway grinds slowly downtown, I look out of a dusty

31

window and watch the stations flash by. I repeat everything I said to myself and to Eddie. I tell myself that it won't be too different or too difficult, that going back to my undergraduate school adviser and beginning a part-time premed program should be manageable. I am prepared to tell the premed adviser why I want to be a doctor and why I think I can do it. I hope he won't ask questions I can't answer, such as how I will manage with my child and my marriage, and how I can expect to perform in math and science with nothing but the most basic education in either one. I know I can count on my father, who has recently retired, to help with the care of Evie while I go to school at night, and Eddie will pitch in when he comes home from work. I think that I can make it through all the math and science that I never took before. But I'm not sure. Then I begin to imagine, to see myself as Dr. Greenbaum—confident, educated, efficient, wearing a white coat, taking a pulse, saving a life. I like this picture of myself, and I freeze it in my mind.

I feel a comfortable familiarity settle over me as I walk past the admissions building and up the stone path to the adviser's office. This is, after all, my alma mater, and everything is the same. The old brick buildings are covered with ivy. Walkways cut through the brown winter grass like paved gray arteries. The bare trees jut harshly into the clear sky, their branches knotting into thick brown webs. Nothing has changed, but dressed in my teacher's clothes and grasping my leather handbag, I feel strangely grown-up. The other students look like high school sophomores. No one else is wearing high heels and stockings; no one else is worried if her child has been properly fed and bathed.

I am sure I will be the oldest student in Biology 200, but I am prepared for that. I am also prepared to be told that my ambition is admirable but my chances for success are minimal.

Once again I remind myself that I *do* have a master's degree, I *did* skip two grades, and I always found school easy—so easy that I rarely studied, and I wrote my papers at the very last minute. I am sure that I can go to school one night a week, study before Eddie gets home, and continue being a wife and a mother while I prepare to become a doctor.

Tiny goose bumps ripple along the insides of my arms as I enter an office with a door marked PREMEDICAL ADVISER. I am surprised by what I see: other people. Sitting neatly and patiently on metal chairs, there are several men and women; some are older than me. I never thought that on this particular day anyone else in the world might also be planning to become a doctor. The coincidence makes me smile. Then I begin to wonder and to worry. Does anyone here have a graduate degree in science? Are these women married? Do they have infants at home? Does anyone here have a father or a brother or sister who is a doctor? Can they afford tuition? What were their grade point averages? I realize that some of these furrowed brows and nervous, tapping fingers may have a better chance than I do. Some of these bodies may take *my* place in medical school. I turn my face away, trying not to confront the competition.

"Mr. Gold will see you now." An elderly secretary leads me into a small office. Mr. Gold stands up and holds out his hand to me. I notice that the crumpled tail of his shirt has worked its way free from beneath his blue pinstripe vest. His face is ruddy and flushed, and his voice booms with an ebullience I had not expected.

"Hello, Mrs. Greenbaum," he says, smiling. "May I call you Dorothy?" he asks, not pausing long enough for me to answer.

"So you want to begin a premed program?" he says. I watch as his chubby fingers move steadily across an open folder containing my college transcripts. A thin gold wedding ring is embedded in the soft fold of skin beneath his knuckle. I can't help wondering if our meeting this morning will be repeated tonight when Mrs.

Gold asks him how his day went. I can almost hear him laughing, telling her about the mother with a master's degree in English who wandered into his office wanting—of all things—to become a doctor.

But Mr. Gold isn't laughing. In a slow, even voice he is explaining what I will have to do.

"Dorothy, your undergraduate and graduate grades are respectable but not exceptional—a solid *B* average. In order to be considered by any medical school you'll have to prove you have a facility for math. Your science background is what we call 'science for poets'—amusing but hardly the stuff from which doctors are made. I suggest you begin by taking calculus." Calculus. The word ripples through the tiny office. Calculus! I haven't taken any math in nine years. How can I begin with calculus? That was always a forbidden territory, a world where symbols replaced numbers and strange wiggly lines were part of a special language only math majors could understand. I was thinking I could start with science—something medical, like anatomy or biology or cytology. I didn't expect to begin with calculus.

"And another thing," Mr. Gold is saying, "I think you should take a biology course, just to see if this is really what you want." I breathe a sigh of relief. Biology. I am back on familiar ground. Mr. Gold is writing in a slow and steady hand across a yellow pad. He is creating a program for me. He tells me that I will need about forty-six premed credits in order to present a solid application to medical schools. The absolute minimum for completing this program will be two years. Med school is another four years, internship and residency are three more after that. He explains that I can start immediately even though the semester has already begun. He doubts that being a week or two behind will matter much.

"Here's the program I suggest, Dorothy," he says as he pushes the yellow pad across the desk. I look down at the neat little black squares, the careful handwriting. I'm not sure what I am seeing. Four nights a week *and* Saturdays! This is not what I had in mind at all. I repress a desire to request a lighter schedule, to explain that I have a child, that my husband works full-time, that we can't afford child care. But I can tell as Mr. Gold's smile hardens into a rigid line that he is not considering babies, husbands and financial worries.

"Dorothy, I must be honest with you," he says in a soft voice. "Your chances are not terrific. You have a great deal of catching up to do. You have a child, and you have virtually no background in this field. It won't be easy. But I'm not saying it's impossible."

I recognize this as a form of encouragement. I feel buoyant, hopeful. I stand up to leave, holding the program he has written out for me. I am grinning blindly into the white glow of the fluorescent office lights.

"Oh, and one more thing, Dorothy," Mr. Gold booms as he walks me to the door, "one *B* and it's all over."

I sit on a flagstone wall watching as flecks of clouds move slowly across the afternoon sky. It smells like snow. A thin sheet of ice begins to form on the walk beneath my feet. I am still reeling from Mr. Gold's parting words. I repeat them aloud now: "One *B* and it's all over." I know without having to be told what this means. I have to prove that an English major with a *B* average can become a medical student, and to do that I must earn an *A* in every subject, even calculus.

As the white flecks merge to become the shapeless beginnings of clouds, I look down at the yellow paper. Four nights and Saturdays. I breathe in the smell of damp wool. I am perspiring through my sweater and my winter coat.

Breaking this to Eddie won't be as easy as I had thought. When he agreed to my plans, medical school was far in the future. We both assumed premed would be a part-time involvement, one night away from home, one night sandwiched in between home-cooked dinners and Saturdays together with our child.

By the time the gold Chevy arrives I am composed and well rehearsed. I know how to weigh my news with excitement, enthusiasm and hope. I can hardly restrain myself as he reaches over and opens the door for me.

"How did it go? Tell me everything," he says.

"Great, just great," I say. "Gold thinks I can do it. I already have a schedule. Can you believe it? We're on our way. Eddie, it's like a dream come true. I know this is the right thing for me. I can feel it."

I watch his eyes grow wide with excitement. I knew this would happen, my enthusiasm has become contagious.

"That's great! When do you start?"

"Yesterday—tomorrow!" I say, laughing. "The semester has already begun, but Gold says I can still be admitted. I'll just be a week or two behind, but I can catch up."

Eddie nods his head in agreement. "This is terrific. What night will you be in school?"

I pause, looking at Eddie sideways as he drives along the congested city streets. Carefully, I measure the words.

"It's not just one night a week, Eddie. I have to put in a real effort if I'm going to catch up with all this lost time. I have to go four nights a week and Saturday."

We have stopped at a light. Eddie is repeating my words. "Four nights *and* Saturdays! We'll never see each other!" he shouts. "I don't believe this!"

"But Gold says this is the only way. They'll never take me seriously if I don't take calculus and biology." The words *calculus* and *biology* form a thick paste. They are glued together in a permanent configuration. Even the idea seems weighty and difficult now.

Eddie turns the wheel of the car and sighs. "What can I say, Dorothy? This is what you want. Four nights and Saturdays is tough. I'm not happy about it, but that isn't enough of a reason for you not to try."

I relax into the seat. I've convinced Eddie. All he has to worry about is taking care of Evie and filling in the time until I come home. *I* have to face calculus. And then there is the greatest threat of all—the words I keep hearing again and again as the car moves toward the Bronx: "Remember, Dorothy, one *B* and it's all over."

That evening as I brush Evie's blond ringlets, give her "magic kisses" from the top of her head to the top of her toes (to keep her safe), sing her the Yiddish song "Sholom Aleichem" and tuck her into her crib, it hits me: Even premed will make big changes in our lives. Eddie will have to shoulder all sorts of new responsibilities. Maybe it isn't fair. Maybe we should reconsider now, before I even begin.

Once again, I find myself sitting on the blue couch looking out at the dark winter sky. I am worried that my decision may be selfish. It may cost my husband more than he is willing to spend.

Eddie is standing in the doorway.

"We need to talk," I say.

He sits down beside me.

"Eddie, this is a big step—a big risk. We need to discuss *your* feelings. How will you react to doing housework, helping more with Evie than you do now? How will you feel when people make remarks about me being in medical school while you're teaching junior high in the South Bronx? This isn't going to be easy."

Eddie leans back against the cushions and closes his eyes for a few minutes. I can tell he has been thinking about this, too.

"Dorothy," he begins, "do you remember what it was like being in my house as we were growing up?"

"How can I forget?" I smile. "It was the happiest place in the world. There was so much love and fun there, I never wanted to leave."

"You weren't the only one," he says. "Everyone loved being around my family. I had a friend once who came to stay overnight and who wound up living with us for over two weeks! But the important thing is that *I* loved growing up in that house. My parents enjoyed each other. They laughed together. They knew how to share. And if you remember, Dorothy, my mother always worked."

I did remember. Eddie's mother was a top-notch secretary, and she loved her career. At a time when women didn't work unless they were forced to, Thelma worked, not only to help out financially but also because it gave her a sense of importance. She enjoyed the business world. I never remember Eddie or his brother, Al, feeling ashamed or resentful.

"The important point about my mother's career," Eddie continued, "is that my father was so proud of her. Sure, he knew she worked so I could go to college and we could afford a few extras, but he thought it was terrific that she had so many skills, that she could go into an office, get a job with responsibility and bring home a decent paycheck. And he made sure we did everything we could to help her. When she cooked dinner, he set the table and shopped for groceries. And on the weekends, do you know what we did together?"

"I can't remember," I said.

"My mother would rest or knit or visit relatives or even cook, and my father would put on some ridiculous outfit—cutoffs, one of his nutty pins with some funny saying on it—light a cigar, put an Al Jolson album on and humor me into helping him vacuum, wash the floor, paint the stoop or do whatever chores needed to be done. I know it's hard to believe, but he made it *fun!* He'd tell jokes, laugh, reminisce, and we'd spend the entire afternoon like that, listening to music, talking and helping my mother out. My dad made it so special that I never envied other kids whose idea of a day with their father was going to a football game or playing ball in the park."

I couldn't help laughing when I tried to picture Eddie, a strapping six-foot-tall teenager with curly auburn hair and long sideburns, pushing a vacuum cleaner across the worn carpets, while Harry, his father, puffed on a cigar and Al Jolson crooned in the background.

"Dorothy," he continued, "*I* never thought it was unusual. I thought this must be how all men behave. This must be how all families live. It seemed fair, and it was actually fun. My dad is a happy, funny guy. He adores my mother. They never fought over who made more money or whose turn it was to shop or clean. We were a family. It seemed natural that we should all pitch in."

I remembered Thelma sitting curled up in one of the worn easy chairs, laughing at Harry's jokes as she knitted Eddie or Al a sweater.

"I'm not saying my parents were perfect, but they were happy, and that's what I've always wanted for us. My folks never had much money, but in 1967 my father went out and bought a new car—the only new one he was ever able to buy—a gold Impala. We drove the car home together. I remember feeling so proud and excited. When we pulled up in front of our building, my father took out a little envelope he had been keeping in his coat pocket. Inside were those stick-on letters. Right there he glued my mother's initials on the dashboard—T. V. G. When I asked him why he had done that, he answered, 'Because this is mother's car. She worked hard so we could buy it. She deserves some recognition!'

"What can I tell you?" Eddie asked. "That's how I was raised. My father was my role model, the man I admired most. Just before our wedding my father took me aside and said: 'Once you get married, your wife should be the most important person in the world.' I believed him. I still do."

As Eddie spoke, I realized for the first time how much his family had shaped his dream for our life together and how much their love had contributed to ours.

Eddie continued: "Some men buy their wives jewels or furs.   ·
Some men want to make a lot of money. I never *wanted* to be a
lawyer or a doctor. I enjoy teaching—it's what I do best. But I can
see it just isn't that way for you. *You* want to be a doctor. That
doesn't make you less of a woman or me less of a man. But I
wouldn't be honest if I didn't admit that there was one time that I
felt bad about not making a lot of money or being in a high-
powered profession."

"When?" I asked, almost afraid to hear his answer.

Eddie looked down. "This isn't easy for me to say, but I might
as well admit it. Do you remember when we got engaged?"

How could I forget that day?

"Well, I wanted to give you something—a diamond ring. It
hurt when I realized I couldn't afford it."

"But Eddie—" I began.

Eddie gestured for me to listen.

"I'm realistic. I may never be able to buy you those luxuries,
but I've been thinking about it, and last night you gave me the
opportunity to give you something more valuable than the biggest
diamond in the world—something few men are able to give their
wives. I can help you become a doctor, and it's something *no one*
else can do. It's something I want to do."

Tonight I had learned so much about my husband. I knew that
his decision to help me had not been impulsive.

"Promise me one thing," I said. "Promise me that if things get
too rough, if you feel we have made the wrong decision or that our
marriage may be in jeopardy because of this, you'll tell me."

Eddie smiled. "I'm not one to suffer in silence," he said. "If I
think we're in trouble because of this, you'll be the first to know."

4

Commitment

The lecture hall is stark and modern. Bright lights embedded in a cork ceiling illuminate an empty stage, and rows of orange seats wait to be occupied by the students of Biology 200. I had expected something different: the old-fashioned lecture halls I had always seen in movies, the kind with a skeleton hanging in one corner and a dusty blackboard suspended in the center.

There is something about this bright, unprotected atmosphere that frightens me. It makes me think that tonight I will finally be discovered—exposed by a knowing professor in a gray suit and rimless glasses who, in one definitive gesture, will point a finger at me and ask a question I cannot possibly answer. As I walk slowly and tentatively through the door, I realize that there are no hiding places here.

I slide into a soft orange seat. Two rows down, to my left, there is another woman, an older woman—someone who looks like a doctor. She is wearing a dark woolen suit, her hair is caught up in a gold barrette at the nape of her neck, and she adjusts her glasses with authority as she leafs through pages of neatly written notes. I immediately assume that this woman knows everything the professor has taught in the two weeks I have missed and that she will get the coveted *A*—the one I must get in order to continue the program.

Almost everyone in this class is a premed student, and they are all aware that achievement is measured on a bell-shaped curve. We are pitted against one another in a competition that is designed to sort out prospective medical students from dabblers, dreamers and general incompetents. As I stare at the woman in front of me, I think that I probably fall into all three categories simultaneously.

When the professor enters, I am relieved to see that he is a young man, dressed casually in a sweater and slacks. He writes the word *cancer* on the chalkboard. I relax and lose myself in the discussion of cell mytosis and the endocrine system. This is material I had studied while I rocked Evie in her carriage in the park.

The two-hour class passes quickly, and when it's over, my notebook is filled with hastily scrawled diagrams and descriptions. I am feeling light-headed and excited. As I pack up my books, I pause long enough to picture myself peering into a microscope, staining a slide, making a diagnosis. The image dissolves slowly in the bright auditorium lights. I remember that there are two full years of premed, then four more years of medical school before that can happen. I try not to think that my daughter will be seven years old when I become a doctor. I try not to think about the days and the nights I will miss.

The other students are filing out of the auditorium in orderly clusters. I watch as the woman who looks like a doctor talks quietly to the student beside her. I maneuver myself until I am standing directly behind her, staring at the gold barrette. She is speaking in a quiet voice, and I strain to hear. She is not talking about medicine or biology. She is talking about children—her children. I smile when I realize what we have in common.

Outside the building some of the students are still talking, comparing notes, arranging times to meet and study. I am almost walking in step with her now. As we pass the other students, I lurch ahead.

"I couldn't help overhearing you," I say. "I have a child, too." A blast of cold night air turns my words into a visible cloud of warmth. The woman with the gold barrette smiles at me from behind her glasses. Before reaching into her coat pocket for gloves, she pauses and holds out her hand.

"I'm Myra," she says.

Within minutes it becomes evident that Myra and I have much more than our children in common. We are both premed students, and this is the first biology class we have ever taken. Walking slowly toward the parking lot, we exchange brief autobiographies. Myra is thirty-two years old and has two sons. She lives in the suburbs with her husband, who is an accountant. Her father had been a doctor, and after his death last year, Myra decided that she wanted to follow in his footsteps. She has been in the bio class since it began two weeks ago and offers to share her notes with me. We develop an easy camaraderie. She understands my worries about leaving Evie while I attend class and when I will have to study.

"I have *two* children," Myra explains, "so I can sympathize. But this is important work. I intend to specialize in pediatrics when I finish."

I am impressed and encouraged. I ask Myra if she will be in my calculus class, and a look of disapproval passes behind the horn-rimmed glasses.

"Oh, no!" she says. "You didn't let Gold talk you into *that!* Calculus is a trap. It's a way to weed you out of the program before you have a chance to make it. You know if you get a *B* in that, you're out!"

Those words again. Obviously, this is the standard warning he gives all his premed students. Suddenly the night seems threatening and cold. I bury my face in the warmth of my scarf. It seems that I have fallen into a trap, one that Myra, more determined, confident and knowledgeable, has managed to avoid. When I open my mouth to say good night, my voice sounds small and far away. Myra says something about getting together to study before she disappears into the darkness.

When I get home Eddie is waiting for me in the kitchen. He sits impatiently beside a steaming teakettle as I wearily peel off my heavy winter clothes. Once I begin telling him about the class I forget the tedium of the long drive home. He listens, totally absorbed, as I describe the room, the professor, the material we covered. He wants to know everything. Through the steam that rises from our coffee cups, I see that his face is filled with curiosity— and with love.

We sit side by side in the soft light, surrounded by baby bottles, toys and dishes. Now that I am in school our dinner conversations are filled with events from *both* our days. Eddie begins to ask me questions about my class. He wants to know which glands perform which functions, why cells behave in certain ways. I'm surprised how easily I can answer all his questions. During the next few hours we review the class together. As we talk I begin to feel that anything is possible.

When we are finally in bed, listening to the gentle hum of the traffic outside our window, I tell Eddie about Myra. I have saved this special news for last. He is relieved that I have made a friend and that I am not the only woman with a child who has suddenly decided to take premed.

"See, Dorothy," he says, "everything is working out just fine." I smile back at him as he rolls into a sleepy ball. There's no sense telling him what Myra has said about calculus.

Last night's snow has already hardened into a thick crust, and my boots make crunching sounds as I push against the wind on my way to the mathematics building. It has been nine years since I last studied here. I am terrified to face the bleak, obtuse world of calculus.

I am early, but the class is already half-filled. This course is a requirement for math majors. Their books are open to page 50. I stare down at the used textbook I have purchased. I see that the equations are highlighted in yellow marker. This route has been traveled before.

The teacher is a young woman, pleasantly dressed. She writes symbols and letters on the board. This seems to be a signal to the students, who begin working on solutions immediately. Myra's words take on an ominous ring as I watch everyone around me working furiously to solve problems I cannot even identify.

I find myself staring at the teacher's mouth, hoping that if I stare hard enough and long enough, the words she is speaking will suddenly begin to take on meaning. But she is using a vocabulary I have never heard before. Despite my efforts to pay attention, I find myself drifting, moving backward, floating out of the classroom into the snowy night. I am back in kindergarten in the Bronx. The second week of school, a smiling Chinese boy was led by the hand into our play group. He could not speak a word of English. He said nothing, only listened, while he clung to a worn flannel blanket. Miraculously, and seemingly without effort, by the end of the term he was speaking English. We could all understand him perfectly.

The teacher's lips have stopped moving, and I begin to copy the symbols she has written on the board. If this is a foreign language, then I will learn to speak it.

There is no exhilaration after this class. When the last student has left the room, I approach the professor. She understands when I explain that I feel lost. Then, without meaning to, I confess that I haven't had any math in over nine years. She narrows her eyes and suggests we meet before and after every class so that I can catch up. I'm too afraid to ask her if she thinks I have any chance at all—not just to pass, but to get an *A*.

As the months passed I hardly noticed that the harsh winter was softening, fading into a mild and welcoming spring. During the day, I took care of Evie and talked with Suzie as I always had. Now my conversation was sprinkled with facts about the human endocrine system or information about how normal cells become malignant. Suzie was interested and asked me questions. Neither one of us noticed that the dull drone of the television had disappeared from our afternoons together. While Evie napped, I studied. Biology was a joy. I felt as if I were reading a novel with twists of plot and subtle shades of character. As midterms approached, I paid a local teenager to sit with Evie while I struggled with calculus. I remember trying to solve equations as the laughing strains of Big Bird seeped beneath the bedroom door.

Eddie continued to be fascinated with biology, but to him calculus remained impenetrable. Whenever he saw the letters and symbols, a blank look clouded his eyes. I joked that he had a "math block." He laughed and remembered how he had struggled with algebra in high school.

"I guess I do have a math block," he said. "But then, I'm not the one who has to get an *A* in calculus."

By midterm I began to feel more confident. I couldn't be absolutely sure, but I thought I had a chance at an *A* in bio. Whenever I could, I bundled Evie up, packed the stroller in the gold Chevy and drove out to Myra's comfortable house in the suburbs. We'd sit in the kitchen, drinking coffee and reading our notes aloud. Now I had a friend who could challenge me, ask questions, provide answers.

Being with Myra was both stimulating and disconcerting. She was so sure, so determined that she would succeed. If anyone should become a doctor, I thought, it was Myra. She had a generosity of spirit, a sharp intellect and a totally unselfish motive for becoming a physician. As I got to know her, she revealed to me how much she wanted to work with what she called "special children." She was interested in congenital birth defects, mental retardation and Down's syndrome. Somehow her dedication and strong sense of direction made me feel superficial. I hadn't yet thought beyond passing my first semester of premed, and here she was, already projecting seven years into the future!

As spring blossomed, so too did the city streets. It seemed that the entire Bronx moved outdoors in celebration of their freedom from the confines of cramped winter apartments. My father began to take Evie on what we laughingly called "urban nature walks." Somehow he managed to find flowers, shrubs and all sorts of greenery where I had thought there was only painted concrete. When Evie came home she would proudly point out the window and identify a chrysanthemum, a daisy or a geranium. As happy as the walks made Evie and my father, they also served a very important function—they gave me forty-five minutes alone without the TV, without having to listen until Evie's breathing came slow and steady and I knew she was finally asleep so at last I could study.

My father was glad to help me. He thought I was a dreamer and that my goal was unrealistic, but he told me again and again, "Dorothy, you've got *shpilkes*." I laughed at this Yiddish expression that intimated I had ants in my pants. But my father meant much more than that, and he made it clear when he told me, "Dorothy, if anyone has the energy for a child, a husband and a medical career, it's you." I was grateful for his vote of confidence. Other people weren't nearly as charitable.

I remember my mother proudly telling the other women in her office in the garment center that her daughter was going to be a doctor. She refused to listen when they told her I'd probably never make it or that I belonged at home with my baby. My mother had always worked, and she knew that having a family life and a career was possible. Still, it disturbed her when relatives—people I had known all my life—grumbled that by attempting to get into medical school I was likely to incur great financial debts, and that my marriage would never stand the strain. "What kind of a husband will be happy teaching junior high school when his wife is a big-shot doctor?" they would ask. When Eddie came home from school he'd tell me how the other teachers asked him what he planned to do when I finally became a doctor. "Will you be her nurse?" they'd ask. Other friends asked how he'd feel when I began making more money than he did. I remember the fears and the worries I felt as I leaned over the dinner table and asked Eddie how he answered these questions.

"It wasn't so hard," he explained, hardly looking up from his meal. "For one thing, even when we were *both* teaching, you always made more money than I did. Why should I mind that? It will improve both our lives. And as far as the guys in the faculty room, I just said, 'I'm surprised. I never would have believed you'd be jealous of Dorothy's ambition.'"

Eddie certainly seemed to have all the answers. Somehow he managed to sound absolutely sure about issues that puzzled everyone else. I was grateful, but I knew that Eddie was far from perfect, and I reminded myself that this was just the beginning. Neither one of us could really know how we'd react or what feelings we'd have once medical school, internship and residency finally became realities.

One evening Eddie's mother called and told us that the women in her office wanted to know who did the dishes in our house. Eddie took the phone from my shaking hand.

"Tell them it's none of their business," he said through gritted teeth. "And Mom, this is no time to work against us, we need all the help we can get."

"So far, so good," I thought to myself as Eddie slammed the

receiver back in place. After that night there were no more jokes about Eddie becoming a "doctor's wife," and both our families were careful to censor any disapproval that was voiced by the outside world.

Although our time together was limited, Eddie and I seemed to be managing with our new arrangement. We had a happy celebration when I received an *A* on the biology midterm. But our happiness was short-lived. Despite the long hours of studying and the extra tutoring, I got a *B* on the calculus midterm. I was sure it was all over.

That night, as the sweet scents of spring filtered through our partially opened window, I asked Eddie if he would lose all respect for me if I didn't get an *A* on the final.

"That's the only possible way I can get an *A* in the course," I explained as he threw off the covers and propped himself up on one elbow.

"If you don't make it, it won't be for lack of trying," he said.

"How will I face everyone if I don't pass?"

"You'll face everyone. We'll go on. We have each other, and we have Evie. Whether or not you become a doctor, you'll still be the woman I love and you'll still be Evie's mother. Besides, why think about the negative side of things? You'll get that *A*. I know you."

During the weeks between midterms and finals, Eddie's confidence helped keep me going. His unswerving optimism made the long nights of studying worthwhile. The thought that I might have to face certain truths about myself—that the great potential I was always told I had might be highly overrated, or nonexistent— gnawed away at me. It was a dark shadow that crept into the sunny spring days, a gray cloud that hovered over me while I walked the now familiar path to the mathematics building. I was terrified that I would fail Eddie and my family. I longed for an escape valve, a way to get out gracefully, to be excused for not making it. Immediately after the calculus final—even before I knew my grade—I found that escape.

Sun streaked through our open kitchen window. It was a Saturday. My parents were visiting. They talked and joked while I fed Evie from a bowl of green peas. Suddenly, the green peas took on a yellowish cast. The room began to tilt in strange circular motions, and I felt a familiar nausea rise in the pit of my stomach. I ran into the bathroom and vomited. When I stood up and looked at myself in the medicine chest mirror, I saw that my face was ashen, my eyes puffy. In the corner of the mirror I saw a reflection of my mother. Her arms were folded across her chest, and she was framed by the bathroom door. She didn't have to say a word. An unspoken mother/daughter language existed between us.

"How late are you?"

"Mom, I haven't had my period in seven weeks. My breasts are tender. I'm nauseous. I must be pregnant."

"What about school?" she asked.

I shook my head. I didn't have the answer.

By this time Eddie and my father were jamming into the tiny bathroom. "What's wrong?" they asked.

My mother put a protective arm around me and led me back to the kitchen. Now it seemed that the sunny day had been erased. All the laughter had disappeared. Three faces searched mine, waiting for an answer.

"I think I'm pregnant," I said.

It seemed there were only two choices—having the baby or having an abortion. Both involved tremendous sacrifice. My mother remained silent. My father watched as Evie pushed a stray green pea across the table.

"Please don't even consider abortion," my father pleaded. "It will haunt you for the rest of your life. So what if you have to give up school? A child is a great joy, a full-time career."

I looked at my beautiful daughter. What if her brother or sister was growing inside me? How could I take that life? I looked into Eddie's eyes.

"It can't be true," he said. "You can't be pregnant."

"What if I am?" I asked, challenging his confidence. "I don't see why I have to make the choice. Why can't I do both?"

The kettle began to whistle, slicing like a sharp knife through Eddie's angry silence.

"Dorothy," he said, speaking with a slow, deliberate voice, "there is no way we can manage what's ahead with two infants. We can't have both. We have to make a choice."

I couldn't believe what I was hearing. This was the first real obstacle Eddie had ever put in my path.

I knew that he was right. There was simply no way I could handle a heavy course load and medical school with two babies. Eddie's income put the food on the table and paid the rent and my tuition. There wasn't a cent left over for full-time child care.

The next few days moved in slow motion. I waited for a sign that I wasn't pregnant, and I waited for my calculus grade to be posted on the bulletin board in the main hall of the mathematics building. On Monday, Myra and I both received our final As in bio. On Tuesday, she whispered to me that the calculus grades were up. She placed a sympathetic hand on my shoulder and offered to go with me to the mathematics building. I waved her away with a shake of my head.

My hand trembled as I followed the computer dots that ran from my name across the page to the grade column. My heart sank at the irony of what was happening. I was still in premed. I had learned the forbidden language. I had gotten an A on the final.

I ran coatless and shivering to the subway and downtown, preparing myself for the doctor's office. I knew that I was no closer to making this decision than I had been before. I longed to have Eddie beside me.

The doctor was the same one who had delivered Evie, the same doctor I had hugged and kissed in a moment of joy when he told me, almost two years before, that I was pregnant. He was not prepared for the bedraggled, dejected, coatless woman who straggled slowly into his office.

"What's wrong, Dorothy?" he asked me immediately. "How's our future doctor coming along?" His words could not have been more mocking if he had planned them. Slowly, without emotion, I told him why I was there. My voice was flat, expressionless. The symptoms were so clear that I felt that going through with the examination was a pointless charade.

After the brief physical, I dressed and walked tentatively into the familiar beige office, where the walls were decorated with photographs of babies. Beautifully framed degrees hung directly over the large glass-topped desk. I tried not to think of the world that within minutes would be beyond my grasp forever.

"I can't be sure from the examination," the doctor said. "It's too early to tell. You may be late because of all the pressure and stress. On the other hand, there *is* a chance that you might be pregnant. I'm going to run a lab test. I'll have the results for you in twenty-four hours."

The subway ride back to the Bronx was endless. As I sat on the stained plastic seat, I thought about the type of single-minded commitment I would need to become a doctor. I remembered the rigid expression on Mr. Gold's face when he told me I would have to go to school four nights a week *and* Saturdays. I remembered Myra with her two children, studying constantly, remaining determined even though the odds seemed so much against her. I reminded myself that this was only premed. I vowed that if I wasn't pregnant, if somehow I was given a second chance, I would begin next semester with an even stronger determination. I realized that in looking for an escape I had given in to my own self-doubts and that those self-doubts would gnaw away at the foundation of my dream. They could destroy everything I wanted to build if I let them.

The next twenty-four hours became an agony of waiting. When the news came, Eddie was home. We were sitting side by side, drinking coffee and watching the clock. I let the phone ring twice before picking it up. The doctor's voice sounded fuzzy and far away.

"Dorothy," he said, "the lab tests are in. They're negative. You're not pregnant."

Eddie could tell at once what the doctor had just said. He gave a whoop of joy and picked me up in his arms. His reaction proved that he wanted me to become a doctor as much as I did—maybe even more. Yet instead of unbridled joy, I felt strangely disappointed. In the midst of Eddie's excitement I stopped and looked seriously into his eyes. There was one question I had to ask.

"Eddie," I said, "does this mean that we can never have another child?"

I knew as I looked over his shoulder at my beautiful daughter that being an only child could be a lonely experience. I knew that someday I wanted to give Evie the sibling I had lost. I realized that in many ways the memory of Albie was still with me.

"Of course not!" Eddie said, laughing. "We'll have as many kids as you want, only not now. There's something you have to do first, something I *know* you can do."

"What's that?" I asked.

"Become *Dr.* Greenbaum."

5

The Eagleton Summer

The summer of '72 arrived in a sweltering fury. The heat seemed to bake into the streets. It seeped through the screen windows, making our nights restless, and burned like a branding iron, leaving its mark on our unprotected shoulders. It slipped between the slits in the blinds, making our days long, sticky and unbearable.

For me, it was the summer of premed chemistry. With calculus and bio completed, I had signed up for an accelerated course that condensed a full year of lectures and labs into eight weeks of class held from nine to five every weekday *and Saturday.* For Eddie, it was his first summer at home. He had full responsibility for Evie and the apartment while I sweated over steaming flasks and boiling beakers. For the rest of the world it was the summer of the presidential conventions. And it was, finally, the summer when Eddie and I came face-to-face with the toll my career could take on our personal happiness and our marriage.

I knew that the eight-week course would help get me through

premed faster. I knew that going to school five days plus Saturdays was a lot, but as I said over and over to Eddie, "It's only for eight weeks. Once fall comes, everything will return to normal." I didn't know it then, but a lot can happen—or almost happen—in eight weeks.

Staying home was a dramatic change for Eddie, who had been employed every summer since high school. His temporary jobs included everything from school bus driver to assembly line packer of school uniforms. He was used to working, and he had come to enjoy it. But he agreed that eight weeks was not very long, so he consented to take my place and care for Evie full-time.

I loved chemistry. Being in the lab was like being on the set of an old Frankenstein movie, complete with foaming beakers and test tubes filled with steaming chemicals. I loved the order and structure of it, the acrid odors of boiling chemicals, and even the heavy white lab coats we wore in the sweltering lab. Myra and I were lab partners. Together, we huddled over our experiments, measuring carefully, making sure we didn't forget to throw boiling chips into our flasks and test tubes. I remember Myra yelling across the crowded lab: "Chips! Chips!" as I hurriedly threw a handful of small porous rocks into my experiment. These silicone pebbles prevented the boiling liquid from overflowing the flask.

During that scorching summer, Myra and I became closer than ever. We often joked that we were spending more time with each other than we were with our husbands and children. But being lab partners was more than a lark or a convenience. It was also a protection. This class was for premed students intent upon getting a seat in a medical school. The competition was sharp, and it was not unusual to leave class for the cool relief of the Student Union, only to return to an experiment that had been tampered with, destroyed or thrown out entirely. Whenever I left the lab Myra guarded my test tubes and beakers, and I did the same for her.

Organic chemistry was more than a test of ability—it was also a test of survival.

Now that calculus was behind me and my confidence was restored, I found that the chemistry lab and lectures weren't as hard as I had feared. I was in love with my work, so in love that when I returned home to a messy apartment, a crying, cranky baby and a sullen husband sitting amidst a pile of scattered newspapers in a dark, stuffy apartment, I didn't say anything. I took a shower, dressed and went out to do the grocery shopping. That summer it seemed that my energy was limitless. I wanted to do everything: cook, clean, shop, tend to my child *and* earn straight As. Since all that wasn't possible, I delegated some of those duties to Eddie. At first I was surprised by his inertia. I wrote it off to the constant, unyielding heat and to the events of the Democratic convention, which kept him glued to the TV set, or to my own guilt. "After all," I thought, "what can I expect if I'm out of the house every day till well after five P.M. *and* all day on Saturday?"

It seemed that Eddie and I talked less and less, and at night he sighed and rolled himself up in the sheet while the grinding air conditioner droned on and on.

In the morning, long before class began, I sat in the kitchen studying my notes. I was more intent, more determined to get an *A* than I had ever been before; this time there were no escapes and no excuses. The other students in the class seemed equally determined. One young man, a twenty-two-year-old whose father was a surgeon, worked nearby while Myra and I chatted, measured and mixed. Rick was tall with long, sandy hair. He had an easygoing way about him and was so friendly and helpful that both Myra and I liked him at once. Soon Rick began walking with Myra or with me during our breaks, and his experiments were guarded by whoever had to remain behind in the sweltering lab.

Rick was an exceptional student; he was also under great pressure from his family. For a doctor's son not to become a doctor was unthinkable, and so Rick rarely stopped to think what he might do if he didn't get accepted in medical school. But he had a better chance than Myra and I did, and we all knew it—he was single and could easily adapt to the long hours of studying and internship. We envied him, but we never said it aloud.

After class, Eddie picked me up at exactly five o'clock. If I had to work a little longer, I'd find myself nervously checking my watch, hoping Evie was not getting cranky in the scorching sun, and that Eddie was not becoming impatient and resentful. As I walked one day from the smelly lab out into the pungent summer air, I watched as two students lightheartedly threw a Frisbee back and forth over the sun-dried grass. For a moment I stopped and imagined them returning to the dorm or to their parents' homes where dinner was prepared and the laundry was washed and neatly folded. I envied them their quiet rooms and their simple student lives. As I watched the white Frisbee sail across the amber sky, I walked toward my husband and my baby. Eddie was leaning against the car wearing a torn T-shirt and a pair of stringy cutoffs. Evie was dressed in a striped blouse, plaid shorts and mismatched socks. It was more than I could bear.

"How can you dress her like that?" I shouted, yanking Evie out of Eddie's arms. "Just look at her! Don't you remember how I always dressed her? Everything matched perfectly. She always looked so beautiful. How can you leave the apartment looking like this?"

Eddie shrugged his shoulders and looked past me as the students chased the gliding white disk.

"It's not important," he said. "Do you think a baby knows if her socks are matching? What difference could it possibly make?"

My hands still smelled of sulfur as I opened the car door and slid angrily into the front seat. I wasn't sure what was happening here. Did it really not matter to Eddie how Evie looked, or was this a way to sabotage me—show me how angry and demeaned he felt staying home all day with Evie, the laundry, the diapers and the television?

All the warnings that had been voiced last semester haunted me as I walked through the newspapers that littered the living room floor. When Eddie cooked dinner, it was a dried-out hamburger or a few hastily scrambled eggs. One evening, I blew up and shouted at him.

"Why do you lock yourself up in the apartment all day? Why don't you get out?"

"Where do you suggest I go with an eleven-month-old baby?" Eddie asked sarcastically.

"Look, I know we don't have any extra money right now, but you can take Evie and go over to Suzie's house. I used to do it when I was home. She can be pleasant company. She also sits in the park with some of the neighbors during the day. It can be a nice break, really."

Eddie nodded as he shuffled into the living room to watch the evening news. I wondered if he was getting fed up with all this, if one simmering afternoon when he was diapering Evie for the fifth time or trying to do the wash while she cried in the stroller, he would be transformed into an irate husband who demanded I trade in my aspirations to become a doctor for something more realistic and short-term like a medical technician.

It wasn't easy for me, a compulsive cleaner, to ignore the dusty furniture, the wrinkled laundry and the crumbs lined up beneath the refrigerator. When Suzie came to visit one afternoon, I watched with embarrassment as she stared at the door knobs. Every one was covered with Eddie's shirts or my summer dresses. The floors were sticky from Evie's last mealtime tantrum, and even the furniture, which I had always lovingly cared for, was now dulled with a thick layer of grime. But as much as I found all this disconcerting, I knew nagging Eddie was useless. He'd look at me from behind his papers or tear himself away from the television just long enough to say: "Dorothy, I wasn't trained to do this!"

"But Eddie," I'd plead, "don't you see how filthy and messy our home is becoming? Doesn't it bother you?"

I knew what the answer was as soon as the words left my lips. He just didn't see or he didn't want to. I couldn't be sure if Eddie was as oblivious as he claimed, or if he was sending me a coded message: "Dorothy, stay home. Forget this doctor thing." In exchange for his silence, I carried the burden of grocery shopping and cooking whenever it was possible. I even tried to lay out matching outfits for Evie every night. But the schedule was becoming just too exhausting. More and more, I'd return home hot and weary, smelling of sweat and chemicals, only to shower, eat, and walk, trancelike, into the bedroom to study before it was time for bed.

But once Eddie dropped me off at school, I entered a different world, one where everything was neat and orderly. Myra was there, dressed in her white lab coat, her beakers and flasks already bubbling with a new experiment. Rick worked at breakneck speed, trying to keep up with everyone. We were all competing for those As, and nothing was going to slow us down.

As midterms approached, I watched Myra's confidence begin to wane. Something was troubling her. She was having difficulty with this course. In the unrelenting heat, it was easy to become careless. Myra was constantly chiding me to throw chips into my boiling chemicals. Rick, too, needed to be reminded. Once we began working on our experiments it was easy to forget, to turn away for a split second and become distracted by a glimmer of light, a sound or even a daydream. Our buddy system was more than necessary—it was essential. The chemicals we were dealing with were volatile. A mistake, a moment of carelessness, could turn into a tragedy.

It happened the first day of midterms. The sun had been beating down on the flat tin roof of the lab for days. Inside, the temperature must have been well over ninety degrees. We were all working intently, trying to distill our chemicals, trying to get everything done correctly and on time for the exam. Myra sat slumped in a corner, wiping perspiration from her face. I looked longingly out of the window, wondering what Eddie and Evie were up to, dreaming of a cool, quiet place where I could rest and study. My mouth was parched, and I remember thinking how good it would be to feel the soothing coolness of a tall glass of iced tea. Suddenly, from a smoky corner of the lab, I heard someone shout: *"Rick, boiling chips!"* I turned around just in time to see Rick's experiment begin to rise out of the beaker in a violent, seething foam. Instead of grabbing the handful of boiling chips Myra waved in his direction, Rick, sweaty and anxious, ran toward his beaker. For a second I saw a look of desperation in his eyes as he watched his midterm, his ticket to med school, boil over the edge of the glass. Without thinking, without even stopping, he grabbed the scalding glass with his bare hands. His agonized screams pierced the heated silence. In an instant, the lab reeked of scorched flesh. People were rushing in all directions shouting for an ambulance. Rick lay writhing on the floor, the smoking chemicals forming a shapeless puddle beside him. His hands were red and blistered; he had suffered third-degree burns. In one moment, an impulsive response had eliminated him from the competition.

After Rick's accident, I approached the lab with more caution and with a knowing sadness. Rick had lost the hard way—by default. But as I looked at the intense faces around me, I knew that many of them would also lose. Only those at the peak of the curve would go on to apply to medical school, and from those few, only a fraction would be accepted and then continue until the final goal—residency.

Somehow I got through midterms. Despite Eddie's sullenness and Rick's accident, I managed to summon the concentration to get the *A* I needed. Myra was not as fortunate.

I remember standing alone in the cool, tiled corridors of the science building, looking at the list of names and grades posted on the bulletin board. I couldn't believe what I was seeing. Myra hadn't just missed with a *B* or even a *C*; she had flunked completely. The *F* stood like a solitary, ominous marker beside her name. I stared at that *F* until the long list of names became a meaningless assortment of black-and-white squiggles. This was incomprehensible. Everyone knew Myra was brilliant. What happened?

The mystery of the *F* was solved the next afternoon when Myra, sweat pouring from her forehead, asked me to tutor her.

"It's that damn math, Dorothy," she confessed. "I just can't get it."

For the first time I realized that her confident demeanor was a mask. Myra had a math block.

"I'd like to ask for your help," she said, "but you know med schools have quotas. How many older, married mothers do you think they'll admit? If I ace chemistry it will affect *your* chances of getting in."

"I know the competition is stiff," I answered, "but there's *got* to be room for both of us."

Myra smiled. We agreed to study together.

As the summer blazed on, Eddie became more morose and withdrawn. I was sure any day he'd tell me he simply couldn't take it and ask me to take charge of Evie and the apartment again. But that didn't happen. Instead, he sat in front of the television watching as George McGovern chose Thomas Eagleton to be his running mate. He was so involved with the events of the nation that he simply ignored such mundane things as shopping, cleaning or dressing Evie in matching outfits.

One rainy afternoon, I came home to a dinner of dry hamburgers and a husband slumped on the living room sofa.

"What's wrong now?" I asked, almost afraid to hear the answer.

"I went over to Suzie's," Eddie said. "We went to the park and sat while the kids played in the sandbox."

"That's terrific!" I said. "You've got to get out of the apartment and be with people."

"I don't know how they do it, Dorothy," he said, looking past me as if I weren't even there.

"Do what, Eddie?"

"Look, I went over there with all the best intentions. I brought the morning paper and asked Suzie and her friend Ruth what they thought about McGovern. I asked them if they thought he'd have a chance against Nixon. You won't believe what they were talking about."

I was afraid to ask. I, too, had sat on that bench. I knew what was coming, and I dreaded it.

"They were talking about their kids' vomit—vomit! One of them saves chunks of it every time her son throws up so she can bring it to the pediatrician to be examined. There is a presidential election coming up, and these women were talking about vomit!"

It was the first good laugh Eddie and I had had since the summer began. But it didn't last. He soon went back to his newspapers and television. Eddie seemed more involved with McGovern and Eagleton than he was with me.

As the finals in chemistry approached, I no longer had time to dwell on how messy the apartment was or how lost Eddie seemed to be. I was intent upon distilling a particular chemical. That single experiment was going to be the basis of my final grade in the course. As much as I worked, and as much as Myra helped me, we simply could not get our chemical more than eighty-eight percent pure. Everyone was working frantically, boiling, distilling, trying every technique he or she could think of. Everyone, that is, except Rudy Woods.

Rudy, a young premed student, seemed to have an edge on the rest of us. But there was something about him that made me suspicious. While we sweated and toiled over our experiments, Rudy spent most of his time in the air-conditioned Student Union. One evening after class Rudy approached me.

"Dorothy," he said, "you seem to be bright. You want med school more than anyone. I think I can help you."

Rudy's solution was simple—and expensive. For a hefty sum, he had managed to find a chemist who could deliver the desired chemical to premed students, already distilled to ninety-five percent. "So," I thought to myself, "that accounts for Rudy's relaxing summer."

I considered his offer. I knew I was doing all I could to purify my chemical—at times I thought it simply wasn't possible to do any more—but here was Rudy with one at least seven percent more pure than mine. If I refused his offer I might forfeit my place at the peak of the curve. With his illegal chemical Rudy would surely upset the order of things. There was a chance I would miss out on my A simply because I *hadn't* cheated!

I turned him down, but the thought that Rudy might be able to cheat his way into med school frightened me. It also frightened me to think that his cheating might cost me or Myra our chance at success.

That evening, as I attempted to pick up the newspapers that littered the living room floor, calm Evie and watch our dinner as it simmered on the stove, I began to wonder if Eddie would ever return to normal. My thoughts were interrupted by Evie's red-faced screaming. Eddie moved slowly into the kitchen. I looked up at him, perspiration standing out in beads all over my face. I was the picture of the frazzled, overworked housewife.

"Do you think she would be calmer if I were home more?" I asked Eddie, hoping that he'd return to himself and comfort both of us.

His answer was short and cutting. "Yes," he said.

"You didn't have to be so blunt," I shouted, bending down to pick up the tiny plastic spoon Evie threw across the kitchen.

"Listen, she'll adjust," Eddie said almost as an afterthought as he returned to the living room to listen to the latest news about Thomas Eagleton.

That night after dinner I said, "The hell with the house," and I threw my dress over the last unadorned doorknob in sight. I tried not to look back at the dirty dishes sitting in the sink or the layers of dust on the furniture. "No one has washed this floor in six weeks," I griped to myself as I stepped over baby-food stains on the linoleum. "But, I simply don't have the time. If Eddie doesn't do it, it just won't be done." I realized that Eddie was not as compulsive as I was. Maybe dressing Evie in matching outfits wasn't that important, maybe the dust and the grime could be overlooked, but something inside kept telling me that Eddie just wasn't coping. The piles of wrinkled laundry and stacks of un-washed dishes were irritating, but they were also symbolic. Some-thing was very wrong.

Eddie's obsession with Thomas Eagleton troubled me more than I could put into words. As much as I wanted this *A,* I didn't want to get it at his—or our—expense. I knew that I had to get be-tween my husband and that twelve-inch TV screen long enough to find out what was really bothering him, yet every time I tried, my own anger, fear and gnawing guilt kept me from talking. Instead, I continued to harp on the messy apartment and the neglected chores. I was angry, too. It seemed that Eddie was reneging on his promise. Sure, it was easy to be encouraging and loving when I was going to school, taking care of Evie *and* doing the cooking and cleaning, but now that he had to go out of his way, Eddie was faltering. I was sure he was punishing me, and I was afraid that any minute I would have to give up my dream.

As the days wore on, it was becoming increasingly clear that

Myra would have to work harder than either of us had anticipated if she expected to get that *A* on the chemistry final. I watched as she battled daily against her math block. She seemed panicked by the thought that she might not make it. In contrast to Myra's hard work, there was Rudy Woods, who seemed to take things more and more for granted. I remember watching as he sat with a contented smirk on his face, mixing chemicals, pretending to work.

During those long, hot days in the lab, I discovered that Rudy had offered to sell the purified chemical not only to me. I overheard two other students talking about similar offers. Obviously Mr. Woods was not content just to get an *A* in chemistry; he also intended to make some extra money while doing it.

One dreary afternoon, when the skies were murky with gray rain clouds, I looked at my reflection in a small pocket mirror. I saw that my hair was matted with perspiration, there were dark rings under my eyes. "Yep," I thought, "this is one day when I look as miserable as I feel." Maybe that was because this was not just another day. It was my baby's first birthday. Instead of being home with Eddie and Evie, smiling into a camera as we blew out that one pink candle, I was trapped in an airless laboratory.

When Eddie came to pick me up in the evening, I tried not to let on how tired and drained I was. As we rode silently up to the Cloisters for Evie's birthday celebration, I looked out of the window and thought about how many more birthdays I would be missing. And I wondered, as I held Evie close, if it would all be worth it.

By mid-August I was so consumed with my work that I no longer had time to worry about my personal life. I was secretly hoping that everything would just get better by itself, but one afternoon, as I walked into the apartment, I could see that things were getting worse.

This particular day Eddie was more than just withdrawn and preoccupied. He was obviously distressed. He sat in the easy chair,

picking at the edges of his raggedy cutoffs. His eyes seemed vacant—empty.

"Okay, what's going on?" I asked as I piled my notebooks on
the small table in the hall.

Eddie answered me with a cold and distant stare. Despite the
heat, I was trembling.

He rubbed his sweating hands up and down along the arm of
the chair. "You've been watching the news," he said. "You know
all about Thomas Eagleton and that breakdown he had. I've read
the statistics. Thousands of men have nervous breakdowns every
year. I've been following this all very closely. I've listened to all
the descriptions of Eagleton's symptoms. They're the same ones
I've been experiencing. I'm sure of it, Dorothy. I must be having a
nervous breakdown."

I didn't answer Eddie immediately. I knew that what I said now
would be crucial. I held back the tears as I looked at the room.
Newspapers were scattered everywhere. An empty glass sat on the
end table. Part of a half-eaten doughnut lay crumbled on a paper
plate on the floor. Eddie's prized record collection was gathering
dust on the shelf.

I realized that my husband needed me desperately right now. I
tried not to smile or cry as I took his sweating hand in mine. I
knew what Eddie was feeling, and somehow I had to communicate
that to him.

"I know exactly what you're going through. You sit here all
day, unable to mobilize your energy. The books are only a few feet
away, but somehow those few feet seem like a mile. It takes every
drop of strength you have just to get dressed and go out to buy the
newspaper or a carton of milk. You feel as though your life is
empty, purposeless."

Eddie's eyes met mine for the first time in weeks.

"How do you know that?" he asked.

"How do *I* know?" I sighed. "That's exactly the way I began to feel when I stayed home those seven months when Evie was born. I don't think you're having a breakdown. I just don't think you were made to stay home all day. You've always worked, and you need to be occupied with something more than the baby, the dishes, and Suzie and her friends in the park. Staying home is good for some people, but it's just impossible for you and me."

"Do you really think so?" Eddie asked as he gripped my hand. It was good to feel close to him like this, to really talk and to hold hands. I assured him again and again that he would be all right. I realized how the past weeks had driven a wedge between us. I had had no idea what the real reason for Eddie's preoccupation with Thomas Eagleton had been all about. And I thought now, as I looked around the tiny, cluttered apartment, that he had no idea how I had been struggling with my own anger and guilt at what was happening between the two of us.

That afternoon was the first one in weeks when the events of the nation did not encroach upon our own private world. Eddie and I talked well into the night. We put Evie to bed and planned how we could both make it through August. After discussing it for some time, we realized we would just have to take it one day at a time. There were only a few more intense and critical weeks to go, then Eddie would be back at his full-time job and I would have school and studying to keep me busy while Evie napped or when my father came over to relieve me. This was a schedule we could live with, but I knew as I looked at the shirts hanging from the bedroom doorknob that we would both have to make permanent changes in our attitudes if our long-range plan was ever going to succeed. For now, it was enough to reassure Eddie that he was *not* having a nervous breakdown, and that he was just experiencing those same stay-at-home blues that I had felt last winter.

I wondered, as I listened to the air conditioner grind away, if my expectations about having the perfect home, the perfect child, the perfect marriage *and* a spectacular career had not been more than a little unrealistic.

After our talk, Eddie was relieved and less lethargic. He began picking up after himself, reading books and cataloging his enormous record collection. Just knowing that he and Thomas Eagleton had nothing more in common than their interest in politics made a big difference. But despite Eddie's improvement, we both knew, as he marked each passing day with a big red X on the calendar, that September could not come soon enough.

As much as I wanted this broiling summer to end, I was always aware that when it did I would have to face that chemistry final. Myra and I worked nonstop, but neither of us seemed to be able to distill our chemicals more than eighty-eight percent.

The days between the exam and the time the final grades were posted were long and uneventful. I took Evie for walks, spent time with Eddie and visited my parents. Everyone treated me with kid gloves. They all knew I was waiting, and they knew how torturous that waiting was.

When I got to the science building the day the results were posted, the long, tiled corridors were filled with students milling around bulletin boards searching for their course number, their names and their final grades. Each murmuring group of students represented a small cast in an eight-week drama that took place in a lab or lecture hall. Each drama would have its happy and tragic solutions right here—right now.

I walked slowly and deliberately up to the computer printout. The list for chemistry was long and difficult to read. My eyes traveled down the column automatically, carefully ticking off the names until I reached my own. I held my breath as I followed the dots across the page. Somehow I had pulled it off. The A seemed to leap out and grab me. As soon as I saw my grade, I instinctively scanned the list for Myra's name. Still holding my breath, I followed the same dots across to the next column. $C-$. My heart sank. All that work and all that worry, and now this. I knew the $C-$ meant she could not go on with the program, but I hoped it wasn't true. Before I walked away from the bulletin board, I remembered Rudy Woods, and curiosity drew me back to the list of grades. It would be unbearable if Rudy had gotten that A, especially now, after Myra had lost so much. The grade next to Rudy's name was clear and startling: F. I reeled. How was it possible? Had someone turned Rudy in? Had his illegal chemical been a phony?

I walked toward the cafeteria. I knew Myra would be there.

I felt an uncomfortable mixture of happiness and disappointment as I entered the noisy lunchroom. Students were congratulating and consoling one another over cups of coffee and glasses of soda. My eyes scanned the room for Myra. I wasn't sure what I would say, or what I could say. I felt like apologizing for my success. I was confused at how things had turned out. I thought of all those long afternoons in her kitchen studying, talking about how she wanted to become a pediatrician. I had always known that Myra had something special to give. I reminded myself that Mr. Gold would see that, too. He just couldn't let someone like Myra slip through his and society's fingers.

Myra was sitting in the same place we had always occupied when we studied. She stared listlessly into a mug of coffee, and I slid into the empty seat beside her and took her hand.

"Congratulations, Dorothy," she said as she turned to me.

Despite the tears in her eyes, I knew she meant it.

"And I want to thank you for all your help," she added as she ran her fingers around the inside of the coffee mug.

"Did you hear about Rudy?" she asked.

Myra tried to compose herself as she spoke.

"It seems that Mr. Woods's plan backfired. That chemical he bought was just a little *too* pure."

"What do you mean?" I asked.

Myra was almost smiling as she spoke. "Well, the professor knew that given our wonderful lab conditions, it simply wasn't possible to distill those chemicals more than, say, ninety percent, so when Woods handed in one that was ninety-five percent pure, it was obvious he had cheated."

"I guess there *is* some justice in this world," I said as I pictured Rudy smirking and pretending to work on his experiments.

"Listen, Myra, if the system can sniff out a Rudy, maybe it isn't so bad after all. Let's go over to Mr. Gold right now. Let's see if you can talk to him. There must be some way you can make this course up. He likes you. Maybe he can arrange something."

Myra was reluctant. She didn't want to fool herself, but at the same time, I could see how she clung to my words. This was her only chance, and we both knew it.

We walked silently across the almost deserted campus to Mr. Gold's office. I waited while Myra went inside. Standing there, smelling the warm summer air, I remembered how only a few months before I had stood on this very spot and repeated the words: "One *B* and you're out." I just couldn't believe that the rules had to be so rigid that no exceptions could be made. I knew the system was designed to weed out people like Rudy, but in the process it might also discard the Myras and the Ricks.

Less than half an hour had passed when I saw Myra walk, then run, from the gray stone building. She almost passed me. I grabbed her by the arm as she strode by.

"What happened?" I shouted.

Myra turned to me, her eyes red with tears. For the first time she was crying openly.

"Dorothy, he told me it was undignified to be a perpetual student. He told me to forget it, that I'd never make it. He said no other school would accept me. He told me to go home to my husband and children."

"Go home? That's it?" It seemed impossible. But I knew that Myra was officially out. There was nothing more I could say.

Myra seemed small and vulnerable as she kissed me and said good-bye.

"Good luck, Dorothy. You're going to make it. I just know it" were her last words.

After that sweltering summer I never saw Myra again. She disappeared from the labs and the lecture classes. When I called her at home, she was polite but brief. She simply did not want to be reminded. Two years later, I heard that Myra had enrolled in nursing school.

The events of the Eagleton Summer became a milestone in my career and in my personal life. After finals, and before school began again in the fall, Eddie and I had a chance to reevaluate what had happened to him and to us. I knew that even though he was back on his feet, optimistic and encouraging, Eddie would never clean and cook with the same compulsive attention to detail that I always had. And I saw, as the summer reached an end, that there was no reason why he should. "As long as everyone is happy and healthy, why should we worry if there are a few crumbs on the floor or if the laundry is wrinkled?" he asked. Finally I had to agree. I realized as Eddie and I talked that we were in a partnership and that meant I couldn't have it all my way, all the time. I remembered when Suzie told me one day that she couldn't go to sleep until all her son's toys were put back exactly the way they were supposed to be.

"I even have to make sure that the little green man is in the little green truck," she had said, referring to a toy that also contained little red men in little red trucks and little blue men in little blue trucks. I knew, as I surveyed Evie's nursery and our living room, that those days were over for me.

I couldn't do it all and I didn't have to try. It was not possible for me to go to school, study, be a mother and a wife without having to give up some of my domestic authority. If Eddie and my parents were going to help me, then I had to learn to live with things that weren't always "just so." It was a small price to pay for having my career *and* my marriage.

The events of this summer had forced us to grow and change, to renegotiate a partnership that had been established upon fairly conventional lines. And we knew, as we sat and watched Evie play in the cluttered living room, that the changes had only just begun. We also knew that there were no role models, no established patterns to follow. We had to make our own way.

"Dorothy," I remember Eddie saying, "remember how you always prided yourself in being so efficient around the house? You used to tell me that people could eat off this kitchen floor. How are you going to feel about that when you come home tired from school and I'm working, and the floor just doesn't get washed?"

I laughed aloud. "After this summer I've learned my lesson. If anyone is stupid enough to eat off this floor, they deserve what they get!"

6

Waiting

I am wearing my brown knit suit for the first time (not counting rehearsals in front of the mirror). The office is noisy and crowded, and I have to wait for a seat. There are many women here. Everyone carries a briefcase.

We are all here to see Mrs. Maloff. At home, her photograph and the interview from the newspaper are Scotch-taped to my refrigerator door. Mrs. Maloff is the woman who helps "hard-to-place" students get into medical school. She is the one to see before beginning medical school applications. She has a reputation for helping older women students. Mrs. Maloff is the person who will tell me what I need to do in order to stand out from the thousands of other medical-school applicants.

There is a mystique about these interviews: a wrong way and a right way. Everyone knows that straight As are not enough. There are certain things I must say and do, and now that I am finally ready to apply, I need to learn these things. That's why I am here. That's why we are all here.

Two women next to me are talking. One has a master's degree in physics, the other a Ph.D. in chemistry. I think about the résumé in my briefcase: a master's degree in English literature, teaching experience in a suburban high school. But that doesn't matter. I remind myself of what I have already achieved.

The waiting seems endless. Here in the reception area, the phone rings constantly. The receptionist, her horn-rimmed glasses resting authoritatively on her nose, dispenses with advice the names of medical schools and course titles. Occasionally I see her nod her head in approval, repeating words that make me uneasy, words like: "Yes, a Ph.D. in biology will be very helpful. Yes, why don't I schedule an interview for you?"

When my name is called, I am not visibly nervous. I am being interviewed by the smiling lady in the newspaper article. She will tell me how I can get into medical school. There is nothing to worry about.

Mrs. Maloff sits at a desk covered with folders, résumés and applications. She has a pleasant smile.

"Dorothy Greenbaum," she says. *"Mrs. Greenbaum,"* she repeats for emphasis. She is studying the résumé I have placed before her. I explain that I want to take a few more premed courses at this university, but I would also like her guidance and advice, since I will be applying to medical schools this year. Mrs. Maloff looks up at me. I brush imaginary crumbs from my skirt. I remember what Eddie said about looking directly into her eyes. I remember what I practiced in front of the mirror. I force myself to look up. Mrs. Maloff pushes my folder across the desk.

"You have a bastard education," she says.

The words skim across the surface of my skin like a temporary shadow. They don't go any deeper. I feel a funny echo in the back of my head. But I say nothing. I do not even move.

"Mrs. Greenbaum, there are women out there with advanced

degrees in the sciences, with years of study and training. You come here with a handful of science courses and expect me to help you. You are wasting my time and yours. Mrs. Greenbaum, to be quite frank, you'll never make it."

I can hear the sound of my own heartbeat as I gather my papers. If I squinch up my eyes, I can remember how Mrs. Maloff looked in the photograph on my refrigerator door. I can make her small and unimportant again. I look down at the brown knit suit. This is my official interview outfit. Eddie told me it would bring me luck.

I leave the office without saying a word. I have not answered Mrs. Maloff. I feel numb. The As on that résumé are all mine, and they were hard-won. But she is telling me that even they are not enough.

In the waiting room I pause to put on my coat. The receptionist is assuring someone on the other line. "Yes, Mrs. Richards, your son can definitely apply to medical school from that university. Yes, Mrs. Richards, just tell him to keep up the good work. Of course he has a chance!"

So this is the final sifting out process. It appears, as I sadly close the door, that I am one of the rough grains, one that has to be discarded.

On the ride back to the Bronx, the tires of my car, the noise of the city streets, even the radio, all form a chorus that chants the same two words again and again: "bastard education." They are words that follow me up the cement steps and that sit beside me on the blue couch as I wait for Eddie to come home from work. The words cling to me, even after I have removed my interview suit and hung it up in the closet. There is nothing to do but wait for the echoing sound in my head to subside. I try to think. What do I do now?

Despite Mrs. Maloff's opinion, Eddie and I decide that we must go on. Somehow we believe that I can slip through the cracks in the system. Somehow the medical school applications that we have worked on together will impress someone enough to request a personal interview. My husband and my mother reassure me that after that, I'm in. "Once they meet you in person, you'll be accepted immediately," they tell me as I shake my head, wanting so much to believe they are right.

Eddie and I work nonstop polishing the essay: "Why I Want to Be a Doctor." He types and retypes for me, until everything is perfect. Each application costs twenty-five dollars, and some days the canceled check arrives simultaneously with the rejection letter.

It is 1973, and Eddie has a new interest. He has been following the trial of Jim Garrison, the New Orleans attorney who claimed to have new evidence on the Kennedy assassination. Eddie has read every book ever written on this topic. Now he has decided to subscribe to the *New Orleans Times–Picayune* so that he can follow Garrison's trial for accepting bribes. The paper is delivered to our apartment in the Bronx every day. When I try to reach the thin white envelopes with the university emblems, they are always behind the *Times–Picayune.* My knuckles are scraped and bleeding as I jam my hand anxiously into the small mailbox in an attempt to retrieve the newspaper and the mail. This morning ritual becomes so uncomfortable that I wind up waiting in the hallway for the mailman. After several weeks, he and I begin to get acquainted. Because of his bright red hair and beard, I joke and call him "Firebeard." He sorts through our mail, handing me first the *Times– Picayune,* then a pile of thin white envelopes. I never read past the "Dear Applicant, We are sorry, but at this time we have no opening in our medical school . . ." It is Eddie who carefully reads and files my many rejection letters.

Today, Firebeard is waiting for me and smiling. He hands me the inevitable *Times–Picayune* and then an envelope with an impressive return address. This one is from a prestigious Ivy League school. "Probably another rejection," I muse. Firebeard hovers by the door as I tear open the envelope. It is a request for an interview. He pats me encouragingly on the shoulder as he wheels his cart down the steps.

On the day of the interview I am well rehearsed. I have spent many hours in front of the mirror watching myself talk, monitoring the expressions on my face until I am sure I'm ready.

The address is an elegant town house in Manhattan. I check myself out one last time before I press down on the polished-brass door knocker. An elderly man in a dark suit opens the door. "Mrs. Greenbaum," I say. He ushers me past the rich mahogany furniture, the Oriental carpets and the fireplaces that glow with burning logs. Suddenly my suit looks cheap, flimsy. It is obvious I do not belong here. I have never seen a room like the one in which I am now sitting. Leather-bound books are arranged impeccably in a bookcase; a gilt-framed oil painting hangs directly in front of me. There are stacks of medical journals, and strains of Mozart are piped in from a speaker I cannot see. I remember that I am Dorothy Greenbaum from Creston Avenue and my first impulse is to explain to the gentleman in the dark suit that an error has been made. The letter was delivered to the wrong Greenbaum. The interview is all a mistake. My hands are shaking. I remember what someone told me about these interviews. Sometimes there are tricks. One student was interrupted by a man shouting *"Fire!"* When he ran to open the window, the student found that it had been nailed shut. He panicked and was immediately rejected for responding poorly in an emergency. I wonder if there will be any tricks this afternoon.

"Dr. Jonathan Green will see you now." The man in the dark suit leads me up the thickly carpeted stairs to a small room. I am shivering. A young man sits behind an enormous desk in a room

that is strangely bare. "Hello, Mrs. Greenbaum," he says. He does
not shake my hand, and I am relieved since it is trembling with
cold. "I see you're shivering," he remarks. "There doesn't seem to
be any heat this afternoon." I wonder if this is a trick. Casually, I
drape my coat over my shoulders.

Dr. Green asks me if I mind if he tapes the interview. "So I can
remember you later," he explains as he presses the "on" button of a
small tape recorder. He begins by telling me that he too grew up
in the Bronx. He has fond memories.

Dr. Green's first question is about my child.

"What plans have you made for the care of your daughter?" he
asks. I explain that my mother is planning to retire and that she
will care for Evie, who will be in nursery school part of the day. I
add that my father is also retired, and he has offered to pitch in as
well. I am not ready for what comes next.

"Mrs. Greenbaum, what provisions have you made in the event
that both your parents die while you are in medical school?"

None of my rehearsals with Eddie has prepared me for this question. I turn in my seat.

"My parents are in perfect health. I have not made plans for
their simultaneous deaths," I answer. My voice sounds strained. I
know I have said the wrong thing. But I do not know a right
answer for this question. I sit with Dr. Green for a total of two
hours. He asks me how Eddie will react to my elevated status, how
he will feel when I make more money than he does, even how I
think medical school will affect my "intimate moments" with my
husband. After we are through, I am led to another room where
Dr. I. Richard Coleman, an elderly man with silver hair, asks me
more questions.

"What would you do if a patient who needed to have a leg
amputated refused and asked you to prescribe sleeping pills instead?"

I answer that I could not be the instrument for anyone's murder.

Again, I feel that my answer is wrong. Dr. Coleman taps his fingers on the desk top. He asks me how I feel about a recent development that was reported in the news, in which a physician admitted to engaging in sexual activities with several of his patients. I answer that I feel such behavior is "inappropriate and unprofessional." Dr. Coleman leans over the desk and looks me right in the eye.

"What I'd like to know," he asks, "is what makes you think you would be so proficient sexually that a patient would desire to have relations with you?"

This must be a trick. I say, "Frankly, it never crossed my mind." Dr. Coleman straightens his bow tie. He asks me something else. I say, "What?" and ask him to repeat the question. Now I know it is all over.

Within two weeks, I received a formal letter of rejection from that first interview. But now there were more requests for interviews. There were more gray-haired men in white coats who wanted to know what plans I had made for the care of my child and how my husband would feel about having a doctor for a wife.

"Just for once," Eddie said, laughing, "when they ask you about your plans for Evie, why don't you say, 'My daughter! Oh, my God! I never thought about my daughter! What in the world *am* I going to do with her?'"

One interview actually began when the doctor admitted that he had chosen my application and wanted to see me in person because he was curious to meet someone who could get a *C* in tennis. I remember answering: "I'm a klutz when it comes to athletics, but I'm a terrific chess player." My interviewer flinched and told me I was being aggressive. Within ten minutes I was back on the subway to the Bronx.

The interviews became grueling and tedious, and not once did one of the gentlemen in the white jackets ask me the question I was so eager to answer: "Mrs. Greenbaum, why don't you tell us why you want to become a doctor?"

By June, I had been turned down by eleven medical schools. Eddie joked that we could paper a small room with my rejection letters, but I was not in a laughing mood. I had completed organic chemistry and physics and was enrolling in embryology and genetics for the summer session. I continued to get As, but the fear grew until it became a hard, immovable knot in my stomach. I remember staring listlessly into my morning coffee cup thinking, "This is a terrible thing. I'm twenty-four years old, I know what I want. I've worked hard and I'm not going to get it." But Eddie refused to give up. He made a list of twenty-five more medical schools. He urged me to apply to universities in Mexico and Italy.

"What about you?" I asked. "How will you manage in a foreign country?"

"I'll learn the language. I'll teach or work at something else. Don't worry about it," Eddie answered.

By late July, the bulk of the rejections had arrived, and the waiting was almost over. There was only one school left to respond. Firebeard was discouraged when he handed me a few thin envelopes wrapped in the *Times–Picayune.* He had become a character in our little drama, but his gentle words of consolation barely touched me as I shuffled back upstairs.

That afternoon Eddie decided it was time to take a more aggressive approach to our problem. "We're going to get organized and start all over again," he announced. He urged me to come with him to the stationery store, where he picked out red, blue and green folders. He bought colored pens, yellow pads and erasable typing paper. Next he drove to the bank and took out a personal loan for $1,500. "For medical school applications for my wife the doctor," he told the bank manager.

I was skeptical, but I let Eddie's enthusiasm wash over me.

In early August, Firebeard handed me a thin white envelope. I stared at the university seal before I tore it open. It was a request for an interview.

"One more silver-haired doctor in a white coat asking me what I plan to do with my daughter or how my husband will feel about our being addressed as 'Mr. and Dr.,'" I thought. But Eddie was more optimistic.

"We still have a shot," he reminded me.

Eddie took the day off from work and drove me to the interview himself. He assured me he would be right down the block playing with Evie in the park. I needed my family close by; I needed to know they would be there when this was over.

For the first time I am not facing a man with gray hair and a white coat. My interviewer is a woman, and she is smiling at me. I relax. But then I remember Mrs. Maloff, and I feel the tension begin to build. I am already anticipating her opening question when she says: "Mrs. Greenbaum, I am not going to offend you by asking what plans you've made for the care of your daughter. Obviously, you've had a great deal of time to work that out. I'm a mother myself, and I know that must be your first concern. Let's talk about medicine."

For an hour, Dr. Elizabeth Wolf and I talk about science, medicine and medical school. Now I am actually saying all the words I have rehearsed in the mirror. There are no questions about my husband, my child or my personal life. I feel that for the first time I am really being interviewed as a candidate for medical school.

When I leave Dr. Wolf's office, I am soaring. Eddie and Evie are standing by the car. My thumbs-up sign is all they need to see. Now the waiting begins.

For the next three weeks I greet Firebeard expectantly every

morning. "Nothing here but this damned *Picayune*," he announces
sadly.

One afternoon Eddie is home from work early. I have been out
all day with Evie and have missed the morning mail. When I enter
the apartment, Eddie's face is glowing.

"We did it! We did it!" he shouts, grabbing me in his arms.

Tears stream down my cheeks. "Where's the letter?" I shout.
"Let me see it."

Eddie stops suddenly. His face is frozen, his voice small and
weak.

"Dorothy, God, I'm sorry. I mean that Garrison was acquitted.
There was nothing for you. No news from medical school today. I
didn't think . . ." His voice trails off.

I am speechless. The hard knot in my stomach makes me nauseous. How long can the waiting go on?

It is a cloudy day in September. Evie stands beside me as Firebeard opens the building door. He is smiling.

"I have a certified letter for a Mrs. Dorothy Greenbaum," he
says.

"Fat or thin?" I shout.

"You'll have to sign first, Mrs. Greenbaum," he teases.

My hand shakes as I sign my name. I never get past the first
words: "We are pleased to inform you that we have an opening . . ." I have been accepted in medical school.

"Congratulations, Doctor!" I feel the rough red beard against
my cheek as Firebeard hugs me. He waves good-bye.

I rush upstairs to call Eddie. Evie squirms in my lap as I dial the
number. He is in class and cannot be called to the phone.

"Is there a message?" the secretary asks.

"Yes, tell Mr. Greenbaum his wife called." Then I pause. "Give
him this message: Just say, 'We made it!'"

Thirty minutes later, Eddie calls me back. I can hear the sounds of the school echoing in the background. He is standing at a public phone booth in the corridor. All he says is my name. We both cry tears of joy.

"I'll be home soon, Dorothy," he says. I am trembling as I hang up the receiver.

I sit on the blue couch and look down at the streets below. This is how it all began. It has been a long time, and it has not been easy. But I have made it. No one can take this away from me. I am going to be a doctor.

7

Albie

The days before I began medical school were filled with anticipation and activity. I was still finishing up my last premed courses, but now I had time to catch my breath and think about what I had been and what I was about to become.

It is a Sunday afternoon and I am in my parents' apartment. I remember looking at the narrow stripes of afternoon sun streaming in between the half-closed venetian blinds. Eddie is reading the Sunday *Times,* and Evie is playing cards with my father. I listen to the singsong rhythm of her little voice as she announces each number, color and suit.

I walk into my parents' bedroom. The closet door is open. Behind the shoe boxes and handbags I can see the corner of an old carton. The cardboard is pinkish and soft to the touch. I remember this carton and it stirs a primitive memory for me. I can tell that it has been hidden for a very long time.

I have never looked into my parents' closet before, but today something is urging me to pull the ancient box from the darkened interior.

I open the box and see baby pictures, photographs from twenty years ago. There are no dates on the pictures, but I recognize myself. I am three years old, wearing a tan spring coat with a matching brown velvet collar and feeding pigeons in the park. As I look closely at the photograph, I see that the park where I spent so many days is suddenly familiar. I have been there recently on an interview for medical school. The big gray building in the background is a hospital. A strange uneasiness comes over me. I feel I am about to unearth a terrible secret I have never wanted to know—something that has been waiting for me.

My movements are automatic as I leaf through the photographs. There are black-and-white pictures of an aunt, an uncle, my grandmother, cousins, someone's bar mitzvah, someone's wedding. I know at once when I have found it: a photograph of two children. It is a moment that has been frozen for twenty years. Tiny bits of memory filter through my mind like the light seeping through the half-opened blinds. I recognize myself even though my back is facing the camera. I see the long, dark curls, the short, pleated jumper, the chubby, dimpled thighs. I am standing on tiptoes peering over the top of a black baby carriage. Inside is another child. He is facing the camera, barely smiling. The child is pale and blond, and his lips are strangely dark. He is propped up by several pillows in a homemade infant seat. What I know about medicine tells me that I am looking at a very sick child, someone who is cyanotic, unable to get the oxygen he needs to grow and to live, a child who can neither walk nor speak. I know that he has a fatal heart disease, that he has been born with a terrible deformity. The core of his heart is missing. He cannot possibly live.

His pale eyes are staring. It seems that he is staring through the photograph, through twenty years, through death and through life—at me. I hear the words he was never able to speak: "I am your brother. I am your twin. Help me, I'm dying."

Albie and I were conceived at the same moment. In that mysterious instant he inherited a heart that could not sustain life, and I grew organs that were strong and healthy. In the darkness of the womb where we floated together in blissful symbiosis, we shared a dreaded secret: one of us would live, one would die. Born only minutes before Albie, I entered a world that promised hope and joy. Albie was delivered into a world of pain and helplessness.

I had almost forgotten my twin brother. I could no longer conjure up images of his golden hair or his pale eyes. The photographs had been hidden to help dull my parents' pain.

Now the memories take shape. I see the nursery and the two cribs side by side. I hear the rasping, desperate breaths that cut through my dreams. I remember the worried faces, the trips to the hospital, the twin who was always too small, too silent.

I hold myself and cry as I stare down at the photograph of Albie. I think of the brother who never had the chance to share with me his sweet, secret dreams. I cry for the brother who became, finally, a few photographs hidden in a carton in the back of a dark bedroom closet.

The pieces finally fit. I understand my parents' anguish, their arguments, the year my mother and I slept alone on the foldout couch. I remember the dark look that passed behind my mother's eyes when I told her I was pregnant. Albie and I were twins. His disease was congenital. It could have been me. It could have been my child. I see my daughter, with her fair coloring, and I can feel my mother's silent agony. I see my father as he sways back and forth in desperate, urgent prayer.

None of this has been an accident. There is a reason I have been obsessed with medicine and with finding answers, and it has lingered on the edges of my consciousness until this moment. Albie died, but he has been here with me all this time. For twenty years I have known, somewhere in a shadowy corner of my mind, that I have a debt to pay. Now, as I prepare to become a doctor, I know that debt is falling due.

PART II

8
Anatomy

On a warm September day, when the clouds were twisting like white threads in the afternoon sky, I walked purposefully into the Student Union with a list of equipment. Using the money I had just received from what would be the first of many loans, I purchased a scalpel, forceps and several probes. The instruments were delicate and well made. They felt solid and professional. I liked the weight of them in my palm, the way my fingers curled around the handles, the way they shone in the light. These were precision tools, and I was going to use them to dissect a dead body.

Although I was also taking courses in biochemistry, physiology and cell biology, for me, as for most medical students, anatomy was the real beginning. Here in a basement lab that reeked of formaldehyde, I would be initiated into the mysterious rites of cadaver dissection. Along with one hundred fifty other anxious students, I walked down the long, sterile hallway from the lecture class where just minutes before, Dr. Parsons, the anatomy professor, had cautioned us that, "In no way could we be prepared for what would come next."

I remember thinking to myself that he had sounded disconcertingly like Vincent Price when he had leaned forward and warned: "What you are about to see will shock many of you. . . ." But this was no movie. I knew as I moved slowly down the corridor that it was all very real. I only hoped I would not do the expected—faint, vomit or run away.

I had imagined anatomy class many times before this: images of cadavers being slipped out from human filing cabinets and lifted delicately onto gleaming stretchers. I could see myself masked and gloved, gently and deftly dissecting layers of skin, revealing organs and muscles. Dr. Parsons was right. I was not prepared. The lab was large and bright. There were no metal filing cabinets, no sterile gowns and surgical gloves. These bodies were dead. There was no need to fear infection.

The cadavers lay on metal tables, beneath giant domes of stainless steel. At the top of each cover two handles met. I could see that when the handles were released the covers would slide down.

My mind began to wander as I squinted into the bright lights of the lab. What if the body was a child's? What if it was a woman my age? What would I do if I was overcome by shock or embarrassment?

Before I had much time to anticipate and to dread what would come next, I was assigned to a table. There would be five of us working together. I stood at table number six while four other students arranged themselves in a semicircle around the cadaver.

The introductions were brief. Standing next to me was Richard. He was tall and lanky with dark hair and heavy, black-rimmed glasses. Next to him stood a shorter man with blond hair and a small crocheted yarmulke on the back of his head. His name was Simon and he looked nervously at the stainless steel covers. Simon seemed uncomfortable, dreading what he was about to begin. Fern was the other woman in the group. It was clear she was young and straight out of college. She shyly twisted her auburn hair around her index finger and tried to avert her eyes from what was obviously the center of everyone's attention. Eric stood to my right. He was tall and strikingly handsome, and he wore a look of supreme confidence. While everyone shifted nervously from one foot to the other, Eric leafed through his anatomy text, underlining sentences, starring words and paragraphs.

Dr. Parsons walked briskly over to our table. I watched his hands as they grasped the two steel handles. I held my breath. The covers slid down with an ear-splitting *slam!* My most vivid memory of that instant was the smell. The formaldehyde in which the body had been soaked seared my eyes and nostrils. All five of us reeled backward from this unexpected assault to our senses. Then we looked at the body. I tried to avert my eyes from the face, as Dr. Parsons had told us to do in his introductory talk. I stared, instead, at the body of a thin, frail female in her late sixties. Her skin was grayish tan. It had an unreal quality about it, almost as if by being pickled in a briny chemical it had been drained of the color, odor and texture of life. The bloodless cadaver could not have weighed more than eighty-five pounds. Small, withered breasts lay like two deflated balloons across the narrow chest. The hands were gnarled and clenched in tight, arthritic fists.

I tried not to think of the body before me as a person. I tried not to imagine how she had died and whom she had left behind. I told myself, as I gripped the side of the table, that she was made of plastic or modeling clay. "It's not real, it's not real," I repeated again and again.

Richard was the first to pick up his scalpel. Dr. Parsons had just begun to give the directions. We were to begin with a dissection of the neck to the breast. Before any of us could stop him, Richard was slashing away at the grayish skin. His technique was clumsy

and destructive. Fern and Simon instinctively moved back from the
table. It was Eric who moved forward and took command. He
immediately christened Richard with a name that would last all
term: the Slasher.

Eric warned Richard to slow down and wait for directions. We
all knew how important it was not to destroy the tiny and delicate
nerves and veins we were supposed to uncover and learn to recognize.

Gradually, as we became accustomed to the smell and the sight
of the cadaver, we each took our turn at dissecting. Simon laughed
when he held his scalpel over the body. "My first patient and she's
dead," he joked. Then he began to talk to the cadaver. "I'm going
to cut you now," he said. "This won't hurt. Hold still." Simon's
sense of humor unnerved me, but it seemed to relax him, and he
made a neat, careful incision. Fern was next. Her hand trembled
slightly as she moved her scalpel deftly over the clavicle. When she
finished, she nodded to me. The moment had arrived. I felt a wave
of nausea move up from the pit of my stomach. I was actually
going to cut into human flesh. "It's modeling clay," I reminded
myself as I gritted my teeth and moved my brand-new scalpel over
the lifeless body. The skin was tough and leathery, and it was not
easy to make the incision. I remembered how, only a week before,
I had touched my finger with a sharp kitchen knife and in a second
bright red blood had bubbled up from the small tear in the flesh.
But this skin was different. It was thick and bloodless. I applied
pressure until I had made a neat and satisfactory incision. I felt
triumphant. I was here to do a job and to learn. This was the
beginning.

Eric hardly waited for me to finish before he was working away
at the breast dissection. He had already read most of the textbook
and had mapped out the approximate locations of the major organs
and arteries. Eric, who already knew he wanted to be a surgeon,
was well organized and prepared. We deferred to him—all except

Richard, who was studying for an M.D. and a Ph.D. in bio-chemistry simultaneously. It was clear that Richard was brilliant, but it was also clear that he was no surgeon. He hacked and slashed away at the cadaver so brutally that we made him promise, right there in that first lab, that he would never work on the cadaver unless all five of us were present.

The whole purpose of anatomy was to study the body and to learn to identify every muscle, vein, artery, bone, nerve and organ. We all knew that one unsupervised dissection by Richard would result in an indistinguishable mass of flesh, tissue and bone.

As the lab progressed, it was obvious that most of us were be-ginning to relax. At another table, one student had briefly left the room, but he had returned a few minutes later, pale and perspiring but ready to continue. No one fainted that first day, and as we became more accustomed to the task before us, we lost track of time.

We were all in awe of what we were doing—revealing the con-struction of the human body. I was amazed how compactly every organ, muscle, vein, bone, nerve and artery fit neatly into the small body. Despite my initial discomfort, I could not help but marvel at this compact design, which was at once magnificently simple and incredibly complex. I remember looking for the first time at fascia, the connective tissue that pads one muscle to the next, one organ to the next, and that connects bone to muscle. This white, puffy, airy tissue is the body's Styrofoam. It has a tensile strength, yet when I held it in my hand, it shredded like fragile tissue paper. Discoveries like this one made the four hours pass quickly. At other dissecting tables, students became so in-volved that no one even left the room for a break.

After the lab was over, we put our scalpels, forceps and probes away. Then table six walked together toward the cafeteria.

The stench of formaldehyde did not dissipate in the September air. It seemed to follow us as we made our way across campus. Fern was the first one to admit it would be impossible to eat. She was honest, bright and aggressive. Simon, fresh out of jokes, admitted that he too had lost his appetite. Only Eric and Richard ventured as far as the food line before they turned back and decided they really weren't very hungry after all. Fern, Simon and I stood outside in the busy courtyard. Although we had all made it through the first lab, we still needed to regain our composure *and* our appetites. Simon seemed to be trembling. "That was something, wasn't it?" he asked. Before I had time to answer, he broke out in a big smile. "Well, it was a little dead in there if you know what I mean." With that, he waved good-bye, turned on his heel and walked toward the dorms. I watched as his yarmulke disappeared behind the trees.

"I have a date tonight," Fern said when we were alone. "Do you think I'll ever get this smell off my skin?"

"Try a long bath," I suggested. "Only don't start daydreaming. That could be dangerous."

Fern nodded her head in agreement. "I know what you mean," she said. "I just hope I don't have any nightmares tonight."

I could still see the gray skin, the wilted breasts, the gnarled fingers. I dreaded sleep.

"Are you going out tonight?" Fern asked.

I answered that I would be going home to my husband and daughter.

"You're *married?* You have a *baby?*" Fern was incredulous. "How do you expect to get through medical school? Is your husband a resident?"

I dreaded explaining everything again. After those endless interviews, I thought all the questions would be over. I answered Fern as briefly as possible.

"A husband *and* a baby. I don't know how on earth you'll make it." She shook her head in disapproval.

· Fern waved a quick good-bye and hurried across campus, trailing a scent of formaldehyde behind her. I knew I had not made a friend. "Well," I thought, as I shifted my anatomy book to my left hip, "we only work together. We don't have to like each other."

"Can you smell it?" I asked Eddie as I slipped into the front seat of the gold Chevy.

He was there to pick me up after my first day as a medical student.

"Smell what?" he asked as he leaned over to give me a kiss. I held my hand close to my nose. "Formaldehyde. I can still smell it," I mumbled as I rolled down the front window.

As usual Eddie wanted to know everything.

"But not now," he said. "Wait until after dinner," he warned as we bucked the evening traffic and headed home.

No amount of soap and water could wash away the odor of the lab. Finally, reluctantly, I pulled myself together and decided it was time to eat. Eddie had prepared a simple dinner, but I thought I'd have a snack before we all sat down. Chopped herring. I knew we had some in the house. It was my favorite food, and tonight I craved something familiar and comforting. The instant I opened the container, I knew I had made a mistake. The nausea rose up in waves. The herring was the same color as the cadaver. Gray. I was flooded by images I had hoped I could leave behind in the lab. I could still see the leathery flesh, could still feel it hard and resistant beneath my scalpel.

"Maybe Fern was right," I thought. "Maybe I will never eat again."

After the dinner I couldn't eat, my parents came by for a visit. They had taken an apartment in our building so they could be nearby to help care for Evie. They looked curiously at me as they stirred their coffee.

"What was it like?" my mother asked. "Was the body really dead?"

"Were the eyes open?" my father asked.

For an instant, I felt like Charlton Heston in *The Ten Commandments*. Today I had been allowed to look into the secrets of the universe, to analyze death from a position of safety. They asked, but they really didn't want to know.

"Enough! Enough!" Eddie said as he waved his hands and got up to check on Evie.

"Yes, let's talk about something else," my mother added as she pushed her untouched coffee cup across the table. I was glad to have them all there, glad that I could postpone sleep and dull the images that threatened to return the instant I closed my eyes.

Once my parents had said their good-byes, I turned to Eddie.

"How was *your* day?" I asked.

He lit up his pipe and crossed his arms across his chest.

"The usual stuff: a fight in the cafeteria, a kid suspended for carrying a knife, and a fire in the wastepaper basket."

"With all this did you manage to teach anything?" I asked.

"Somehow I always manage. Once I get the kids interested, you'd be surprised how responsive they are. Today we began the unit on President Kennedy. I think my social studies classes will really go for this. They've heard about him, but they were just babies when he was president. I want to make it exciting, I want them to feel like they're really living through it. But I don't just want them to learn it as history. My main goal is to get them to start asking questions. God knows, I've never stopped."

It was obvious that Eddie was stimulated by his work. "I wish I had had someone like you for a teacher when I was in the seventh grade," I said. Eddie smiled and went into the other room to prepare his lesson plans. It was getting late and I had only a few more precious hours to study.

That night my sleep was dreamless. There were no haunting

images of death, no visions of gray flesh or twisted hands. Some unconscious mechanism, something deep inside my mind, was protecting me, allowing me to close down for the night, so that I could face the next day and the lab.

In the morning, as I prepared to leave the house, my father sat with Evie. She read her picture books and he thoughtfully stirred his coffee. It was a pleasant scene, but as I approached the door, Evie grabbed my leg and began crying. "Don't go, Mommy—please!" I was gripped with guilt. My father cajoled her back to the kitchen, but I could still hear her cries as I walked to the elevator. I could still hear her voice calling me again and again.

By the time I got to school, I was frazzled. I had to face a delicate and demanding dissection, and all I could think of was my child. Even though it would make me a few minutes late, I ran to the phone and called home. My father was reassuring.

"Dorothy, as soon as you left, she stopped crying. She's playing now and is as happy as can be. Don't worry about it."

But of course, I did. Evie was all that was on my mind.

Today it was Eric who released the metal handles as we all stood poised and ready around the dissecting table. I was not prepared for the jolt I felt as I looked at the now partially dissected body. I thought I had become accustomed to the sight and the smell, but I found that today, and for many of the weeks that were to follow, that initial *slam!* of the metal covers would be just as shocking and disturbing as it had been that first time.

As usual, the Slasher was the first to begin the dissection. We were to begin by looking for the femoral vein. Dr. Parsons explained how to slip the scalpel carefully under the vessel and take note of how it passed adjacent to the artery. Without hesitating, Richard clumsily gripped his scalpel and ripped the femoral vein out of the body. He stood smiling as he held the shredded vessel in his bare hands.

"That's *it!*" shouted Eric as he grabbed Richard by the shoulders. "If you *ever* do that again I'm going to beat your head against the wall!" Simon had to pull Eric's hands from Richard's throat. The whole lab stopped and looked to see what was causing the commotion at table six. We were all angry. We were losing precious time, and Richard had almost ruined the entire lesson for us. We would have to study this part of the dissection on another cadaver if we were ever to learn it properly. Eric was right, but his violent outburst frightened us. Even Simon became serious and subdued. We all worked silently and intensely for the next three hours.

As the weeks passed, the lab and the lecture classes became increasingly demanding. There was so much to learn and to remember. The situation at table six did not improve. Richard continued to be careless and crude. Although he knew more about biochemistry than any of us, his ability to interact with people was as poor as his surgical skills. Eric became more competitive, tense and determined. He organized study groups, photocopied other students' notes and made extra visits to the lab. Simon made steady progress, but his constant jokes got under my skin. In the midst of all the pressure and competition, Fern and I developed an uneasy alliance. I knew she still didn't "approve" of my marital status, or my child, but when I was absent from class, she was the one who offered to spend four extra hours reviewing the leg dissection I had missed. It was the first show of friendship from any of my lab mates, and I was grateful for it.

At home, the time Eddie and I spent together was now qualitatively different. There was always some household chore to take care of, and once that was done, there was always something to study or to memorize. At night, when most couples curl up in bed or in front of the TV, Eddie and I sat side by side on the blue couch. I studied anatomy or physiology, and he listened to music through an inexpensive pair of earphones. After a while, I began to find this ingenious arrangement somewhat comforting. Here I was, safe and secure with my husband by my side and my daughter peacefully asleep in the next room. There were no demands for my time or attention, and I was free to concentrate on the material I would have to know before midterms. Eddie rarely complained. He, too, disappeared into his own world. Occasionally, a strain of music would escape from the headphones, and I would hear the familiar, faraway voice of Al Jolson float through the silence between us.

My life was pared down to the barest essentials: Eddie, Evie and school. There was no time for socializing. On Saturdays I put my books away and devoted myself to my family. It was, Eddie and I agreed, essential to have this one day, untouched by thoughts and preoccupations with medical school. On Sunday, I'd grab half an hour of studying time by locking myself in the bathroom while Evie played and my parents or my in-laws visited. Even the household chores were streamlined. After that disastrous summer, we dealt with domestic responsibilities in the simplest way possible: whoever was closest to the dishes when the sink was full washed them. The same went for the laundry and the cooking. During the weeks before midterms I was careful to keep a respectful distance from the sink, the stove and the hamper. And Eddie understood.

By midterm all of us at table six suffered from exhaustion and overwork. The anticipation of our first important exams had everyone teetering on the edge. One afternoon, as I donned my lab coat and approached the cadaver, I noticed that at table four a group of students were huddled, whispering and shaking their heads. When I joined them, I was genuinely shocked. I had heard stories of sabotage in medical school, but I never would have believed that anyone would go this far. The cadaver at table four had been destroyed. Part of the dissection had been purposefully slashed so that the tissue, veins, arteries, organs and muscles were unrecognizable. It looked as if a giant eggbeater had macerated the vital organs. Eric took one glance at table four and suggested we protect ourselves from a similar fate. He decided that we should all chip in and purchase a combination lock. The lock, Eric explained, would be affixed to the steel handles and only the five of us would know the combination. I was impressed by Eric's rather quick and well-thought-out solution to the problem, but something about it made me suspicious. I could see, as I caught Simon's glance, that he too was just a little uneasy about Eric's "spontaneous" response.

With midterms less than two weeks away, Fern broke out in a horrible rash. Her face and hands were covered with oozing pimples. Her hair had to be pulled back to keep it from touching her irritated skin. When he saw her, Richard pulled back and shouted, "UGGH! What happened to you?"

"It's an allergic reaction to the formaldehyde," she whispered to me as she turned her back on the Slasher.

"I'm absolutely miserable. On top of this rash, the guy I've been seeing told me he couldn't take my schedule anymore. Now, with this face, and midterms coming up, I've got to worry about my social life!"

I reassured Fern that the rash would go away and told her to ignore Richard's insensitivity. After all, *her* problem was only skin-deep!

On the day of midterms, I left the house and glanced momentarily up at a calm, pastel blue sky. It would be a long, tedious day. I would not be outdoors again for several hours.

The practical portion of the anatomy exam reminded me of a butcher shop. Dr. Parsons had selected various organs and placed them on a table. Beneath each organ was a little sign which read: "What am I?" "Where am I located—right or left side?" "Am I healthy?" Each student stood several feet apart from the next, and Dr. Parsons timed us at each station. After fifteen seconds he'd shout: "Move! Move!" By that time, we were to have written the answer to all three questions.

It was a relief when the exam was over, and I hurried away from the students who stood outside comparing notes. I didn't want to know which answers I had missed and which ones I had gotten right. I just wanted to pass.

Everyone showed up at table six the next day. We had all made it. Only Simon looked depressed. He had gotten a 70. It was a close call, and if he didn't do better on the final, he would be out of medical school before the second year.

I realized, as we finished that day's dissection, that four hours had passed without a single joke or wisecrack from Simon.

As I walked across campus to the cafeteria, Simon walked beside me. I had always avoided him, but it was clear that today he was seeking me out. "May I join you for coffee?" he asked. There was no way I could refuse him. Together we made our way through the crowded, noisy cafeteria.

We sat at a corner table. Simon slowly unwrapped his cheese sandwich. He had the same thing for lunch almost every day, he explained. It was difficult to remain kosher on a university campus.

"I'm sorry about your grade," I blurted out. But deep down I was thinking that Simon had joked around too much.

"Dorothy, I knew it bothered you that I fooled around a lot, but if I hadn't, I would have dropped out that first week."

"How do you figure that?" I asked sarcastically.

"My father died two weeks before school began. It wasn't easy to work on a cadaver so soon after the funeral."

I felt ashamed. I had never seen Simon as anything but an annoying clown. But his jokes had been a protective armor. And they had served him well.

"Simon, I'm sorry. I didn't know."

"Forget it. You couldn't have known. Maybe you're right. Maybe I *did* take the jokes a little too far."

"I have an idea. Why don't we put in some extra time at night? Eric doesn't have any after-lab groups planned yet, but we could go together, on our own."

"I can't. Not right away, anyway."

"Are you afraid?"

"Afraid of what?"

"You know, the lab, alone at night."

"Dorothy, this is science. There are no ghosts in the lab."

I felt a little embarrassed. My own fear had inadvertently slipped out. Of course, I had studied in the lab after class, but I had always been with a group of students. I had been avoiding working there alone at night, and I had never known why until this moment.

Simon touched my hand. "Look, don't be embarrassed. I know how you feel. It's not that. It's just that I have so much studying. And I have to give my weekends to my brothers and sisters."

Simon explained that he was the eldest of seven children. His mother had died several years before, and now, with his father gone, he felt responsible for sharing what little time he had with his family.

"But I know that's no excuse," he said. "I can't flunk out now, not after getting this far. I'm going to buckle down. Just watch me."

We smiled at each other over our half-eaten lunches. This was not the same Simon I had met in September; or maybe it was, and I just hadn't seen him there under all that armor. It felt good to have made a friend.

That night Eddie drove me to the lab. "Are you sure you want to do this?" he asked.

"Don't be silly," I assured him. "It's perfectly all right."

The halls looked the same as they had during the day: beige tiles, marbled linoleum, lab door slightly ajar, white-jacketed students sitting beside partially dissected cadavers, drinking coffee, studying anatomy books and comparing what they had read to what they were looking at.

The lab door was open, but no one was there. I turned on the light and walked slowly over to table six. It seemed strange to be there without Simon, Richard, Eric and Fern. My foot bumped against an empty milk container. Yes, we had all become so used to the lab and the cadavers that some of us actually ate lunch while we worked.

My hands were steady as I whirled the combination lock and slid the metal doors slowly downward. I looked at the cadaver. It was just as I had left it—gray, leathery, dead. For the first time, an image slipped past my inner censor. I remembered my grandmother's funeral. The coffin had remained open, and I had peered anxiously at the waxen figure. "So this is death," I had thought.

Now I looked at the cadaver. Its face was expressionless. The partially closed eyes were empty sockets. The eyeballs had been removed and placed in an eye bank. It was no longer difficult to look at the face, to notice the tiny wart on the left hand, the hysterectomy scar across the abdomen, the barely visible pinpricks in the earlobes that had once held earrings.

"When you're dead, you're dead," I whispered to myself. "This is it." I had not found a soul in this bloodless body. There was nothing my scalpel would unearth that hinted at an afterlife— something that would live on. Sitting here alone in the dark, wearing my white jacket and gripping my dissecting tools, I found it difficult to reconcile my religious feelings with what I saw laid out so concretely before me. But as I began to concentrate on my work, I had another thought. Something so perfect, so efficient and highly organized, could not have been created by accident.

Simon was right, there were no ghosts in the lab, but that didn't mean we knew all the secrets. It just meant we knew some of them.

In the weeks that followed, Dr. Parsons made a brief and ominous announcement. Several students had cheated on the midterms. He was aware, and so were other professors, that an elaborate system of "taps" had been developed and used during the written parts of the anatomy and physiology exams. His lecture was stern and sobering. He had his suspicions, and if they could ever be proved, the students responsible would be expelled immediately. I remembered hearing feet tapping frequently during the anatomy midterm, but I had never suspected. Everyone at table six looked stunned except Eric. I couldn't be sure, but he seemed visibly uncomfortable. I knew he was competitive, but I wasn't sure just how keen his competitive spirit was, just how much he was willing to risk losing in order to win.

This week we were to begin the genital dissection. It was an uncomfortable moment when we began to work on that area of the cadaver. I felt, somehow, that this was the ultimate violation of privacy, the final invasion. Fern stood beside me. She had become openly friendly in the past few weeks and had seemed more involved, happier, more eager to ask questions and offer help. Only Eric remained aloof and uninvolved, except for the warning looks he shot the Slasher, who continued to live up to his name.

The cadaver's ankles were tethered by ropes which were attached to hooks in the ceiling. My first impulse was to turn my head away, but I reminded myself that this was science. It was Simon, serious and unsmiling, who began the dissection. The lab was silent except for the voice of Dr. Parsons giving directions, telling us what to look for and what to be careful of.

Then Simon's voice filtered through a fog of discomfort and dread.

"What the hell is this? What's going on here?"

Simon waved us all closer to the cadaver. There was some sort of fleshy obstruction in the vagina, something we had never read about or seen in the text. We had been told that when any abnormality was found, we were supposed to call it to the attention of Dr. Parsons, who would then explain it to the rest of the class. At table three earlier in the year, the students had found a hideous brown dermoid tumor composed of teeth and hair in the pelvis of their cadaver. Dr. Parsons had explained that such tumors were not uncommon. They were benign and rarely the cause of discomfort or illness. Even so, it had been hard to work that afternoon after seeing the grotesque tumor spilling forth its chocolate-colored contents into the pelvic cavity.

For some reason, none of us thought to call Dr. Parsons. Perhaps we were all too engrossed in what Simon had discovered. Maybe we were too embarrassed. Or maybe it all just happened too fast.

The fleshy obstruction inside the vagina was a dismembered penis.

"Someone's idea of a joke!" murmured Simon, red-faced and furious. Fern moved back from the table and covered her eyes. Before we could say anything, Eric disposed of the organ and told us to just go ahead. I was so angry that my hands began to shake. "This is medical school," I thought. "Everyone here has worked hard to be admitted, but still the system has failed to weed out the cheaters, the saboteurs and the insensitive practical jokers." I wondered, as I looked around the room, who had been responsible for this and if he or she would someday become a practicing M.D.

Fern and I, angry and disgusted, walked in silence toward the cafeteria. It was pointless to discuss the afternoon's lab. We pulled our plastic-wrapped lunches from the glass shelves and moved along with hundreds of other students down the noisy line to the cashier. Fern began to smile.

When we had wedged ourselves in among several other students at a large round table, Fern began asking me questions about marriage.

"Do you really think you can have a relationship and be a medical student? How do you divide your time between your husband and your studies? Is Eddie jealous? Does he help you around the house?"

By this time I knew that Fern's questions were more than idle curiosity. I also knew that her improved attitude and attempts at friendship had to do with someone new in her life.

"I might as well tell you," she said. "I've met someone and I'm in love. I'm thinking about getting married, but you're the only woman I know who is actually managing both school and marriage. I just had to ask you."

"I also have a child," I added.

"But that shouldn't be too much of a problem," Fern said as she waved her hand in the air. "They have that wonderful nursery here on campus. I hear it's terrific."

I had to laugh. "Sure, it's terrific—if you're the *wife* of a medical student."

"What do you mean?" Fern asked.

"That wonderful nursery is only open from nine to twelve. What am I supposed to do with Evie for the rest of the school day? If I was married to a med student and didn't have a full-time job, it would be no problem."

Fern tilted her chair backward and frowned. "I guess this world just isn't ready for us yet."

"Don't let it discourage you. I wouldn't want to face an empty apartment every night. Going home to my family is the bright spot of my day—especially a day like this one."

Fern nodded in agreement. Then she drifted off into a private silence. I had a feeling we would have a lot in common before medical school was over.

By second semester, I became more adept at dissection and more involved in my studies. It took my father to point out that Evie had changed, too. "Dorothy, she doesn't even cry when you leave anymore. Haven't you noticed?" It was true. Evie had adjusted just as Eddie said she would. I no longer left the house feeling anxious and guilty. The family had adapted to my being a full-time student (out of the house at seven, home by seven, six days a week) so well that every night Eddie automatically put on his earphones and held me in his arms while I studied. It became a pattern we were so used to, I wondered if it would later become difficult to break.

Even though things were going well at home, I felt that familiar dread as finals approached. I lived on coffee. I doubt that I had more than twelve hours of sleep in five days. I studied early in the morning before anyone woke up, and late at night after everyone was asleep. Only Saturday remained untouched—sacred. It was reserved for my family and nothing, not even finals, was going to change that.

The pressure was beginning to build for everyone at table six. Medical school wasn't a snap for anyone—not even the Slasher. Although he probably needed to study less than the rest of us, I could see by the circles under his eyes that he too was burning the midnight oil. Eric became increasingly jittery, talkative and driven. Simon thought he was taking speed, and he was right. In a gesture of generosity, he made his large and varied supply of amphetamines available to everyone at the table—for a price, of course. There were no takers. Fern, Simon and I stuck to what we laughingly called the poor man's amphetamine—coffee. Richard, who now seemed to live on another planet entirely, withdrew from all of us. We still had to watch him carefully, and we were constantly shaking our heads and clucking our tongues when his turn came to dissect.

When the exam schedule was posted, and I realized that I had all three finals in one week, I was sure I'd never make it.

"I'm going to crack up right there in the classroom," I told Eddie. He only smiled, put his arm around me and placed the headphones over his ears. In the silence of the night, as I sat close to him, I'd hear the strains of an old Al Jolson song.

"Can't you make that a little lower?" I'd ask as I lifted the headset so Eddie could hear me. But no matter how low he turned down the volume, I was sure I could hear the happy voice crooning, "There's a rainbow 'round my shoulder."

On the day of exams, I felt as though I'd been through a war. My eyes were bloodshot and my back ached from sitting up all night. I tried to remember the location and name of every organ, bone and artery, but I couldn't do it. "No one is capable of remembering and recalling all this information," I thought.

By the time the anatomy exam was placed before me, my aching eyes could barely focus. I had to read slowly, underlining every word with my finger. Then I began to hear it. "I must be going mad," I thought. I put my fingers in my ears. It did not go away. That damn song. Somehow Al Jolson had followed me into the exam room. I could hear him in that familiar faraway voice, happily singing: "There's a rainbow 'round my shoulder."

"This is all Eddie's fault," I thought. I wanted to kill him. But the music did not stop. I was sure any moment I would become hysterical. But someone else did instead.

Suddenly an ear-splitting scream echoed against the bare plaster walls. Eric. He covered his face with his hands, but I recognized his perfectly arranged blond hair immediately. Maybe it was the amphetamines. Maybe it was the compulsion to be the best. I sat stunned, silent, frightened as he was led quickly from the room. For an instant, I looked up and caught Simon's eyes. We had never expected him to break. But there was no time to mull over what had happened. The exam was strictly timed. The large clock on the back wall warned me that nothing and no one could distract me now.

Simon was waiting for me as I walked, exhausted, frazzled and drained, from the room. We didn't need any words. We had become friends months ago when he had decided it was time to become a doctor and stop being a clown.

"How did you do, Dorothy?"

"It if weren't for that damn music, I would have done okay," I said, snickering.

"What?" Simon tilted his head to one side. "Are you all right?"

"I will be. I will be. As soon as I get home."

"How did *you* do?" I asked. Simon really had buckled down since midterms, but we both knew he had to do very well just to stay in school.

"I worked hard. I damn near studied my brains out. I think I passed, but that's about all I can say."

I smiled weakly. Neither of us said a word about Eric. We were too tired and too worried.

That evening I curled up beside Eddie on the old familiar couch. As we sat side by side, I released an enormous sigh. This was the first night in ten months that there would be no barriers between us—no anatomy, no physiology or biochemistry and no earphones. Just the two of us. But Eddie was still on automatic. He slung his arm around my shoulders and put on his headset. I was too weary to object. I just began to cry. Midway through the song, Eddie turned and saw me, with my bloodshot eyes, crying silently. He took off the earphones.

"This is our first night together without the books. How can you do this?" I cried.

"Dorothy, I forgot. I honestly forgot."

Then Eddie held me in his arms, and I cried against his chest. When he held me close, I felt the tension ease. I had made it through the cadaver dissection and the exams, and I had learned a great deal not only about medicine but also about the people who chose to study it. Now it was time for us.

As the light wove spidery webs across the bedroom wall, Eddie and I made love. It was a night I hoped would never end. When we lay silently, side by side in the darkness, my mind wandered back to Creston Avenue—to the little boy who collected monster posters and pictures of presidents. His love for me had never faltered—not for a minute. He had been with me all this time, and I knew, as my hand reached out and grasped his, that we would be together for whatever would come next.

When I went to look up my grades, I was pleased to see that Fern, Simon and I had all passed. No one was sure if Eric would have a second chance. Richard had done well in all his finals, but his name was not to be among those in the medical school program next year. The Slasher had decided to drop medicine and study for his Ph.D. in biochemistry instead. Perhaps he would become a professor. "As long as he doesn't decide to become a surgeon!" Fern said, laughing, as we walked across campus to congratulate Simon.

He was sitting on the lawn with a teenage boy he introduced as his brother Jacob. Simon had gotten the highest grades in the class in anatomy, physiology and biochemistry. For a few minutes, we reminisced about how nervous and how afraid of the dissection we had been the first day.

"We're old pros now," Fern said with a smile.

"No bad dreams," I added. That whole term my nights had been strangely dreamless.

Simon gave me a warm hug before he wandered off with Jacob. Fern and I walked toward the cafeteria together.

"I think we're going to have a lot in common, Dorothy," she whispered as she squeezed my hand.

It is two weeks after the anatomy final. I am lost in a dark and hazy dream. I am in a car with Fern, Simon, Eric and Richard, and we are moving. We are all straining to see. There is a yellow line down the middle of the gray highway. The night is smoky black, but we can see something. Someone is calling—waving us down. We move closer, straining forward to look through the rain-soaked windshield. The car begins to slow down. We are approaching something familiar. A gnarled fist is outlined against the opaque sky. A woman, her silver hair blowing wildly around her face, is beckoning us closer. I know I have seen her somewhere before. Her mouth is contorted in a frozen, silent scream. She stares at me through vacant eyes. Her skin is crisscrossed with red slashes. Her organs spill grotesquely in a pile on the pavement. It is the cadaver.

"I felt *everything!*" she screams.

I bolt up in bed, sweating and shaking. The early morning sun filters in through the blinds. I know that anatomy is over, but it will be a long time until I can distance myself from what I have seen. Once more I repeat Simon's words: "There are no ghosts in the anatomy lab." He was right. The ghosts were not in the lab. They were here, inside my head, waiting until I was ready to see them.

9

Initiation

Anatomy class was followed by two years of studying, memorizing, taking notes and writing papers. I knew my courses in neurophysiology, epidemiology and microbiology were essential, but I was anxious to actually touch a real patient.

By the end of my second year of medical school, Evie was five years old. She had been placed in a program for gifted children and would be entering first grade in a nearby school in the fall. After long, weary days in class, I looked forward to that special moment when I could hold my daughter in my arms, cover her face with kisses and listen to her read aloud in either English or Hebrew. Time was moving so quickly that now every moment I shared with Evie was precious. Eddie continued to pick me up after school so that we could all be together that much sooner.

Some days I was surprised to find Evie sitting silently on Eddie's lap, absorbed in her reading. Other days she'd be running in little circles, her corkscrew curls flying around her face like a platinum halo, her singsong voice bringing life to the dark, silent hallways.

For two years, Evie was everyone's "little darling." Even the most serious student found time to stop and touch her hair, to see what she was reading or just to smile. She was a delicious child, and some evenings after I had tucked her into bed and kissed her good night, I would find myself tiptoeing back into her room just to look at her or kiss her one more time. During those early years, I collected all of Evie's drawings, and I tape-recorded her as she sang her rhyming songs and recited the Pledge of Allegiance. I took endless photographs of her dressed for school, climbing into bed, or smiling, naked and innocent, in the bathtub. Every "first" was recorded on tape or on film. I was determined not to miss a word, a step, a second of her growing up. My favorite possession became a poem she presented to me toward the end of my second year of medical school:

> *I love to be with my mommy*
> *Even shopping with her is fun.*
> *When I look at my mother's smile,*
> *It's as big as the sun!*

Slowly, my anxieties about being away from home began to lessen. Evie certainly seemed to love me. Although my family life was settling into a comfortable routine with both Eddie and Evie finding delightful ways to fill the time until I came home, I feared all that would change as soon as I began working in the hospital for my clerkship. For the most part, the class work was over, but the real challenge was just beginning. During the third year of medical school I would be examining patients and spending my days (and nights) in the hospital.

The summer of 1976 became a time of transformation and change. I was slowly, tentatively testing the waters, seeing how it really felt to act like, talk like and *be* a real doctor. The transformation did not come naturally. At the end of the term, Eddie and I drove to King's Plaza, a large shopping center in Brooklyn. We were going to buy the two white "doctor's jackets" and the name tag that were required when I began clerking in the fall. Although the jackets came only in men's sizes, we finally found a style that fit me well. Eddie joked that it was lucky I was tall; otherwise, we'd have to spend even more money on alterations. But for me, it seemed that the jackets would never quite "fit," probably because I couldn't imagine ever being ready to wear them.

My feelings intensified when it came time to choose a name tag. As Eddie mulled over the colors, I began to experience a disturbing confusion. I wasn't really a doctor, yet I would be working with patients, treating illnesses, spending all my time with the hospital staff. In preparation for this clerkship, my professors had stressed the importance of professional confidence. They had made a point of saying that for some of us, "Doctor" would be a title we would have to grow into. They were right. My "growing pains" began as I stood staring at the blank name tags.

"Eddie," I said, "I don't know what to write. If the tag reads, 'Dorothy Greenbaum, M.D.,' it will be a lie. If I just write 'Dorothy Greenbaum,' it certainly won't inspire confidence. I'm just not sure."

While I paced back and forth, Eddie suggested we concentrate on choosing colors. We agreed that a serious-looking black tag with white letters would be best. And then Eddie helped me decide: my name tag would read, "Dr. Dorothy Greenbaum."

All that summer the two jackets hung in my closet. Occasionally, as I folded laundry, brushed my hair or underlined a phrase in my textbooks, I'd look up and catch a glimpse of white. Then I would remember. Some afternoons I'd find myself standing in front of the open closet looking at the jackets with the same longing and expectation I had felt so many years ago when I had stared at the raspberry bridesmaid's dress in my room on Creston Avenue. Deep down I knew it was only a matter of time, yet I wondered, as I touched the cool white sleeves and the neatly pressed jacket lapels, when I would begin to *feel* like a doctor.

I examined Eddie and Evie every night. I searched for their pulses, I listened to their heartbeats, I looked into their eyes and ears. The gleaming new instruments I had recently purchased felt awkward and heavy in my hands. When I took Eddie's medical history, something we were told to practice as often as possible, I broke into nervous laughter.

"What's so funny?" Eddie asked, a look of annoyance spreading across his face.

"Eddie," I remember saying, "no one will ever believe me. It's like playing a game. It just doesn't feel natural."

"Get a grip on yourself," Eddie cautioned. "There's nothing funny about this."

I knew he was right, but as he talked, my mind wandered back to the tiny backyard behind his mother's house, the one we had played in as children. When I closed my eyes I could still see the red oilcloth his mother had kept on the outdoor table. Twenty years earlier Eddie and I had played "Doctor," and he had been the patient. It seemed we were doing it all over again, but now, as I held the ophthalmoscope in my shaking hand, it hit me—this time we were playing for real.

Sensing my growing insecurity and my need for "new patients," Eddie suggested I begin my official debut as "Dr. Greenbaum" at the annual family barbecue.

"Come on, Dorothy," he urged, "my folks will get a kick out of it!"

I looked down at my brand-new black doctor's bag and reluctantly admitted that it was time to carry it past the front door.

Everyone I loved would be at the Greenbaum family picnic, both sets of parents and grandparents, Eddie's brother, Al, Al's wife, Helene, and their two daughters, Debbie and Rae. This

time, as in all the times past, the girls would play with Evie while
the rest of us crammed onto the tiny terrace, but unlike all those
other times, this year I wouldn't be there at all. A stranger, someone wearing a white jacket and carrying a black bag filled with
shiny new instruments, someone named "Dr. Greenbaum" would
be taking my place.

I half expected the family to laugh when Eddie led me cere-
moniously into his parents' bedroom and told each member of the
family that he or she would take turns in the "doctor's office."

While Eddie closed the blinds to ensure privacy, I sat obediently
on Thelma and Harry's bed and stared down at the familiar patch-
work quilt. The room was hushed, and the sun seeped in between
tiny cracks in the blinds. I rubbed my hands along the smooth
grain of my black bag and checked my instruments, hoping no one
would comment about how nervous I was or how awkwardly I
handled the blood-pressure cuff, the stethoscope and the tongue
depressors. When I sat up straight, I caught my reflection in the
oak-framed mirror. I seemed unfamiliar, an impostor in a white
jacket.

"Am I believable?" I asked myself as I squinted at the image
shining back at me.

One by one, my "patients" walked slowly, tentatively, into the
bedroom. My mother-in-law was first. She fidgeted and made
small talk while I placed the stethoscope on her chest. I was so
involved with what I was doing, so anxious about locating her
heartbeat, that I never looked up. If I had I would have seen the
questioning, concerned look in her eyes. As I struggled to adjust
the blood-pressure cuff, she began to ask me questions.

"Dorothy, I have this little lump here," she said as she pointed
to a small bump near her shoulder. "What do you think?"

I was stunned. "Mom," I felt like saying, "how should I know?
I'm only a second year med student." But when I looked up at her
worried, nervous face, I knew that she wasn't asking her daughter-

in-law, she was no longer talking to the woman she had known as a little girl. She was asking "the doctor." I ran my fingers across the bump. "It's just fatty tissue," I assured her. The look of relief in her eyes surprised me. Didn't she know this was all a game, that I was still little Dorothy from Creston Avenue?

Eddie's father wanted to know about a persistent itch. Eddie's grandmother pulled a container of pills from her purse and asked me if I thought she should continue taking them. Al wanted to know if his blood pressure was normal. Helene wanted to make sure the girls' eyes and ears were healthy. No one seemed to notice how often I dropped the stethoscope or how long it took me to find a pulse. They just wanted me to listen and to reassure them.

By the time I left my in-laws' bedroom, the instruments began to feel more comfortable in my hands. I was less self-conscious about my skills and more aware of what my "patients" expected of me. I still felt like Dorothy, but I knew by my family's reaction that something was very different.

"She's a regular Albert Schweitzer!" my father-in-law said, beaming, when I finally emerged from the darkened bedroom. As the smoky scent of barbecued chicken drifted in from the terrace, the rest of the family smiled and nodded in agreement.

"You were terrific," Eddie said, placing a paper plate piled high with chicken, potato salad and corn in my shaking hands. Eddie was the only one there who knew how insecure I had been. We smiled at each other between mouthfuls. My first "clinic" had been a success. From then on, everywhere I went I traveled with my black doctor's bag. Little by little I began to accept it as part of my identity, part of the baggage I would be carrying with me for the rest of my life.

There were only a few lazy days of summer to rest before clerkship began, and I spent those days with Evie. Together we took walks, went shopping, read childrens' books and peered at slides under a microscope. Evie was probably the only little girl in our neighborhood who could spell and pronounce polymorphonuclear leukocyte, and thanks to her persistence and curiosity, she had a pretty basic understanding of how these white blood cells actually functioned.

More and more, studying medicine became a secure and welcomed refuge. I believed that when I knew enough, everything would make sense. I was sure that medicine was going to give me the orderly world I longed for, the universe where everything fit like so many pieces of a puzzle, where every mystery had a solution.

It was on a muggy, nondescript summer evening when Evie was fast asleep and Eddie and I were huddled over our late-night coffee, planning our budget for the fall, hoping our loans would be approved, that I was thrown headlong into the chaos and confusion of an emergency—forced into being a doctor long before I was ready.

All the neighbors knew I was a medical student. In the small community that was our apartment building, my mother, who lived downstairs, took every opportunity to point to me and boast with maternal pride, "That's my daughter, Dorothy—almost a doctor!" For the neighbors, the word *almost* was never questioned, it became an unimportant disclaimer. And I believe that when Mrs. Goldstein began shouting in the hallway it was because she had not only listened to my mother—she had believed her.

It began as a low, moaning wail and quickly turned into a gut-wrenching scream: "Help me! Help my Ben!" The howling ripped through our calm evening. Eddie jumped up and ran to the door. I hesitated for a second, gripped by an awful terror.

Mrs. Goldstein was kneeling in the corridor, her bare knees scraping against the worn linoleum. She was still wearing the flowered dress I had seen her in that afternoon. Her apron was knotted around her waist. Her cries could be heard up and down the halls. A wave of neighbors began to flow from opened doors.

Someone said something about a doctor, and in an instant I was clutching my black bag and moving automatically through the sea of faces. They dutifully parted as I approached.

The door of the Goldsteins' apartment was flung open. The room smelled of soup and pot roast. Photographs of grandchildren were lined up in neat rows on the old-fashioned Victorian furniture. Everything seemed so neat—so orderly. Except for Mr. Goldstein. Ben lay stretched out on the faded carpet. His face was gray, beads of sweat sprouting like tiny translucent bubbles along his forehead. His voice, barely audible, seeped out between gasps. He was begging for air. Someone was trying to force a tablespoon of Pepto-Bismol down his throat. Another neighbor was tugging at his shirt sleeve, hoping to drag him to an open window. Everything seemed to be happening in silent slow motion.

Eddie freed Ben from the well-meaning neighbors and cleared an area. I approached the old man. "My God, he's dying," I thought as my eyes roamed about the room, picking up random details, hoping to see a doctor, someone who could help.

A voice from the hallway floated through the silence: "Thank God she's a doctor!" I looked down at my black bag and kneeled before the choking man. I checked his airways, took his blood pressure and listened to his heart. He was in shock.

"What drugs has he been taking?" I asked. Mrs. Goldstein pressed some loose pills into my hand. Since there were no prescription bottles, there was no way to identify the medication. When I continued to question her, Mrs. Goldstein tugged at her apron and told me their doctor's name. Within minutes, Eddie had the doctor on the phone. I took the receiver from his hand and gave the doctor the information on Ben's vital signs. The voice on the other end of the phone was calm and self-assured. Either Ben was having an adverse reaction to a new medication, the doctor said, or he was having a coronary. The voice told me to call an ambulance. Between the time I dialed the ambulance and it arrived

at the building, I prayed Ben would not stop breathing. I wasn't
sure I could resuscitate him if he did.

Once the old man was lifted from the living room floor onto the
emergency stretcher and taken to the ambulance, the sounds returned. Neighbors pumped my hand. They slapped me on the
back. A deafening roar of voices made me want to clap my hands
over my ears.

It was well past midnight when Eddie and I returned to the
kitchen. Our coffee cups were right where we had left them, but
nothing was the same. I broke down in tears.

"Eddie, that was the scariest thing that ever happened to me. I
felt completely useless. That man could have died right then and
there!"

Eddie looked stunned. "You're wrong," he said. "You calmed
everyone. You took over like a pro."

Eddie's words floated past me like flecks of dust. I was convinced I could have done something more.

The next day Mrs. Goldstein called to tell me that her husband
had indeed had a coronary and that he was responding well to
treatment. She thanked me for saving his life. I couldn't tell her
that I felt like an impostor.

The memory of that emergency was still fresh in my mind when
my clerkship, two years of working with patients on the wards
while under daily supervision, began. Like all the other students I
had been randomly assigned to a hospital and was told to report to
a local facility that primarily served an elderly Jewish population. I
was hopeful that under the guidance of my preceptors, real doctors
who had real answers, I would no longer feel unsure. I was ready to
stop playing doctor and begin saving lives.

My first patient was a ninety-four-year-old man with a history of
strokes, heart disease and severe organic brain syndrome. He had
been sent to the hospital from a nursing home because of his con-

tinued dehydration. He was toothless and horribly emaciated, his skin hung in translucent, wrinkled folds from his thin skeleton. A few strands of silver hair clung to the sides of his skull-like head. When I bent over and introduced myself, he merely wheezed, "Ah yee," as if he hadn't heard me at all. A friendly intern took me aside and told me to rap on the old man's forehead with my knuckles and scream, "Good morning, Mr. Blum!" to get him to respond. Mr. Blum would then respond briefly before falling asleep, stopping intermittently to vomit and/or aspirate.

Although it was disheartening to find that my first patient could not appreciate my well-rehearsed bedside manner, I was shocked when I discovered that I could barely keep from fainting during his examination. Mr. Blum was covered with ulcerous, oozing bedsores. When I saw them for the first time, I was overcome with nausea. A large one on his sacrum needed to be debrided. The procedure was one I had read about. It meant that the thick scab had to be surgically removed. But my readings had not prepared me for the actual sight of the opaque green pus that oozed from the wound. Along the fissures in the scab, not too far beneath the surface, I could see the glistening white bone with a thin film of muscle attached to it. The intern, obviously unmoved by the sight, suggested that I begin the debriding procedure. Grasping the metal handrail beside the bed to steady myself, I slowly shook my head and stumbled into the nearest bathroom.

I didn't eat the lunch Fern ordered for me in the hospital cafeteria. I hadn't seen her since anatomy class, and she was excited to tell me that she had gotten married over the summer. While she chatted happily about her wedding and her new apartment, visions of Mr. Blum and his awful bedsores flashed through my mind.

"Dorothy, where are you?" she asked as I stared down at my untouched tuna fish sandwich. Again the feelings of being a fake became overpowering. I began to talk in a flood of words. I told Fern about poor Mr. Goldstein and how I had only gone through the motions, and how his wife had thanked me for saving her husband's life.

"But it wasn't true," I said sadly as I shook my head.

Fern listened intently.

"You did everything we have been told to do. You checked his airways, his pulse and his heartbeat. You even asked to see his medication. That was the right procedure." Fern's words became a tiny ray of light illuminating my dim view of what had happened. Somehow her words began to sink in. I was beginning to feel better. I pushed the memories of Mr. Blum's bedsores out of my mind. I was ready to face my next patient. I was going to pull myself together. This time I was going to be a real doctor.

That afternoon I met "the Kid" for the first time. Our preceptor, the chief of medicine himself, was taking us on rounds. Dr. Feldman was a brilliant man who loved to teach. We were all looking forward to meeting him. His specialty was peripheral vascular diseases, so he made a point of presenting the Kid to us. We were a small group of third-year med students, and for most of us, this was our first exposure to such a young patient.

The boy's last name was long, Russian and difficult to pronounce, so we came to affectionately call him "the Kid." It was a nickname he responded to. He spoke little English but seemed to have some basic understanding of what we said, and he could make his objections known. At nineteen, he was the youngest patient on the floor, but at first glance, he did not seem to be terribly sick. He had developed gangrenous ulcers—some infected—on his fingers and toes. Since there was no known cause for his condition, he was in the process of being "worked up."

Dr. Feldman led us into the boy's room. The Kid sat on the bed looking thin and frail. His skin was very white, and his hair equally black. I noticed how some dark curls circled his face in a haphazard manner. He had no beard yet, and that, coupled with the fact that he weighed only 115 pounds for his five-foot seven-inch frame, made him look even younger than his nineteen years.

The Kid didn't seem to belong here in this white hospital world. In fact, as I approached his bedside, I began to suspect that he didn't belong to this world at all. His deathly pallor and his resemblance to every picture I'd ever seen of Jesus made him seem otherworldly. I shivered as I stared at his earnest face.

The boy surveyed our little group with a look of apprehension. As Dr. Feldman touched his bandaged fingers, the Kid's fear was replaced by arrogance. He insisted upon removing his bandages unaided. We stood silently as he unveiled the ulcers. I was thankful that I had seen Mr. Blum's bedsores that morning, because by comparison, the Kid's wounds were not nearly so horrible. His fingers were completely consumed by the gangrene, and most of the nails had sunken in or completely fallen off. Dr. Feldman began his demonstration. He squeezed the radial artery of the Kid's hand. Instead of filling with blood, the hand became cold, white, limp. One by one, Dr. Feldman called us up to feel the pale, lifeless limb.

I felt a blackness moving in slowly from the corners of the room. A distant ringing in my ears became louder as Fern moved toward me. Sensing something was wrong, she grasped my hand and whispered, "Think of Evie."

For an instant I was transported from the room. I saw my daughter, her long hair neatly braided and clipped with red barrettes, standing just as I had left her that morning at school. She was wearing the little red-checked dress, the white anklets and the patent-leather Mary Janes. I recalled the mixture of sadness and pride I had felt as I handed her her lunch bag and watched as she walked off to the auditorium. But I didn't leave just then. I stood and I waited. I wanted to make sure, when she turned to check, that I was still there, smiling, waving, just as my grandmother had done for me so many years before.

The vision of Evie sustained me as I walked forward and pressed the Kid's cold hand in mine. Still, I could not look into his eyes.

He was just a child, and even though I wore a white jacket and stethoscope, I was still very much a mother.

As the weeks passed, I became more at ease in the hospital environment. I learned to smile when poor Mr. Blum wheezed, "Ah yee," as I knocked on his forehead each morning. Fern and I became partners; we shared patients, made our rounds of the wards together, and compared histories and physicals. Our attending physician at that time was Dr. Berliner, and almost instantly he became an ominous figure to me. What I found most upsetting about him was the way he led students into giving the wrong answer. Then he pounced on them, grinning from ear to ear, for falling into his trap. I was determined to escape his elaborate tricks. When it was my turn to present material, I memorized everything I could about my patient and his disease. The closest I ever got to an actual compliment was when Berliner turned to a resident and thanked him for briefing me on a case. When the resident explained that I had done all the work myself, Berliner merely shot me a glance and went on to the next topic.

Just before a holiday weekend we were all looking forward to, Berliner reviewed some elements of the Kid's case with us. Some test results had come back, and at last there was a positive finding. They had found some cryofibrinogens, crystallized proteins, in his blood. The boy's condition was getting worse with every passing day. His family became a constant presence in the hospital. They paced the halls, chattered away in Russian, drank endless cups of coffee and rubbed the Kid's arms and legs.

That morning Berliner told us the Kid's stomach contained several small ulcers. No one could explain what had caused them. Berliner, obviously as frustrated as everyone else involved with the case, looked at me and snapped, "Greenbaum, for Monday, review all the literature of the past five years on cryofibrinogenemia and report back to us."

Just before I left that night, I stopped by the boy's room. Language prevented us from saying more than hello and smiling at each other. Tonight he looked decidedly worse, having lost another seven or eight pounds. The translucence of his skin reminded me of watery skim milk. His black eyes seemed less intense, more deep-set and resigned. I gripped my stethoscope as I stared at his fragile body. What the hell was wrong with him?

I tried not to bring my work home, but the Kid was different. I was obsessed with finding an answer. Our plans for a family weekend were canceled by Berliner's request that I review all the literature on what he suspected was the Kid's disease. My parents baby-sat for Evie. Eddie and I drove to the library together. Eddie was always anxious to spend time in the library. He was still intent upon researching more medical findings concerning the Kennedy assassination. That afternoon I went straight to the computer and requested a search on cryofibrinogenemia. The computer's answer was terse and disheartening: "Word not in my dictionary." I was angry. I wondered if Berliner was sending me on a wild goose chase.

After spending nearly the entire afternoon hunting, Eddie and I managed to find eight articles written in English (there were five in Rumanian). The information was fascinating, but none of the syndromes fit the Kid well enough to make a diagnosis.

On Monday, Berliner told me he was too busy to hear my report. Tuesday it was the same story. Finally on Wednesday, I presented the material I had worked so hard to find. Berliner said I had done a good job, but he rejected all the diagnoses, including the one I favored: Familial Mediterranean Fever. Berliner then explained that the most recent tests on the Kid had come back yesterday. He no longer had cryofibrinogens in his blood. There was absolutely nothing about this boy we could count on.

None of the students was actually assigned to the Kid's case, but it was impossible not to be curious, involved and concerned. Somehow, in between write-ups, presentations and rounds, everyone managed to find a few minutes to stop off and see him or to ask someone on his team how he was doing.

That Friday afternoon, the Kid developed seizures and was put on anticonvulsants. After his review of the case, the intern, who would be off for the weekend, looked at the doctor who was covering for him and said, "Don't let that child die." No one had dared say it aloud before, but we were all thinking it.

The Kid was still alive on Monday. He continued to lose weight, and his condition changed from hour to hour. His family maintained their vigil in the hospital corridors. His three brothers were healthy-looking young men, very Americanized in their dress and manner, but the mother looked like a typical Russian peasant woman. She spoke neither English nor Yiddish, and she and the boy conversed in Russian. The child's father was in Israel with her other children. A brother explained that they were all going to join them there as soon as the Kid was well enough to travel.

As the days passed, the Kid's condition continued to deteriorate. He was down to ninety pounds. His hair fell into the hollows of his cheeks and neck. He was very quiet, his arrogance and fear were gone. There was nothing left now but a quiet resolve. His body had been defeated, but his spirit seemed above it all. I stared at him in the silence of his gray hospital room. I longed to hold him, to help him, to find the answers that would make a difference.

On Tuesday, when I was working in the ICU, the Kid went into cardiac arrest. We were all monitoring him closely. There were too many people around his bed, but no one could bear to leave. Finally, he seemed to stabilize, and the crowd dispersed. Only the resident, the intern and I remained. We were watching him closely when it happened. Very quietly, without any drama, the Kid stopped breathing. Immediately, the code was called and we worked on him for twenty minutes before we had a normal EKG and spontaneous breathing. During that time I don't remember hearing a word until someone shouted, "I have a pulse!" All that time I had been "bagging" him, pushing air into his lungs with a special apparatus called an ambu bag, and I was awed by the combination of fear and responsibility I felt. I was determined that the Kid would not die because of insufficient oxygen.

During the attempt to resuscitate him, blood spilled from his mouth, down his neck and onto the sheets. By the time we had a satisfactory response, some of it had already dried. His eyes were covered with white cotton pads.

The intern and resident continued to stand vigil by his bed. Miraculously, the Kid's vital signs were stable. He was still unconscious and looked close to death, but not one of us said it aloud.

Later, when I went to lunch with Fern, I felt the wonder of pulling the Kid out of death into life. I was in love with my work. I had finally touched that feeling, that awesome power of medicine. For the first time I felt authentic. I had truly helped to save a life.

After lunch, I went back up to the ICU and passed the boy's mother pacing slowly, deliberately, in the waiting area. Something drew me back to the small gray room. I was numbed by what I saw. The stained white curtain was drawn around his bed. Knowing that the closed curtain was a sign of death, I didn't need to ask what had happened, yet I felt compelled to know. The intern and resident told me that the boy had arrested again. Blood had trickled out of every orifice of his tormented body. It was hopeless. He had died. Now they were cleaning him up before they told the family.

I left the room and hurried past the mother, averting my eyes. I didn't want to be the one to tell her.

There was a strange quiet on the wards that afternoon. Word of the Kid's death had spread like wildfire. Various attempts were made in Russian and Hebrew to appeal to the mother to allow an autopsy, but she refused. None of us ever knew what had ravaged his innocent body. As I sat staring at the cold tiles of the hospital corridor, I thought of the lines from Blake: "What immortal hand or eye/could frame thy fearful symmetry?"

That evening I carried the Kid's suffering home. I saw his tortured face as I pressed my own child to my breast.

After several weeks, my rotation in internal medicine came to an end. I had become involved with several of my patients, including old Mr. Blum, who continued to wheeze "Ah yee" when I knocked on his forehead each morning. I had learned so much in the past weeks, and they were lessons I would never forget.

Each one of those first patients has stayed with me. Each one was like the mark of a hammer on thin metal. I was neither better nor worse after the experience, just different—indelibly changed.

10

County Hospital

A faint shadow followed me as I made my way across the pavement. I walked quickly through the iron gates of the Gothic building. No one stopped me or asked for identification. This huge, ten-story place with its dirt, scarred concrete, underground tunnels and endless corridors was to be my classroom for the next few months. It was here that I was going to learn how to tie a suture, make an incision, draw blood and deliver a baby.

Everyone knew about County Hospital—about the wards crammed with ten, twelve, even sixteen beds, the orange hallways, the bare light bulbs, the peeling ceilings. And everyone knew about the rapist who had been haunting the dark hallways for weeks. So far, twelve women had been attacked: nurses, doctors, med students. According to reports, he was disguised as a doctor.

The rapist had not yet been apprehended when I told Eddie that the second rotation of my clerkship would take place in County Hospital. He was concerned. The hospital was located in a very dangerous area of the city.

"You're not in this alone," he had explained. "You have a re-sponsibility to me and to Evie. If you're not going to trade out of this clerkship, you'll have to wait for me to pick you up after work. I know that area, and no one walks alone to that subway station."

I thought of Eddie as I walked toward the door marked EN-TRANCE, and I remembered our compromise. On nights when I had to work late, he would park in the line with the gypsy cabs and we would drive home together.

County was just the way they said it would be. Patients propped up against walls, sitting on hard wooden chairs, writhing on tem-porary cots in the busy corridors. In the reception area, a giant water bug scurried across the dingy floor.

My first night in County Hospital would not end until nearly two A.M., and it was to be a night I would never forget. The intern I was assigned to work with was named Eliot. He was young, intense and polite. He was also a bit brusque, but here at County there wasn't much opportunity for chitchat, with the pa-tients overflowing into the hallways and barely enough time to get names, dates and symptoms. Eliot remarked that the motto here was, "Watch one, do one, teach one." I knew at once what he meant. After I had carefully observed a procedure once, I should be ready to perform it myself. I should then be prepared to help an-other student with the same procedure. What Eliot forgot to men-tion was that very often there was no time to "watch one" before I was expected to "do one." That's how I came to take my first blood sample.

The wards were nearly full when Eliot admitted Mr. Blackstone. He was fifty years old, a heavy smoker who had been coughing up significant amounts of blood. Eliot made a list of blood tests we would have to make, twelve in all.

"Isn't that a lot?" I asked as I calculated all the blood we would need to draw from Mr. Blackstone.

Eliot smirked. "We assume that the county lab will screw things up, so we take precautions by ordering every possible test. This way we save time—ours and the patient's." He winked when he explained, "That's what we interns call a 'Countygram.'"

I wasn't smiling. "Eliot, we'll need fifty-five ccs of blood. That's just short of two ounces." I knew from my previous rotation that five to ten ccs would constitute a normal blood test.

"That's right," Eliot said as he took a second look at my calculations. He gestured toward the patient's room. "Mr. Blackstone awaits you!"

Eliot turned on his heel and disappeared down the orange corridor. I was all alone. I had never taken blood before. I had never carefully observed the procedure, but it was fairly routine, and I assured myself that it shouldn't be too difficult—not after what I had been through on my last rotation.

The supply closet was crammed with small plastic syringes, bandages, gauze and catheters. I scrounged around until I found the fifty-cc syringe I would need. The barrel that was meant to hold the blood was enormous, six inches long and about one and one-half inches in diameter. I held it in my hand, and an image of another syringe, a tiny plastic one filled with colored pebbles, flashed through my mind—the one I had played with as a child, the one that had been in my doctor's kit. That was the only time I had "taken blood," and even though the experience was purely conceptual, I assured myself that the "concept" would now be basically the same.

The memory of the toy needle stayed with me as I walked toward Mr. Blackstone's room. "Thank God he can't read my mind," I mused. He was sitting nervously, draped in white, on the edge of his narrow bed. I smiled at my first real patient in County Hospital. He didn't smile back. But then he wasn't exactly in much of a mood for smiling.

Mr. Blackstone's upper arms were thick and muscular. As I tied the tourniquet, I was relieved to see that he had what the interns called "pipes," obvious veins. "With these veins, I can't miss," I thought to myself as I took the syringe from my pocket. I was sure the worst was over when Mr. Blackstone looked away, gazing upward at the cracked and peeling plaster, not noticing the size of the needle. "Lucky for me I've got a calm one," I thought as I stuck one of his large veins with the needle. I couldn't tell how deeply I had inserted the needle or how much pressure I was exerting. My stomach knotted and my jaw clenched. Mr. Blackstone let out a groan. I knew I'd hit oil when I pulled back the plunger and saw the dark red fluid filling the huge syringe. I had never quite reached this point with my childhood game, and I continued to hold steady as the red fluid went past the ten-cc mark. Now all I had to do was sit patiently and reassure my patient, until it went past the fifty-cc point. I fingered the test tubes in my pocket. Soon the blood would be safely sealed in these glass containers and on its way to the lab.

As I kept my eye on the needle, I observed the blood inching slowly upward. It seemed that this was taking a very long time. Mr. Blackstone remained the perfect patient, sitting quietly, hardly breathing, and continuing to look away. Everything was very calm. Drop by drop, the blood moved steadily from the vein into the huge syringe. When the barrel was filled to the fifty-cc point, I was feeling fairly smug. I kept right on drawing blood, certain that this syringe, like the plastic one with the colored pebbles, would have a stopper at the end of the barrel. I envisioned myself untying the tourniquet, neatly blotting Mr. Blackstone's arm with a cotton swab and thanking him for his cooperation. But no such moment ever came to pass.

Just when I was sure I had approximately fifty-five ccs of blood, I pulled back, fully expecting to meet some resistance, but there was no stopper. The plunger came off in my hand. The barrel, which had been full, was now empty. In a flash, blood was everywhere. It poured onto the floor, the sheets and Mr. Blackstone.

His eyes opened wide, and for the first time he looked down at his arm.

"Help! She's killing me!" he shrieked as he waved his blood-soaked hands in the air.

Automatically, without thinking, I tried to ram the plunger back into the barrel and the needle back into Mr. Blackstone's vein. But he was no longer calm. We began to struggle across the narrow bed, me aiming my syringe, him shrieking and waving his bloody hands.

Eliot arrived, breathless and angry. He stopped at the door for an instant before he rushed forward and deftly removed the tourniquet from Mr. Blackstone's bruised arm. I continued my attempts to catch the blood and scoop it up into the test tubes.

"What the hell did you do? Why did you pull the plunger out?" Eliot whispered to me while Mr. Blackstone continued to scream incoherently.

Now Mr. Blackstone was holding himself and moaning, "Oh, my God. Oh, my God," as he stared incredulously at his blood-stained pillow and his arms dripping with red. Small puddles of his blood had begun to accumulate between the cracks in the linoleum.

He pointed at me acccusingly as he rubbed his arm. "She's a murderer—a butcher!"

I didn't know what to tell Eliot. How could I explain about my doctor's kit? But he no longer seemed interested. He was busy comforting Mr. Blackstone and explaining that I had just given him a test to see how well he would "react to bleeding." Mr. Blackstone wasn't buying it, so Eliot simply stroked his brow and called for an orderly to change the sheets and the patient's gown. Then he motioned for me to meet him in the corridor.

"You'll have to go back in there and take that blood again."

"He'll never let me near him! Not after what I just did."

I pleaded with Eliot. He was exhausted, impatient and disgusted after so many hours on call.

"All right, I'll do it. If I send you back in there, the poor guy will wind up needing a transfusion!" Eliot said, as he reached into his pocket. "Here, take this urine sample up to the lab. It'll save me the trip." He pushed a small vial into my sweating hand. "And then you might as well go home. You've done enough damage for one night."

I looked down at my blood-spattered shoes. I'd have just enough time to wash up before I was to meet Eddie. How could I ever explain this to him?

I began to make my way wearily up to the lab. No sense waiting for an elevator, they were too slow. Besides, I didn't think I could look a nurse, orderly or patient in the face. I was completely disgusted with myself.

The lab was two flights up. The staircase was dark, the corridor dimly lit. I nervously felt my pocket. It was empty. I had forgotten the eighteen-gauge needle, the one the admitting nurse had told me always to carry for "self-defense."

"Until this rapist is caught, be careful," she had warned me as she placed the long needle in my hand. I must have left it in the supply room, or maybe it fell out of my pocket during my struggle with Mr. Blackstone.

From the darkened corridor, I could see the yellow lights glimmering through the opaque glass window of the lab door. Only a few yards away, I saw another light, a small, glowing, orange speck. I walked slowly forward, straining to make out what I was seeing. The orange speck flickered and moved. It was about six and a half feet off the ground. I sniffed the air. Smoke. The orange light was a cigarette, and the smoker was standing alone in the dark. He was over six feet tall. The darkness and the smoke moved closer, swirling around me like a long-forgotten dream. And then I remembered. I was back on Creston Avenue, in the building with the yellowed plaster walls and the spiral oak staircase.

I was on my way to see my grandmother when I felt the hands. They grabbed me around my waist. The voices burned in my ears. They held me over the long stairs and laughed. "Look down, girlie," the voices rasped, "this is the last thing you'll ever see." There were three of them, teenage boys. I tried to scream, but a hand clamped against my open mouth. I struggled against a rough sweater as I was pulled, squirming and fighting, to the edge of the stairs. I bit down against the hand and held tight, tasting the salty blood as it ran down my lips. I heard the boys shout and scream, but I didn't let go. A voice yelled, "Forget it. Let's get out of here." The blood was on my teeth, in my mouth. Four hands had to pry the flesh from my jaws. I stumbled through the darkness into the familiar warmth of my grandmother's apartment. Later that night, I remember poking my head out of my room. I saw my mother showing my panties to a policeman. She was asking him if I had been molested. He shook his head and said no, but he told her I had bitten so hard that the boy had to be hospitalized.

Until this moment, the memory had been lost to me. Now it was real again. Feeling the same terror I had felt as a little girl, I approached the flickering orange light. "No one is going to hurt me," I thought as I walked quickly into the lab. There was no lock on the door. I had no defense. I heard feet shuffle in the corridor. I emptied the vials of urine and went through the initial tests. I worked silently, automatically, until I had finished.

When I left the lab, the burning smell was gone—so was the orange light. I walked slowly and deliberately back downstairs. I didn't begin to shake until I slid into the car beside Eddie. Then I couldn't stop.

As I talked and cried, Eddie drove cautiously through the deserted city. The shops were closed and boarded up. Metal gates sealed windows from midnight dangers. This was our own private world. The city was silent, work was over. Eddie pulled up in front of an all-night bagel bakery. I waited, feeling myself unwind, feeling the joy and warmth of being alone with my husband.

When Eddie returned, the smell of the fresh bagels permeated the air. I was safe. County Hospital was far, far away.

After several weeks, I began to call this time with Eddie—the drive home, the bagels, the cups of coffee and the long talks—"big time." The time I spent taking tests, listening to pulses, observing residents and interns was "little time." For the next few years my survival would depend upon the delicate balance between "big time" and "little time."

My first night at County Hospital proved more dramatic than the nights that followed. In the morning I attended a class in parasitology, then reported to Eliot and made rounds. I was learning more every day, and there were no more incidents like the one with Mr. Blackstone. I was determined to ask questions, to observe carefully and to ask for help if I needed it.

In parasitology, I watched films of pinworms, larvae and worm eggs. I tried to remain objective, yet it seemed that danger lurked everywhere—in the foods we ate, in unwashed and unsterile implements, even on our own hands. I shuddered when I recalled my grandmother tasting the raw pike as she prepared her special homemade gefilte fish. "It's amazing that she never got deathly ill," I thought.

By the middle of the term, I had stopped eating rare meat, and I looked askance at anything that had not been cooked under my careful supervision. Even Eddie was beginning to notice. Since we couldn't afford to eat out, restaurants posed no problem—until our special anniversary dinner with my friend Suzie and her husband, Jack. It had been a long time since I sat in Suzie's spotless kitchen and talked about marriage, babies and soap operas. I missed her, and I missed socializing. Eddie was reluctant to make new friends. He preferred our family and the friends we had always known. His attitude had become a source of friction between us over the years. But since I wasn't making too many new friends in County Hospital, I didn't have anything to complain about—yet.

Spending an evening with Suzie and Jack was a luxury we felt we needed. We went to a steak house in the old neighborhood. Suzie hugged me and told me how proud everyone was that I had made it into med school. "But you haven't changed a bit," she said as we caught up on old times, "still the same old Dorothy." Eddie grinned as I began to dip my silverware in my water glass. How could I be sure the implements had been properly washed? I looked at the butter—unwrapped. There could be thousands of worm eggs lurking beneath the smooth yellow surface. Suzie pretended not to notice as I held the coleslaw up to the light, trying to figure out just how long it had been unrefrigerated. As I glanced at the menu, I checked off every worm, every disease that I could contract from eating each particular dish. Eddie shot me a warning look. I forced myself to smile. I didn't warn my closest friends. "After all, ignorance is bliss," I thought as I wiped each tine of the fork with my napkin. Then I took a second look at the prices and decided that for this kind of money, I might as well relax and enjoy. I pushed the images of larvae and worms out of my mind long enough to toast my old friends and listen as they chatted happily about their new apartment.

Socializing became increasingly rare for Eddie and me. After I recovered from my temporary obsession with parasites, I decided that the evening with Suzie and Jack had passed all too quickly, and there was little chance we could afford another one soon. Maybe that's why I agreed to see *A Night With Al*. Mrs. Pearl at the Student Union had posted a notice about the play. It was Off Off Broadway and the tickets were free. Of course, no one was interested. *A Night With Al* was about Al Jolson. Of course, Eddie couldn't miss it, and I longed for an evening out, even if I had to spend it with "Al."

I haunted the ticket office for weeks, until Mrs. Pearl handed me the envelope. "Are these for your parents?" she asked.

"No, actually they're for my husband," I said.

"So, you married an older man?" Mrs. Pearl cackled as she made a little black check in one of her record books. "You two must be the only people in New York going to see this show," she mumbled. Mrs. Pearl wasn't too far off the mark.

Eddie pleaded with me to bring my tape recorder and to conceal it in my purse so no one would notice. But that hardly proved to be a problem. As we entered the dim theater, I observed a handful of people squirming restlessly in the dilapidated seats. "Probably relatives of the cast," I said with a laugh as Eddie eagerly made his way to the front row.

The stage was bare. The actors wore tuxedos and evening gowns. Old photographs of Al Jolson were flashed on a screen in the background. In the foreground, a young man wearing black-face knelt on one knee and crooned "Mammy." There were more songs and more slides. I was ready to leave at intermission, but Eddie wouldn't hear of it. Besides, there was still more room on the tape. I sat patiently until the tape clicked and the final curtain came down.

"That was awful," I complained as we left the theater.

Eddie laughed. "If I can put up with your parasites, you'll have to live with Al Jolson."

I smiled. Some compromises weren't that difficult to make.

Within a few weeks I had made a new friend. Her name was Krissy, and we met in my morning neuroanatomy class, which I had begun as soon as parasitology was over. Krissy and I seemed to have a great deal in common. She was in her thirties, had two children and had also been a teacher. It was almost too good to be true. I needed a friend, and Krissy seemed perfect. She introduced me to a group of older, more sophisticated students. Many were married, and some had children. Since the neuroanatomy course was so difficult, Krissy suggested we all meet at her apartment. She offered to borrow the slides we needed to study and to project them on her movie screen. This way we could all review together.

Spouses were invited. It was to be a night of studying and socializing. I was anxious to go, but I knew Eddie would be reluctant. He didn't like meeting new people. I pressured him. I dredged up *A Night With Al.* He objected. We argued but eventually he relented. I knew it would be a chore for him, but I hoped that somehow, something would click. Maybe he would like Krissy's husband, Ben.

I knew it wouldn't work the minute we arrived. Krissy and Ben lived in a fashionable apartment on Manhattan's Upper East Side. The decor was sparse but chic, everything carefully arranged. The effect was cool and sophisticated. The children were occupied with a full-time housekeeper. Ben was a successful lawyer. Krissy and I didn't have as much in common as I had thought.

I sat in the den with the other med students, taking notes as slides of the brain were flashed across the screen, but I was listening to the "spouses" in the other room. I heard voices and laughter. I didn't hear Eddie.

I could tell without looking that he was slumped in a seat in the corner, obviously bored and checking his watch. I spent the evening straining to hear, hoping that Eddie would loosen up and mingle.

As the last slide flashed across the screen, Krissy suggested that we all get together for a dutch dinner the next week. "Everyone bring a dish, and we'll eat and drink and get to know each other," she chirped.

I was determined that Eddie and I would be at that dinner, but I was careful not to mention it to him until we were safely out of Krissy's apartment. Again, it was a struggle. I begged, insisted, demanded. Eddie withdrew. We drove home in silence while I planned the chocolate cheesecake I was going to make. Eddie pretended not to hear when I gave him the date. I knew he would go, but I also knew he was going to give me a hard time about it.

*   *   *

That week I was assigned to the ICU, the intensive care unit. I was particularly concerned about one patient, a Mr. Pletsch, who had lapsed into a coma after surgery for obstructive jaundice. Mr. Pletsch was a vigorous-looking man in his mid-forties, a truck driver who hauled produce across the state and who had always worked long shifts. His chart listed two phone numbers in case of emergency. Before his surgery, the staff had called both residences.

It was an ordinary afternoon in the ICU. I was checking up on Mr. Pletsch when I spotted two women pacing back and forth. One sat with a teenage son, the other dabbed at her eyes. When I left the room, both women came running toward me.

"How is he?" they asked almost in unison.

"Who are you?" the woman with the child asked as she turned questioningly to the one who was now sobbing openly.

"I'm Mrs. Pletsch," she answered. "Who are you?"

"*I'm* Mrs. Pletsch!" she insisted, pointing to her son.

Within seconds the tranquillity of the ICU was destroyed as the two Mrs. Pletsches began screaming at each other. It seemed our "vigorous" patient had been, among other things, a bigamist.

The two wives shrieked, the nurses chuckled, and the doctors shook their heads. Both wives were escorted from the ICU, and Mr. Pletsch drifted deeper into his coma.

"That's one for the record books," Eliot said, laughing. It was the first time I had seen him laugh. But then I realized he had only been on for ten hours. He had twenty more to go before his shift was over.

That night Eddie helped me bake the chocolate cheesecake. It weighed over a pound, and it was so rich and sweet that we had to restrain ourselves from cutting into it before the dinner party. It was a Sunday, and we were both off, but we vowed not to eat until that night. We wanted to arrive with empty stomachs. That afternoon we talked about all the luscious food we were going to eat.

"I bet someone makes a roast beef," I said.

"Maybe steaks or even lobster," Eddie added.

"I don't care what it is, as long as there's plenty of it, because I'm starving already," I said.

Eddie and I talked and laughed all the way to the East Side, but as soon as we crossed the threshold of Krissy's apartment, he drifted into his usual silence. Right away, I noticed that something was strangely missing. The smell of food. I walked into the kitchen with Krissy and placed my wonderful cheesecake in her refrigerator. All I saw there were bottles of spring water and some lettuce.

"The food's in the dining room," Krissy said as she led me into the lushly carpeted eating area. The banquet was laid out on the dining room table. Everything looked very green. There was guacamole, spinach salad, peas and rice, and several unidentified objects covered with sprouts and soy flakes. Eddie smirked at me across the table. The guests were pecking at the food like delicate little birds. I knew I could gulp down everything on that table and still be hungry. I felt like a vulture. But I pecked like everyone else.

The cheesecake was barely touched. "Too rich," I heard someone say. As I sneaked a second helping, I continued to pretend I was having a wonderful time. Krissy and Ben were chatting about their recent vacation in South America, and other couples were talking about their travel plans for the summer. I mixed, I mingled. I learned about primitive art and the opera season at the Met. Eddie sat in a chair and stared at the guacamole. We made our excuses and left early.

"You did it again!" I shouted as we drove home. "You didn't say a word. You acted bored and mean!"

"Why is it we can't even get into an elevator without you striking up a conversation with a total stranger? Why do you have to talk to everyone all the time?" Eddie asked.

"I can't help it, I like people. I'm curious about them."

"Well, that's how we're different," Eddie said. "Those people tonight were strangers. They don't care about us. I'm not interested in them. Our family and our old, good friends are enough for me!"

"Are you sure you weren't intimidated because they were doctors?" I shouted.

"Listen, I don't care what they do for a living. They were pretentious."

"So they're different. That doesn't mean we can't be friends," I answered.

"What about tonight?" Eddie countered. "What did you think of that meal?"

Now we were back on common ground. My stomach was grumbling. "To tell you the absolute truth, I was disappointed," I relented.

"Great! At least we agree on something! Look, there's a Burger King! What do you say we stop in and get something to eat?"

"Some things never change," I thought. One minute we're on the way home from a sophisticated dinner party on the Upper East Side, and the next minute we're sitting under the glaring neon lights of a fast-food joint, stuffing ourselves with burgers, french fries and Cokes.

"Eddie," I said between bites, "this is not settled yet."

"Somehow I have a feeling that on our fiftieth wedding anniversary we'll still be fighting about the same thing," Eddie said.

And then we laughed.

After the disastrous dinner party, I rarely saw Krissy. Neuroanatomy class was over, I had begun my surgery rotation, and I was in love. The romance began the moment I stepped into the OR for the first time. It was a magical place, a place where the surgeon was in complete control and the patient felt nothing. Surgery was orderly and logical, it was repairing something that had been broken or damaged, and making it whole and functional again. "Sewing and plumbing," was how I had described it to my parents.

In surgery I was free from the patients' pain. They didn't moan, they didn't grimace. When they were anesthetized, I became anesthetized. Then I could concentrate on the "fixing." Of course, as a clerk I didn't do any actual surgery myself. Mostly I held retractors, tied sutures, and observed the doctors and nurses. I was awed by the control and the assurance of the surgeons. I had heard they were tough on interns and clerks, but they were usually helpful to me. But then I didn't dare make a mistake. Sometimes when I had to hold retractors on an obese patient, my hands would shake from the pressure. Other times I'd worry that my sutures weren't tied neatly enough, but no one ever complained. I was doing the best I could. I still hadn't forgotten my awful blunder with poor Mr. Blackstone, and even though Eliot had wished me all the best when I moved on to surgery, I was sure he thought I'd never make it.

Every night I'd come home and tell Eddie all about the control and the almost godlike attitudes of the surgeons.

"They're so secure—so confident," I said. "You'd think that sometimes they'd waver, just for a moment, but I've never seen it."

Eddie was skeptical. "They've just had a lot more training than you have. Men aren't gods," he said.

I nodded. Eddie was getting suspicious. I could tell he was wondering if my "love affair" with surgery might turn into something more permanent. He never said a thing, but I knew he was concerned. Our finances were stretched to the limit. We had applied for maximum financial assistance. This loan would cover my tuition and books as well as affording me a small amount for living expenses. In order to qualify for the money, we had to submit Eddie's W-2 form as well as an itemized list of all our expenses. Mrs. Lewis at the loan office had gone over these expenses with a fine-tooth comb. I even had to justify buying Evie a new winter coat. I felt uncomfortable when she examined my life so closely. If I decided on surgery, it would mean extra years of training, extra years of struggling and counting every penny. It would also mean being on every other night, five days a week. Eddie talked about getting a night job to earn more money, but we knew if he did, our relationship would suffer. Increasingly, our "big time" together was becoming more and more precious. We decided we would both work in the summer, and we figured as long as Eddie's teaching job with the city was secure, we could make it—somehow.

When I was in the OR, even our financial problems seemed far away. Nothing could distract me from my fascination with surgery. I was assigned to an elderly man named James Clark, a sweet, polite patient suffering from a serious liver disease. Dr. Reed, the surgeon, had scheduled an operation to relieve the distended veins under Mr. Clark's liver.

"We'll fix you up, chief," Dr. Reed had assured Mr. Clark. His wife, Emma, smiled as she watched him comfort her husband.

"I'm expecting him to be home in time for Christmas," she said. "That Dr. Reed can do anything."

Like most patients, Emma had complete faith in her husband's surgeon. She had to. Once we all disappeared into the OR, she could do nothing but wait, hope and pray. It was important for her to believe in Dr. Reed. I had seen Dr. Reed work, and I believed her faith was justified. He was a fine surgeon, but somehow Eddie's words echoed in my ears: "Men aren't gods."

The room was cold and the huge lights were adjusted and readjusted to prevent shadows from blocking the surgeon's view. Nurses, interns and clerks stood at attention, ready to retrieve any instrument the surgeon might request. Strains of a Beethoven sonata drifted from the loudspeakers. Everything was so orderly, so perfect.

We had given Mr. Clark factors to help his blood clot and to prevent excessive bleeding during the operation. Dr. Reed worked quickly. Despite the chill, tiny beads of perspiration began to dot his forehead. As he unearthed the distended, fragile vein, it burst. The tissue began to ooze blood. Dr. Reed called for a sponge. As he worked, the veins surrounding the liver began to shred at his touch. Blood was seeping over the sponges and retractors. He worked feverishly, but the hemorrhaging continued. I looked up for a split second and noted with alarm that Dr. Reed was sweating profusely. His hands began to quiver. Suddenly, without warning, he began to sing. There were no words to his song. It was a haunting, almost maniacal tune. Everyone watched in horror as Dr. Reed began uncoiling lengths of intestine from the patient's abdominal cavity. There was no reason for this action, and Mr. Clark began to hemorrhage badly. Dr. Reed was no longer coherent. The OR was in chaos. The attending surgeon rushed in and took over as one of the interns grabbed Dr. Reed, who was now laughing hysterically, and half-carried, half-pushed him from the OR. The IVs were open wide as we made a desperate attempt to pour blood and clotting factors into Mr. Clark's veins, but he lost the blood as fast as we replaced it. His blood pressure was dropping rapidly, and he went into shock. There was no way he could survive. The attending surgeon finally broke the stunned silence. "Let's get out of here," he snapped.

I was badly shaken by what I had seen. I heard via the hospital grapevine that Dr. Reed was transferred to a dermatology clinic and was also receiving psychiatric help. Eddie was right. Surgeons were ordinary men. "Maybe too ordinary," I thought as I watched Emma Clark sob quietly in the waiting room. She would never know what had happened during her husband's surgery, but I could never forget. Maybe the pressure was too much, maybe the price for being a surgeon was too high. I was thankful that my next rotation was in obstetrics. At least there I would belong, a mother helping other mothers. What could be more natural?

Of course, I had heard all the usual horror stories about women-hating obstetricians, but I had always had a good relationship with my own obstetrician. He had never been condescending or rude, so I didn't pay too much attention when Krissy and her friends told me to be wary of Dr. Gross.

"He's supposed to be awful," she told me. "Hates women doctors. He probably hates his patients, too."

Since he was the chief of the department, and since OB was a popular choice for women, I didn't believe what Krissy had told me. I wasn't going to begin my next rotation with a chip on my shoulder. And it was a good thing I didn't, because if I had, I would not have been able to contend with Dr. Gross.

I was nervous as I stood with a group of other med students, waiting in the long orange corridor for Dr. Gross. After my enthusiasm and resulting disappointment with surgery, I was hesitant. I didn't want to be disillusioned again.

Dr. Gross was a large, balding man dressed completely in white. He shook hands with the male clerks and then turned to me.

"So you're Dorothy Greenbaum," he said as he checked his list. "How do you douche?" he asked, cackling.

Suddenly I was back in high school. Without hesitation, without regard to rank or status, I retaliated: "It depends who's asking, a friend or an enema," I shot back.

Dr. Gross was enjoying this little repartee.

"I hear you're interested in OB," he said. "You must like vaginas."

"Mine's always been good to me," I quipped.

Dr. Gross looked pleased. He grinned from ear to ear. He seemed to like my spontaneous replies, and he seemed to like me.

The feeling was not mutual. I despised him instantly, and continued to do so throughout my entire rotation.

"I hate him, Eddie," I complained that night. "He's a classic misogynist. I know I'm going to hate OB."

"I doubt it," Eddie answered as he pulled up in front of the all-night bagel bakery. "Anyway, Evie has a school play coming up next week, and you're off, so let's just put this Gross character out of our minds for a while."

"*Gross* is right!" I mumbled as I bit into my onion bagel.

Evie couldn't wait to tell me. She made Eddie promise not to say a thing. The next afternoon she gave me the news in her breathless little-girl voice.

"Mommy, I'm going to be a star in the play for Hebrew school and you've got to make the costume."

"Wonderful!" I clapped my hands. "What's the name of the play?" Evie told me in Hebrew.

"I don't understand, honey," I explained. "I don't speak Hebrew, only Yiddish. What sort of a costume must I make?"

"A goldfish, Mommy," she answered. "I have to be a goldfish."

I looked at her long yellow curls and decided it was perfect casting. I made up my mind that I was going to design a fantastic costume. There had been a parents' meeting, but I had been at the hospital that day, so I simply assumed that the costume should be as special as I could make it.

Evie and I had a wonderful time. We went to the stationery store and bought oak tag, glitter and gold foil. I had her lie down on the oak tag, and I traced a giant goldfish around her torso. We cut out the fish and made two sandwich boards, front and back, which we covered with the foil. Then we spread some glue and some glitter and created a big blue fish eye and a red fish smile.

"Mommy, it's beautiful," Evie said. The giant fish covered her whole body. Only her little arms and legs stuck out from the sides and the bottom of the glittering creation.

"I can't wait until tomorrow," she said, giggling.

"Neither can I," I said as I tried to hug her without crushing the cardboard fish. At times like this it was easy to forget the hospital and Dr. Gross. Nothing could spoil this moment. I was home, and I was being a "mommy" to my baby.

The morning of the school play, I brushed Evie's hair until it shone. We decided to let it hang loose, adding to the "goldfish effect." The costume was so unwieldy, she could barely walk.

She examined herself carefully in front of the full-length mirror.

"This is the best costume in the whole world, and you're the best mommy!"

Then she tried to kiss me. But the fish got in the way.

Evie walked awkwardly into the auditorium. She had insisted upon wearing the costume to the school. When Mrs. Cohen, her teacher, saw us at the entrance to the auditorium, she came running down the aisle, breathless and frowning.

"What in the world *is this?*" she said, pointing in horror at Evie.

"It's the costume," I explained. "Evie is a goldfish."

"Mrs. Greenbaum"—she cleared her throat—"the name of the play is *The Golden Fish.* Each child is supposed to wear a small colored fish on a chain around her neck. Evie was supposed to wear a gold fish, as opposed to a blue, red or green fish.

"Look," she continued, pointing to a little boy wearing a small purple fish on a paper chain around his neck. "If you had been present at our parents' meeting, you would have known this. I simply can't allow your daughter to go on stage wearing that ridiculous costume!"

Evie stirred behind the foil and oak tag. She looked so cute. How could I let Mrs. Cohen spoil our fun?

"You'll break her heart," I whispered. "Please let her go on."

Mrs. Cohen moved back a few paces. "Can she walk in that thing?" she asked.

Evie took a few stiff steps to show she could maneuver. Mrs. Cohen relented. Evie tried to jump up and down, but all she could muster was a halfhearted swish.

Throughout the performance, the other mothers shot me looks of rage. Just who did I think I was, dressing my daughter in such an ostentatious costume? But I didn't mind, and neither did Evie. She glowed. After all, we both knew she was a star.

That special day with Evie sustained me when I had to return to OB. Eventually, Dr. Gross ceased to be a problem. He never dared to speak so disrespectfully to me again, and I merely nodded whenever I saw him. Obstetrics had everything I loved: mothers, babies, life, joy. There seemed to be no death here, only birth and excitement. In spite of the fact that delivering a baby is not difficult—firemen, policemen and taxi drivers do it all the time—for me it was startling, complex and intense. The first few deliveries were like reliving the birth of my own child. Later, when I had a bit more experience, I noticed I was more interested in and more involved with the baby than with the mother. I began to think about pediatrics. Maybe taking care of children, healing babies, was what I really wanted. I knew I would find out very soon. Pediatrics was my next rotation.

Dr. Goldman, the chief of pediatrics, was everything Dr. Gross was not: warm, supportive, emphatic. He smiled as he watched me weigh babies and give children routine examinations. When I brought one of Evie's little rubber toys to the hospital to distract my young patients, Dr. Goldman grinned from ear to ear.

"You've got the right idea," he said as he gave me the high sign.

But I was doing only what any mother would do, and I knew what all mothers knew: a spoonful of sugar really does help the medicine go down.

Although pediatrics came naturally to me and I felt comfortable with infants, children and families, there was one aspect of pediatrics I was certain I would never come to accept.

It began when Mitchel, a chubby, blond three-year-old, was admitted. Despite his healthy appearance, Mitchel was a very sick little boy; he was suffering from a rare tumor just above the kidney. He would need surgery, chemotherapy and possibly radiation as well. Dr. Goldman was not optimistic. At three years old, Mitchel had already passed the prime age for a total recovery.

I looked at his worried parents and realized how much like Eddie and me they were. They even had a little girl just about Evie's age. I began to identify with them. Their little girl was like my Evie. Mitchel, slowly dying in the next room, could have been my son.

Every morning and every evening, Mitchel's family sat huddled together in the dreary waiting room. They held each other's hands, stroked each other's brows. They had so much love to give and to share. Dr. Goldman said it was time to tell them the truth. He asked me to come with him. "Dorothy, this will be a good experience for you," he said. I wanted to run, to disappear into the anonymity of the crowded wards. I dreaded what I knew would happen next.

Dr. Goldman sat down beside the young parents, and in a gentle voice he explained that at best, Mitchel had a fifty-fifty chance of reaching his fifth birthday. He embraced the sobbing mother, urged the father to seek more medical advice and said he would help in any way he could. Then Dr. Goldman sat with them in the awful, final silence.

I slipped away and walked quickly to the bathroom. I cried in the privacy of a locked stall. "There's no way I can go through this again," I thought. "No way."

I waited until Mitchel's family left, until the wards were quiet and the children had drifted into restless sleep. Then I asked Dr. Goldman how he could do it—how I could do it.

"I can't pretend. I can't remain cool and composed while a child is dying," I said. "Maybe pediatrics just isn't for me. Maybe I'm too involved. Maybe working with children will hurt too much."

Dr. Goldman looked sadly into Mitchel's room. "Dorothy, no one expects you not to care. You *should* care about these people. You *should* be involved. And it's precisely because you are so involved and you care so deeply that I think you should consider pediatrics."

I was surprised. I had expected a macho pep talk, the type I had heard again and again in surgery. I remembered listening when an attending physician had shouted at a nervous intern: "If you can't stand the heat, get out of the damned kitchen!" But Dr. Goldman was telling me that in pediatrics it was all right to sweat. It was good to feel the heat—and the pain.

"Dorothy"—he sighed as he took my hand—"every time a child dies, a piece of me dies. No one ever learns to accept the death of a child."

My six-week pediatric rotation was over.

As I hugged Dr. Goldman good-bye, I realized I had a great deal to think about.

I was still mulling things over when Fern called. She was doing her surgery rotation in a hospital across town. She asked me all about County Hospital. "It's everything I anticipated, and more!" I said, laughingly. "It has everything, including a mysterious rapist who simply disappeared."

"Well, that's one thing we don't have here, thank God." Fern laughed. "But, Dorothy, I have to tell you. I know what I want."

I held my breath. She had decided.

"Surgery! This is it for me. There's nothing like the OR. I'm only happy when I'm in surgery."

My head began to spin. Here I was immersed in pediatrics, and Fern was bringing back all the old longings.

"But what about Jack?" I asked. "What about having a family?

Are you willing to put in those extra five years? Do you realize you'll be on every other night?"

"I'll find a way," she said. "Jack and I want a baby, but I also want to be a surgeon. We'll work it out, we have to."

"I wish *I* could," I said glumly, as my own desire to have another child resurfaced.

Fern was optimistic. She didn't know about the guilt. She didn't know how it felt to have to steal precious moments with a child who needed you. I decided I would be optimistic, too. Internship was just around the corner. My hours would be longer, and my "big time" with Eddie and Evie would be shorter.

That night Eddie and I discussed my conversation with Fern.

"I'm so confused," I said. "Surgery, OB, pediatrics. There are so many choices. I'm just not sure."

"Well, cheer up," Eddie said. "What's your next rotation?"

"Psychiatry." I smiled.

"For you, that should be a piece of cake," Eddie said with a laugh.

"How do you figure that?"

"Just think, you'll finally have your wish. You'll be able to sit and talk to people all day, find out all about them—and I won't be there to spoil it for you!"

"You're right," I said, laughing. "Psychiatry will be a welcome change. No more choices, no more sickness, no more pain."

That night I slept as if I didn't have a care in the world.

11

Psychiatry

I walk through the door, and the lock clicks behind me. There is no way out. Psychiatry has begun.

I don't look back at the nurse who is holding the keys, or at the door. I look at Dr. Rosen, who is standing there smiling and holding out his hand to me.

"We've been waiting for you," he says.

Dr. Rosen is wearing a brown corduroy sport coat. He does not wear a stethoscope. Only a pen peeks out from his breast pocket.

None of the familiar smells are here, none of the sounds or the sense of immediacy I felt in the other hospital wards. Here the walls are painted soft peach. Everything is muted and strangely peaceful.

I am seated at a polished walnut table. Surrounding me on both sides are four other med students. Dr. Rosen speaks softly, his hands folded.

"Our purpose here is to help patients by talking and by understanding. You will probably have problems when you meet some

153

of your patients. In order to deal with these issues, we will review your tapes and notes together and work out a course of treatment. There is a tendency to project your own feelings and motivations onto your patients. There is also a common tendency to identify too strongly with a particular case. Remember, there is a fine line between mental health and mental illness. You will discover by working here in psychiatry just how fine that line can be."

I slump down in my seat and watch as Dr. Rosen unfolds his tent of fingers and begins to gesture in the air. He pauses to answer questions. He urges us to come to him with problems and to share our "projections," our "fantasies and our fears." I try not to think of the locked door. Everything here is so pleasant, so warm, so comforting. But I realize as I look around the conference room that here, none of the familiar tools of medicine will be used. In psychiatry I will have only words.

My first patient meets me in a small yellow treatment room furnished with two soft chairs, a desk, a box of tissues and a few tin ashtrays.

Mrs. Weingarten is in her early thirties, slim, attractive and lightly tanned. She wears no makeup and is dressed in a simple white Mexican blouse and tight blue jeans. Her eyes are rimmed in red, and I can tell at once that she has been crying.

After our introductions, Mrs. Weingarten begins talking. She twists the gold-and-diamond band on her left ring finger. As her lips move, her long fingernails flutter in the air like delicate coral birds. She is used to talking and seems anxious to present her "case."

"I'm depressed, Dr. Greenbaum," she explains, "unable to act, totally paralyzed. To the outside world I seem to have it all: a husband, a six-year-old son, two homes, lots of friends. But still I'm unhappy. My childhood traumas are resurfacing."

I am surprised at Mrs. Weingarten's sophisticated analysis of her own problems. I am even more surprised when she begins to use clinical terms and immediately begins talking about her early childhood. She seems to understand the principles and even the practice of psychotherapy. At the end of our first hour, Mrs. Weingarten slows down. The coral birds rest sadly in her lap. She even knows when it is time to stop. Mrs. Weingarten is a practiced and diligent patient. She has been in various forms of psychotherapy for eight years and has learned much about the process, but she has not yet learned how to get well.

My notebook is full. I have used up both sides of my thirty-minute tape. I am sure I can help Mrs. Weingarten. I believe I can talk her out of her doldrums. Dr. Rosen pops in as I am reviewing my tape.

"How about lunch?" he asks. We have one hour for lunch.

"This place is like a country club," I muse as I nibble at my tuna sandwich. Krissy, who is also doing a rotation in psychiatry, joins us. "We were lucky if we got ten minutes for a Coke in surgery, OB or pediatrics," I say.

"You're right," Krissy says. "This is the life!"

I notice that here in psychiatry, everyone walks very slowly. Everyone mulls things over carefully. There is none of the hustle, the urgency I felt in the other wards. It's as if we are all working on individual puzzles, trying to fit the pieces together. I remember Eddie's words as I drink my coffee: "Piece of cake!" He was right. I smile as I dig into my dessert.

I cannot see Mr. Glass alone. Dr. Rosen tells me he is a difficult patient, so we enter the examining room together. I am expecting a violent, crazy man in restraints, but Mr. Glass is small and sedate. He is a twenty-nine-year-old junior high school teacher, and he tells me his hobby is woodworking. He has been here in the hospital for nearly three months. I can see by his records that he has had no prior history of mental illness. I begin by asking Mr. Glass some superficial questions.

Yes, he enjoys teaching. He has a three-year-old daughter and a lovely wife. He also likes to read.

I lean forward in my seat. This pleasant young man could be my neighbor, my cousin, my husband.

"What seems to be the problem, Mr. Glass?" I ask.

Mr. Glass looks directly at me. He has not been crying. His eyes are clear and blue. They are the kind of eyes that do not cloud with doubt or confusion. Mr. Glass is sane, I am sure of it.

"I'm dead," he answers.

I try not to show any emotion, but I feel tiny goose bumps erupting on the insides of my arms. I look at Dr. Rosen. He is absolutely deadpan. The blue eyes continue to stare.

"What do you mean you're dead?" I ask. "Aren't you sitting right here talking to me?"

"Yes I am," he answers. "But I'm dead."

I try all the logic I can think of. I talk nonstop for ten minutes, but Mr. Glass is absolutely convinced he is dead. This mild, rather ordinary man has had a total schizophrenic break.

Dr. Rosen interrupts the session and tells me I can leave. As I get up to walk away, Mr. Glass grabs my shirt sleeve. Those blue eyes again.

"You're not going to be able to cure me," he says.

It is not a question, it is not a plea; it is a simple statement—razor-sharp words that cut deeply and ring true.

Later, Dr. Rosen puts a hand on my shoulder. "Don't feel bad, I told you he was a difficult case."

"I don't understand," I say. "He seems so normal. How can he be so delusional at the same time? Does he really believe he's dead?"

We walk into the conference room. As he pours me a cup of coffee, Dr. Rosen relaxes into a knowing posture. "Let me tell you an old psychiatry story," he says.

"A patient goes to see his psychiatrist.

"'What's the problem?' the doctor asks.

"'Doc, I'm dead,' the patient answers.

"The doctor figures he can cure this guy in a minute. He takes a needle from his pocket and asks the patient, 'Do dead men bleed?'

"The patient says, 'No.'

"'Then put out your finger,' the doctor says.

"The patient does this and the doctor pricks his finger.

"'What's that?' the doctor says as he points to the pinprick.

"'Blood,' the patient answers.

"'So,' the psychiatrist says, 'if that's blood, what do you think that means?'

"The patient cocks his to one side. 'I guess it means that dead men *can* bleed.'"

I break down laughing. Dr. Rosen smiles. It is a moment of relief, and it helps me to forget Mr. Glass's parting words.

"Remember, Dorothy, *he's* crazy, you're not. You're both speaking different languages," Dr. Rosen says.

I nod. But I realize that in this place words are all I have.

It is four P.M. I wait as the door to the psychiatry ward is opened, and I shiver as the nurse locks it behind me. It has been a short day. But in these few hours, I have stared in the face of depression and insanity. I am exhausted.

The drive home from the hospital transported me back to the real world. By four-thirty, I was sitting absolutely still on the living room couch.

"What are you doing home?" Eddie asked as he came swinging through the door.

"I'm finished for the day," I said, sighing.

"Great!" Eddie said. "I told you this psychiatry thing would be easy. Four-thirty and you're home. Piece of cake!" He smiled as he snapped his fingers in the air.

I stood up very straight and looked into Eddie's eyes. They were a sharp blue. There were no clouds, no doubts, no dark visions.

"Promise me you'll never have a breakdown," I said.

"Oh, no!" Eddie said with a laugh. "Let's have a glass of wine. I can see this is going to be a long night."

Eddie was right. That night we began to talk. I looked into my own past, spreading it out like so many photographs. And then I tried to remember. I talked about Albie. I felt the guilt and the rage I had sealed up inside myself for all these years. How could my parents have kept Albie's condition, and even his death, from me? Eddie listened. And then he began to pour out his own feelings. He talked about being a teenager, about always feeling like the "odd man out," the "loner." We talked, listened and cried for each other. In the morning I felt ready to face Mrs. Weingarten and Mr. Glass.

The door closed behind me with a thud. As usual, Dr. Rosen was there smiling, reviewing cases. He was interested in my notes and in my first tentative impressions. The day passed slowly. What had once been my "little time," the time that flew, that kept me occupied and concentrating every second, now seemed to crawl. As Mrs. Weingarten reviewed her mother's abortion, her parents' divorce, and her own guilt, she sobbed openly, and I began to feel empathy for her. I knew how it felt to be a surviving child, I understood her desperate wish to give birth again, and I commiserated with her when she explained that her depression seemed to deepen when she was unable to conceive.

Once again I filled pages and pages with my notes, and once again I faced Mr. Glass, who stared at me with his ice-blue eyes and told me he was dead.

Dr. Rosen was impressed with my analysis of Mrs. Weingarten. He thought I was a "natural." He encouraged me to take on an outpatient in the clinic. I was relieved to spend even part of my day out from behind that door.

The outpatient clinic was housed in a new and separate facility. There were no locked doors here. Instead, there were six good-sized rooms with tape decks, coffeepots and two-way mirrors for observation. The clinic reminded me of a kindergarten. I felt relaxed and confident as I faced my first "outpatient."

Mrs. Willis was a tall, buxom black woman in her early twenties. She wore a dashiki and large, dangling earrings. She had an open, friendly face, and I liked her at once. She, like all the patients here, came to the clinic voluntarily and was able to live a fairly productive life on the "outside."

Mrs. Willis was the mother of three children, ages five, six, and eight. Some quick mental calculations helped me realize that she must have been a little over fifteen when she had her eldest child, Sharita.

Mrs. Willis had dropped out of high school, but still she had managed to earn her diploma at night. Now she was going to college part-time. She dreamed of becoming a doctor, but life seemed pitted against her. She was divorced, living on food stamps and government benefits, and was constantly one step ahead of eviction notices and bill collectors. Mrs. Willis was caught up in a desperate cycle of poverty and hopelessness. I saw her as a survivor. First, she told me about her youngest children, a boy and a girl, whom she truly loved. Sharita was different. Mrs. Willis explained that the girl was a "difficult child." I didn't press for particulars at the time.

Mrs. Willis was depressed. Some days she could barely summon the energy to dress the children. But still she was coming here. I felt sure what this patient desperately needed was some encouragement, a friend to talk with, a safe place to share her feelings. The world *was* against her. I was sure there was no pathology in this warm, open face. I sympathized with Mrs. Willis. In my own way I, too, knew how it felt to struggle against an ocean of nos.

That afternoon I left the hospital feeling more confident. I shared my notes with Dr. Rosen, and my observation that Mrs.

Willis could be helped and might even make some real changes in her life. "She's a good mother," I remember saying. Then I passed through the locked door, and once again that sinking, frightened feeling returned. Why was psychiatry so exhausting? Why, when I got home every night, did I take out my own life and examine it like an intricate road map of the past? What was I looking for? Why did I encourage Eddie to open up every old wound? Why was I always analyzing?

Words were my only instruments now. They were scalpels and I was learning how to use them.

The words of Mrs. Willis, Mrs. Weingarten and Mr. Glass were swirling around in my head when the phone call came. It was my father. His voice was shaking. "There's been an accident. Your mother. Come quickly." He told me that the ambulance had just left. They were on the way to the hospital. I left a note for Eddie.

By the time I reached the hospital my mother was in the emergency room. She had fallen down a flight of stairs. She lay on a stretcher in the hallway. Her right leg was swollen to twice its normal size. Blood seeped from two open wounds that ran from her knee to her ankle. Her face was drained and gray. She said nothing; she just looked up at me in a helpless way I had never seen before. As I stood there in the ward, the smells and the sounds seemed to push at me until my instincts began to return. I demanded to see the resident on duty. I asked for an intern, a nurse, anyone.

"Sorry, lady," an orderly told me. "We're backed up here. It could take hours." I looked at my mother's leg. She was losing blood rapidly, and I knew she was in danger of going into shock. My father gripped my hand. "Thank God you're here," he said.

I ran toward a nurse. "I'm a medical student," I shouted. "My mother should go into X-ray immediately." I gestured toward the stretcher.

"The X-ray machine is backed up for at least four hours," she said. "You'll just have to wait your turn." She snapped her chewing gum and padded away.

I felt the fragile restraints, the ones that stopped me from screaming and crying and running away, begin to strain.

And then I saw Eddie rushing toward me and I felt his hand brush my face. His presence filled the room. He looked at my mother and asked me what was being done.

"Nothing," I cried. "They won't do a thing!" I was pacing nervously down the crowded, noisy corridor. My father had not moved from my mother's side. He held her limp hand in his and whispered words of comfort and consolation. I knew she was badly hurt.

"No one will listen. She might go into shock." I looked at Eddie and hoped the words would sink in. They were all I had. Eddie moved quickly. He called a private hospital and a private ambulance. Within minutes my mother was on her way across town.

As we followed the ambulance, I watched the familiar streets flash by the windows. I closed my eyes and saw my mother's face.

Eddie's mouth was set, determined. He drove as carefully as ever, his hands gripping the wheel. If he had not shown up and taken control, my mother would have still been lying unattended in the crowded corridor.

When we reached the private hospital, my mother was quickly and carefully whisked from the ambulance to X-ray. The attending physician took me aside and explained that it was not a simple fracture. Shards from the thigh bone had snapped; the kneecap had shattered. There was a compound, comminuted fracture. There were multiple breaks of bone, some of which were protruding through the skin. The patient would need surgery. She was receiving antibiotics through an IV to prevent infection. Barring complications, she would pull through.

"Let's hope she doesn't throw an embolus," he said as he walked down the quiet corridor. An embolus is a blood clot that might result in a stroke, a coronary, brain damage, death. This was my mother. I knew I could not be objective.

"Why can't they just put a cast on her leg?" my father asked as he walked out of the waiting room. "If it's just a break, why can't they fix it and let us take her home?"

My voice was coming back. The paralysis began to melt away. I held my father's shaking hand and explained that my mother would need surgery. I said she would have to stay here for a few days. I didn't mention the embolism or the shattered kneecap. I knew how to filter out the bad news.

"She'll be dancing in a week," I said, smiling.

Eddie watched me from a corner of the room. He could hear the words I wasn't saying. He sensed the danger, but his face remained a mask of composure.

The words I had learned in psychiatry meant nothing to me now. They tumbled out and broke apart in the air, turning into syllables—sounds. Only medicine could help.

The next few days passed in shadows and light. Eddie, Evie, my father and I moved, fed ourselves and watched the bright afternoon sun fade slowly through the hospital blinds. My mother was scheduled for surgery, and Dr. Rosen had granted me three days of freedom from the psych ward.

The surgery was supposed to take one hour. Four hours later the surgeon emerged from the OR.

"She pulled through," he said. "Barring any complications, she'll make it." There were other words, too. She would need time to heal—weeks. He couldn't say about walking again soon. There were risks. There might be problems.

The next day, Mrs. Willis was animated. She had missed me. She began to talk in a flood of words. Sharita, her eldest daughter, was "acting up." As she spoke, anger played around the corners of her mouth.

"That girl is evil," she said.

I probed, pushed and poked. I used my words to try to open the skin and find the resentment I sensed growing there. I met only resistance. "She's just no good, is all," Mrs. Willis said over and over again. When I asked for particulars, I discovered that Sharita had not picked up her clothes, that she had not gone to bed on time. This ordinary behavior stirred the caldron of Mrs. Willis's rage. There was obviously something here I was missing. It was a hate I had never seen before.

"Dr. Rosen," I said after my session with Mrs. Willis, "I'm worried. This could be a potential case of child abuse. There could be something dangerous about to happen."

Dr. Rosen chewed the end of his pencil. "I wonder why you feel the impulse to act so quickly?" he mused. "I wonder what feelings Mrs. Willis stirs up in you?"

Dr. Rosen was turning the tables. He was manipulating the words. Suddenly I was the patient, not Mrs. Willis.

I went directly from the psych ward to the private hospital where my mother was slowly recovering. Here there were no ghosts, no demons. The enemy was real, and although my mother was weak, she seemed ready to do battle.

Although the private hospital had excellent doctors, it was terribly understaffed. My mother needed private duty nurses around the clock—three shifts a day at fifty dollars a shift. My parents' medical insurance did not cover this expense. My father, Eddie and I huddled together in the waiting room.

"We'll take it day by day," Eddie said. "Your parents have some savings, and we have ours."

"She'll get whatever she needs, and the best—no matter what!" my father added. We decided my mother would have the nurses, and later, the physical therapists.

Within three weeks we had gone through my parents' savings and most of ours. The nurses had to be paid in cash at the end of each shift. There was no credit and no way to delay payment. My mother's medical insurance covered only part of the hospital costs. I had never before confronted the economics of medicine. Now, as I tabulated the numbers in my head, I realized that these very economics were threatening to destroy my career as a doctor. There was no way I would have the money for next semester's tuition.

That afternoon I visited Mrs. Lewis at the loan office. I bit my lip and curled my toes up inside my shoes as I explained our situation. She agreed to grant me a temporary postponement of my tuition payment.

"But this will be the only one," she cautioned as she made some scribbles in my folder.

Despite the reprieve, Eddie and I were worried. We weren't sure where the money for the next nurse's shift would come from. I felt guilty. Here I was, taking, not contributing. If I had been working full-time, there would be no problem. Being a medical student was expensive, and now the price did not seem worth paying.

That morning Mrs. Weingarten was scheduled for electric shock treatment. Dr. Rosen asked me if I would like to observe. I had watched amputations, cesareans and all manners of surgery, but I knew I could not watch as Mrs. Weingarten, now thin and pale and deeply depressed, was lashed to a table and shot through with electric current. Dr. Rosen shook his head and mumbled something about my "resistance."

In the outpatient clinic, Mrs. Willis spoke about packing her belongings in the middle of the night and throwing them in the back of a rental truck so that the landlord wouldn't catch her. She talked about her eviction notices and lashed out bitterly at a system that granted economic security only to the privileged few. I nodded in empathy. Mrs. Willis saw me as part of the system. She couldn't possibly know that I was preoccupied with thoughts of how I was going to pay for that afternoon's nursing shift. I listened as Mrs. Willis railed on and on. I waited for her to begin talking about Sharita, but she didn't. Finally, I asked, "How is your daughter?"

Now the words were stronger: "bitch, evil." Mrs. Willis leaned across the table: "That child's out to do me in!"

"What do you mean?" I asked.

"That girl is eating garbage. I caught her eating stuff off the floor—carrot tops, orange peels, candy wrappers. She's trying to shame me."

Something clicked inside my head. Mrs. Willis was describing pica, a syndrome I had studied in pediatrics. It was a symptom of iron-deficiency anemia. I asked Mrs. Willis to bring Sharita to our next session. I had to see this child for myself. I wasn't sure what I expected to find.

The next afternoon Sharita, a small, skinny eight-year-old, was led into the clinic. Her hair was hastily combed, and she wore a stained dress. I longed to examine her, to run blood tests, to have her worked up, but this was psychiatry.

Sharita didn't answer when I asked her questions. She nodded her head. She played listlessly with the toys the clinic provided. I could not engage her. As Sharita sat and colored, Mrs. Willis rambled on about the system. The child never once looked up. She seemed dulled; no little-girl lights danced in her brown eyes. She was closed up, sealed against the world.

I thought of Sharita and her mother as I sat over my afternoon coffee. At the next table, Krissy and some of the other med students compared notes and discussed patient pathology. But today I needed to be alone. I was fitting the pieces together. My mother had always been there for me. She had encouraged me every step of the way. Now, with funds running low, with the medical insurance tapped out, and very little cash left for the private-duty nurses, I was still taking. I knew it was time to contribute.

That afternoon Eddie and I talked. I explained that I could take a leave of absence for one semester. I could find a part-time job and care for my mother the rest of the day. The burden was too great for Eddie to carry alone. My father could not find work. There was nothing else to do. "A leave of absence won't be so bad," I said. "I could use the rest." Eddie nodded sadly. Psychiatry was draining him, too. He could no longer tolerate the constant analysis. He was growing impatient with my unending scrutiny of every move, every word. We decided to tell my mother that afternoon.

The nurse at the private hospital greeted me as "Dr. Greenbaum." By now everyone knew I was going to be a doctor. My mother had told my story to every nurse, doctor, intern and orderly. They all smiled when I came to visit. I guess they had mothers, too.

Her head was propped up on pillows. The grayness was slowly draining from her complexion. She had been doing some mild physical therapy and had been able to wiggle the toes of her right foot that day. But we all knew there would be many more weeks here in the hospital, then physical therapy and nurses at home.

"Dorothy, this must be costing a fortune," she said as she added some figures on a piece of paper.

"Don't worry about it, Mom," I answered. "Eddie and I have thought this thing through. I've decided that it's time I began making a contribution to the family. I'm going to take a little time off from med school, just a few months, and get a part-time job. This way I can help out financially and spend more time with you."

My mother was very quiet. She looked at the ceiling, then at her hands, examining every crease and line. When she was ready to talk, her eyes were riveted to mine.

"Over my dead body," she said. "We're not quitters. We'll make it, and you will not leave med school, not for a month, a day, or an hour."

I knew there was no talking to her when she was like this. There would be plenty of time to bring the subject up again. In the meantime, I prepared myself for another day behind the locked door. Not even my mother's illness could release me from psychiatry.

The next morning I told Dr. Rosen about Sharita. I talked about my sessions with Mrs. Weingarten, who had only grown more disconnected after the electric shock treatment, and Mr. Glass, who stubbornly continued to be dead.

"No one seems to be getting better," I said. "They just go on and on."

"Oh, there's definite progress," he answered, smiling. "It's very slow, but there is progress. What you should think about is your need to see immediate results." I felt the web tighten, but this time I was not going to let myself get trapped.

During lunch I remembered the Yiddish word my father had used: *shpilkes.* "Dorothy," he had said, "you've got *shpilkes.*" This meant, as I understood it, that I was on pins and needles, unlimited energy. I needed to feel that energy—that strength—again. Every day when the door locked behind me, I was feeling more drained, more paralyzed. The words were threatening to suffocate me. Even Eddie was disturbed. "Dorothy," he had said, "I'll put you through med school. If you want to be a surgeon, I'll help you with that, but forget psychiatry. I will not live with you if you go for psychiatry. I can't stand it anymore. You analyze every word. You're impossible to live with. You're just not yourself."

I had laughed aloud. There was no chance I would choose to do this an hour longer than I had to.

A day passed. I was on my way to see my mother. A nurse stopped me in the corridor. "You can't go in there yet," she said.

The door to my mother's room was closed. I felt a numbness move through me. "What's wrong? What happened?"

"Nothing is wrong," the nurse said sternly. "Your mother has something to show you. You'll have to wait here."

After a few minutes, someone poked his head out from my mother's room.

"You can come in now," a voice announced.

The door to my mother's room was wide open, and the shades were up. The afternoon sun rotated like a giant crystal in the silence. I squinted against the light. My mother was standing, leaning on the metal bars of a walker. Her body swayed tentatively, painfully, but she was smiling.

"I'm standing for you, Dorothy," she said. "I'm not a quitter, and neither are you."

The image of my mother glinted off the crystal.

She had pushed herself to the limit for me. Despite her injury, her weakness, her age, she was standing. Soon she would be walking. She was not a quitter. I knew as I moved into her arms that tomorrow I would return to the psychiatric ward. Somehow we would pay my tuition. We would make it. The pain was not important. Only the courage mattered. Nothing could stop us.

12

Hard Times

The room was decorated with colored crepe paper and balloons. A cardboard sign hung over the door. Evie had written the words herself: "Welcome Home, Nanny."

As my father wheeled my mother over the threshold, she smiled, then began to cry. It was finally over. We were all together again. My mother laughed through the tears and promised us she would never again leave on such short notice.

Eddie and my father beamed. Evie tried to hoist herself into the gleaming wheelchair. She had missed my mother more than any of us, and now she couldn't seem to get close enough.

My father cleared his throat and made a toast: "As long as we have our health, we're rich," he boomed.

Eddie and I exchanged glances. We were far from rich—in fact, we were broke—but my father was right. We did have our health, Eddie did have his job, and I even had my temporary tuition deferment. Now we were ready to pull our lives together.

My mother's illness had brought unexpected chaos into our carefully ordered lives. It had made us aware of how vulnerable we all were, how fragile the surface of our world could be. But now I was back on firm ground again. The family was intact, and through it all I had managed to keep up with my studies and to continue working with my psychiatric patients. But even now, during this happy celebration, I could not escape Mrs. Weingarten, Mrs. Willis and Mr. Glass. They had slipped through the surface. They were still down there floating in the confusion and the grief, and I had not yet found the opening through which I could pull them back to safety. Despite my sleepless nights and my daily preoccupations, I began to fear that it was hopeless. I would never help any of them.

"Dorothy, come join the party!" Eddie shouted as he handed me a piece of cake. Then, as if he could read my mind, he whispered, "Let's think about tomorrow, tomorrow." I knew that Eddie was referring to money. He was wondering how we were going to pay for the nurses, the physical therapists and all the special equipment my mother would require. But as usual, Eddie was optimistic. When our eyes met, he gave me a knowing look. "We'll find a way," he said. "Haven't we always?"

I found comfort in his words, and as I sipped my wine and ate my cake, I forced myself not to think about tomorrow.

"Tell Nanny about your new friend," my father urged as he held Evie on his lap. She hardly needed encouragement. Within seconds, she was chattering away about her new playmate, Michele. Evie was in the second grade now, and Michele was her first "best friend." While my mother sat in rapt attention, Evie explained how she and Michele shared their lunch in the cafeteria and how they played with their dolls after school. My mother smiled and shot me knowing looks. My little girl was growing up.

I was grateful that Evie had found a friend to give her the companionship and stimulation she needed. Michele had come just in time. Lately, I had been too exhausted and too absorbed with my tapes and my notes to do anything but change the channels as Evie stared at the television. At best, I could listen as she read a few pages from *Pippi Longstocking* before I tucked her into bed. This was not the way I had planned to raise my daughter. But how could I have known how much these psychiatric patients would intrude upon my most private moments with my family?

Now, with both my parents home full-time, maybe Evie wouldn't notice how distracted I had become.

Before Eddie and I began to clean up after the welcome home celebration, we sat down and had a glass of wine.

"She really looks good," he said, smiling at the decorations we had piled in a corner.

"My mother?" I asked.

"Who else?" Eddie said.

"Sorry," I mumbled. "I just can't seem to concentrate on the happy times now. I wonder why that is. I wonder what it means."

Eddie cleared his throat. I was analyzing again.

"Dorothy, I can't wait until you finish psychiatry and we can have a normal conversation."

I nodded as I scraped the last bits of food from each dish. As the plates sunk slowly beneath the sudsy water, I let my mind drift. After spending eight hours a day with my patients, I was no longer sure just what a "normal conversation" was.

The next morning when I arrived at the clinic, Mrs. Willis was waiting for me. We began our session in the usual way. She complained about the degradation and the poverty. I sympathized, then she lashed out at her daughter Sharita. But today I decided to try something different. I asked her a question I had never asked before.

"Mrs. Willis," I said, "why don't you tell me something about Sharita's father?"

In the course of my midnight musings, I had come up with the possibility that perhaps Sharita was not the real target of Mrs. Willis's rage. Maybe Sharita represented something—or someone—else. Asking about the girl's father seemed a logical place to begin. I realized I was stumbling in the dark, and I couldn't be sure my theory was even close to the truth.

I was not prepared for what happened next. Mrs. Willis jerked back, almost as if I had touched an open wound. Her smile hardened into a thin, mean line, and her eyes became angry slits.

"What do you want to know *that* for?" she asked.

Even her voice was different, transformed by fury. I found myself cringing, moving away from my bristling patient. I forced myself to continue.

"Would you like to talk about it?" I asked.

The answer was a terse no. She turned her face to the wall.

Silence filled the space between doctor and patient. For the first time, I could feel what Dr. Rosen had called "the patient's resistance." It was an impenetrable wall behind which the patient felt protected and invulnerable.

Mrs. Willis was not going to give an inch, and her refusal to talk told me more than all the words she had spoken so far. This resistance was my first real clue. Maybe it wasn't Sharita Mrs. Willis considered "evil." Maybe it was more complicated. A lot more.

I was tempted to hammer away, to flood Mrs. Willis with questions, but I knew I would get no further during this session. I had found an opening, but it was so small, so fragile, I dared not continue for fear it would close up forever.

"That girl's just plain bad," were Mrs. Willis's parting words.

I walked back to the hospital slowly and thoughtfully, watching as the clouds shifted in the gray afternoon sky. "So this is how it happens," I thought. "This slowly, this tentatively."

Dr. Rosen was waiting for me in the conference room. I presented my cases, carefully trying to piece together what my patients had said and what I thought they had meant. I told him about Mrs. Willis. I was sure I had seen a glimmer of something behind that resistance. He encouraged me. "Keep it up, Dorothy. You're doing just fine. You're a natural," he said as he chewed on his pencil and began to listen as the next student presented her cases.

That afternoon I sat with Mrs. Weingarten as she again obsessed about her life. I watched helplessly as she ran her fingers through her hair. Mrs. Weingarten no longer wore her diamonds; she no longer manicured her nails. "I'm nothing," she sighed as she looked past me and out the small window.

Mrs. Weingarten and Mrs. Willis seemed so completely different, yet they shared a secret, a mystery that immobilized them. I felt I had to find the key. That's what I believed medicine was all about.

The sky was darkening as I walked up the stairs of my apartment building. It was good to feel the old familiar banister under my hand, comforting to be out of what I had come to think of as "the prison." At least here everything was normal, predictable.

The apartment was strangely silent. I checked my watch: four P.M. I had finished up at the hospital an hour early. Evie was upstairs with my parents. My father had picked her up from school. These days she looked forward to milk and cookies with her grandparents. My mother insisted that having her around was "the best medicine in the world." I smiled now as I thought of Evie and how she had asked to see my mother's scar. It was comforting to know that some wounds could heal, and even if they left marks, the scars were tangible proof that the person had suffered and had recovered. If only that were true of psychic injuries. They left scars, but it seemed that they never fully healed.

A batch of letters was piled neatly on the white Formica table.

My father had stopped to take in the mail before he picked up Evie. I leafed through them dutifully—bills. Then an official-looking envelope caught my eye. The return address read "The New York City Board of Education." Since Eddie and I both opened the household mail, regardless of to whom it was addressed, I didn't hesitate.

The letter was typed on pink paper. It began: "The Children and the Citizens of New York thank you for your past years of service." There was a budget crunch. The public schools had to cut down. Eddie had been fired. Today was Wednesday. As of Friday, he would be out of work.

I read the letter a second time, just to be sure. I walked to the window and stared down at the street below. The gray sky had darkened to an ominous black. Everything was the same as it had been only minutes before. People scurried busily by—tiny ants involved in their own tiny worlds, but up here a world had just fallen apart.

I folded the letter neatly and placed it back into the white envelope. Eddie had been fired. Now there would be no money at all.

Something forced me to move quickly out of the apartment.

I rang my parents' door bell. My father had taken Evie out for a ride. My mother, surprised to see me, grinned eagerly from her wheelchair, but in an instant the grin melted.

"What's wrong?" she asked.

The words slipped out by themselves. I listened to myself explain, heard my voice tell my mother what I was sure I could not say aloud.

"Eddie's been fired. That's it as of Friday."

My mother stiffened. Then she went into action. Her voice was firm.

"We'll go to the board, we'll appeal, maybe they'll reconsider. And if that doesn't work, then we'll sit down and make a budget. We'll figure out just how much money we can all scrape together until Eddie finds work or is rehired."

"Dorothy," she cautioned, "this is no time to abandon ship. I've been through this myself when your father lost his job. It's not the end of the world."

The end of the world. Those were the only words that stuck. My mother was talking, but I couldn't concentrate. All I could think about was what I hadn't told her. We had spent all *our* savings and all *her* savings on the hospital bills. We had applied for a loan for her home care. There was nothing to budget. In two weeks the rent would be due. We didn't have it.

I walked downstairs and waited for Eddie to come home. I decided to make it as easy as possible for him. When my father returned with Evie, I bathed her and tucked her into bed. As my lips brushed her forehead, I felt a painful sadness. I had wanted so much to give her a safe and secure home. Now everything was changing. I couldn't be sure what would happen next.

Eddie was late, putting time in after school to tutor some of his students. "Life just isn't fair," I thought as I put dinner in the oven and looked anxiously at the clock.

When Eddie came home, I avoided his eyes. I moved mechanically, pouring him a glass of wine, hoping somehow that the letter would disappear, or that when he read it, he would laugh and tell me it was all a joke. I felt as if I were walking on glass. It would be so easy to slip now, to say the wrong thing at the wrong time.

After his shower, Eddie sat down at the kitchen table. He sipped his wine and closed his eyes. He was tired. He had put in a long, hard day. How could I tell him?

A ray of light spilled across the table. Soon it would be dark. I knew I had to begin.

"You know I love you very much," I said. "Nothing is as important as our love and our family."

I was trying to soften the blow, but the words weren't linking up properly. They seemed disconnected. Empty sounds that floated like fragments of dust in the milky light.

Eddie took my hand.

"What happened?" he asked. "Is it your mother?"

He knew. He could tell something was wrong.

I cleared my throat. "Eddie, you got a letter from the Board of Ed today." Now the words were connecting. His face froze. Something inside him was pulled taut. He snapped to attention. "Let me see the letter," he said.

"Whatever it is, we can handle it," I said, hoping I sounded like my mother.

I sat silently in the gloom as I watched Eddie skim the letter. Like me, he read it twice.

The chicken was baking in the oven. I could hear the sounds of traffic out on the street. Everything seemed so ordinary, so normal. I tried not to move. I thought that if I sat there perfectly still, Friday would never come.

Eddie looked around the kitchen.

"Dorothy, do you know what this means?"

I know he didn't expect me to answer, but I couldn't help myself.

"Maybe it's a blessing in disguise," I said. "Now you have a chance to start your own business, to get out of that classroom. To hell with them," I said. "If they want to fire you, it's their loss."

I knew my words were meaningless. Eddie had had several opportunities to leave teaching, but he had always turned them down. This was his profession. He loved what he did.

"Look, it isn't the end of the world," I added. Those words again. "Eddie, we'll figure something out. We'll make it. Haven't we gotten this far?"

Eddie looked up at the ceiling, then down at the floor. Then he fixed his eyes on me.

"Dorothy, how are we going to pay the rent?" he asked.

The next morning, the people on the street, the cars, even the buildings—all seemed drained of color. Ashen. I moved mechanically toward the hospital. I nodded to the nurse who unlocked the door and then locked it quickly behind me. Mr. Glass was my first patient.

We sat together in the peach-colored treatment room. He puffed on a cigarette and talked about his teaching job. For an instant I wondered where Mr. Glass had taught. I wondered if there was an opening in that school and if Eddie could get his job. It didn't matter that he was talking and smoking and tapping his foot against the metal chair. He was dead.

After my session with Mr. Glass I drifted down to the cafeteria and drank a cup of coffee. Next to me, Krissy and a few of her friends were laughing and talking.

"Dorothy, why don't you join us?" Krissy asked.

Usually I wouldn't have hesitated, but today I was so drained, so exhausted, that I really preferred to sit quietly by myself. But Krissy insisted. I moved to her table. No one seemed to notice that I was skipping lunch. The thought of eating just didn't appeal to me. Everything tasted like paper. Everything looked flat and dry.

"Dorothy, is something the matter?" Krissy finally asked.

I wanted to cry, to tell her everything, but I remembered what my mother had always told me about showing a brave face to the world.

"Well, actually, we did have some bad news yesterday," I said.

Krissy cocked her head to one side.

"Eddie lost his job. You know with the city layoffs, and the budget crunch and all," I began to mumble.

"That's too bad, Dorothy," Krissy said. "What are you going to do?"

"I guess we'll just have to cut down for a while." I smiled. "No more champagne in the afternoon." Krissy didn't pick up on the sarcasm. She smiled and nibbled at her dessert.

"I'm sure he'll find something soon," she said.

Mrs. Willis was waiting for me when I arrived at the outpatient clinic. She didn't want to talk about Sharita or Sharita's father. That topic was closed. Instead, she talked about food stamps and welfare checks.

"You rich folks just don't know what it feels like to have to ask for food money, to have to count out stamps at the supermarket," she said. Tears came to her eyes.

I held myself back. I wanted to tell her that in two days my husband would be unemployed, that we had so many loans we would probably be in debt for the next twenty years, that we had no way to pay our rent or buy our groceries. Instead, I asked about Sharita.

"She's still eating that garbage," Mrs. Willis said as she shook her head. And then, as if on cue, she repeated what had become a familiar line: "She's trying to do me in. She's evil."

I watched as Mrs. Willis left the clinic and walked to the bus stop. She was intent upon improving her life, and I admired her courage. But I was concerned about Sharita. Trouble was brewing—I was sure of it. I knew I'd have to win the mother's trust in order to meet the child.

In the days that followed, Eddie began a long and involved appeal to regain his job. He put his name on every substitute teacher list in the city. Then he waited. Each morning he got dressed and sat grimly by the telephone. But the budget crunch had everyone frightened. Even teachers who might normally take a few days off for a cold or for "nerves" were reluctant to miss work. The firings were widespread. Only those who had been in the system for many years felt secure.

On mornings when the phone *did* ring, it was the Board of Ed asking Eddie to report to a school in a dangerous area of the city. I would beg him not to go, but Eddie said he could take care of himself. And we both knew how much we needed the money. Soon word spread that Ed Greenbaum was big and strong and a tough disciplinarian, and the phone rang more often. Eddie had become more of a cop than a teacher. "Baby-sitting for hoodlums," he called it, but he never once refused to go.

We didn't know it then, but sub pay came at the end of every month. Although Eddie was earning some money, by the end of four weeks we still hadn't paid our rent. Afternoons, when I took in the mail, I would pile the bills in a bundle and place them, unopened, in my desk drawer. There was no sense even looking. We had nothing to send them.

It was raining the day I came home early and found the note. Eddie was working as a temp in a department store and wouldn't be home till well after six. I checked my watch as I walked wearily up the stairs. I had spent so many hours talking and listening, and still nothing had changed. No one improved. There were no breakthroughs.

From one end of the dimly lit corridor, I could see the white note on the door. Evie. She had left me a little picture before she went upstairs to my parents' apartment.

As I approached my apartment, I narrowed my eyes and tried to focus. The white paper glued to the door wasn't a drawing from Evie. I was standing in front of it now. The words were printed in large black letters. They were unmistakable. It was an eviction notice. We were being ordered to "vacate the premises."

Without thinking, I began to scrape at the paper with my fingernails. I couldn't let Eddie see this, not after a day of working in a department store. When I saw that the glue was stubborn, I opened the door and rummaged through the kitchen drawer until I found a straightedge razor. I stood in the hallway, still dressed in my "doctor clothes," and scraped away until the eviction notice was nothing but a pile of torn and shredded paper.

And then I began to cry.

I walked upstairs and handed my mother the tiny shreds of paper. This time I didn't say a word.

"What's this, Dorothy?" she asked. Behind her in the kitchen, I heard my father humming as he set the table. Evie was doing her homework in the bedroom. I didn't want her to hear our conversation. I began to whisper.

"It's an eviction notice," I said. "We're behind in the rent. Eddie doesn't get paid for subbing until the end of each month."

My mother put her finger to her lips.

"Dorothy, let me take care of this. I'll call the landlord in the morning. We'll arrange for some kind of extension. When I talk to him, he'll understand."

"What about Eddie?" I asked. "How can I tell him?"

"You'll tell him," my mother said. "It's not the end of the world."

During the next few weeks, the gloom followed me to the hospital and waited for me as the door to the psychiatric ward was unlocked. It sat beside me as I studied. It curled up next to me as I slept.

The landlord granted us a temporary extension for our rent payment, but the bill collectors were not as gracious. Our credit cards were canceled, and collection agencies called day and night demanding payment. Eddie hung up the phone and stared at the television. He was still looking for work, still reporting to sub whenever he was called. But more and more he seemed to be losing hope. One night I caught him looking sadly at the T-shirt his seventh-grade social studies class had given him. The words WORLD'S GREATEST TEACHER were printed across the front.

He had appealed to the Board of Ed, but they had turned him down. He was told he would just have to make ends meet until he was rehired.

Making ends meet was now harder than ever. Eddie and I had taken to eating bagels, spaghetti and raisin bran for dinner. Evie had her chicken or her hamburger and her favorite vegetables, but we learned to make do on less. Much less.

I was living my life in a long, dark tunnel. Each day came and went. My patients remained unchanged. Yet in the hospital I couldn't allow my problems to affect my work. Dr. Rosen continued to reassure me that I was doing well.

From time to time, Krissy inquired about Eddie. I always smiled and said we were "making it" and that it was just temporary. Then she told me about her friend Jane. Jane was a single mother whose medical school tuition and rent were paid for by the university.

"How can that be?" I asked. "Jane's father is a surgeon."

"Yes," said Krissy, "but she's emancipated. Since she's not married and is independent from her family, she falls into some sort of hardship category. Maybe you should look into it."

I wasted no time getting over to Mrs. Lewis's office. She wasn't happy to see me. "Dorothy," she said, "I hope you're not going to ask for another loan or another extension."

I told her about my hardships and explained that like Jane, I would like to be made eligible for a subsidy.

"I'm afraid that's not possible, Dorothy," she explained. "You see, you are still married. The fact that your husband is recently unemployed is unfortunate, but he is still capable of supporting you. In order to qualify for this type of subsidy, you must prove that you have absolutely no means of support."

I shook my head sadly.

"But there is an alternative," Mrs. Lewis said. She doodled on her desk blotter as she spoke.

"Now, if for some reason you were *not* married and had custody of your child, then you would qualify."

Not married. "How could I be *not* married?" I started to ask. Then I began to understand. I had heard the term "paper divorce" before, but I had never given it much thought. Eddie and I could get divorced, but we could still live together. Everything would be the same. Only now all my expenses would be paid.

Krissy was having coffee when I returned to the cafeteria. I told her I had just come from the loan office.

"How did it go?" she asked.

"I can qualify for all the grants they have. All I have to do is get divorced," I said.

Krissy nibbled her doughnut. "Listen, don't be so miserable," she said. "Lots of students do it. I happen to know two couples right now who are living together and who have kids. The divorce is only on paper. It's not like it means anything."

But I knew it would mean something to me.

Eddie was sitting in front of the television when I got home. He had been laid off at his department store job, and he hadn't been called to sub for over two weeks. My parents had given us some money that we knew had been set aside for their daily expenses, but that, too, was almost gone.

I could see that Eddie was locked in a battle with apathy and depression. It was the "Eagleton Summer" all over again. "Or worse," I thought as an image of Mr. Glass flashed through my mind.

"Eddie, I think I owe it to you—to us—to tell you a way we can ease our financial burdens."

His eyes lit up. I explained about the paper divorce. His sad, hopeless look returned. He was almost crying now.

"Dorothy, all we have is our love and our marriage. I won't let them take that away. I won't trade it for all the free tuition in the world. And what about Evie? How could we possibly explain that we got divorced just so we could pay our bills? When she's old enough to understand, what sort of example do you think that will set?"

"I know, I know." I nodded my head in agreement. "I just felt I had to tell you. I knew what you'd say."

Eddie smiled. It was the first smile I'd seen in a long time. "But it *is* tempting," he said, laughing.

I threw a pillow at him. And for a little while we forgot all about money, bills and tuition payments.

As time passed, Eddie and I became increasingly desperate. We had just finished a dinner of milk and cereal and had tucked Evie into bed with one of her favorite dinosaur books when we finally admitted we needed help. We had to borrow money from someone. We had no choice.

"I'll call my brother, Al," Eddie said. "Who else is there?"

I nodded miserably. Eddie had never asked his brother for anything before. Al was far from wealthy, and he had a wife and two children to support. But, as Eddie had said, who else was there?

I listened from the next room as Eddie dialed the number and spoke to his brother. He was asking for food money.

This was not supposed to happen. During the day patients looked up to me. They called me "Doctor." I sat in the staff cafeteria. I presented cases. I ate lunch with psychiatrists and interns. But here at home I was eating cold cereal and hoping my brother-in-law could lend us enough money to buy tomorrow's groceries. The irony of the situation made me flinch. If only Mrs. Willis could see me now. If only she knew how much we had in common.

Al arrived within the hour. I was sitting on the bed with Eddie. We were trying to make lists, trying to figure out how much to give the landlord and how much to put aside for food.

Al greeted me with a nod. Without saying a word, he spread the money out on the bed. Four hundred dollars.

"I wish it could be more," he said. "I'm so sorry. I feel so helpless."

He and Eddie embraced. I began to cry. The two brothers talked quietly for a few minutes in the living room, then I heard the front door slam. Eddie sat down on the bed and gathered up the twenty-dollar bills.

"I never even got to thank him," I said, sobbing.

With the extra money Al had lent us, and the trickle of checks that Eddie received from occasional substitute teaching, we were able to stave off the landlord and scrounge up enough to buy food. All the other bills went into the drawer, which was now crammed so full I could barely close it.

I thought about money almost all the time. When I sat with Mrs. Weingarten and she talked about her two homes and her jewelry, horses, art and investments, I felt a pang of sadness. Perhaps it was true that money could not buy happiness, or in this case, peace of mind, but poverty produced its own brand of stress, humiliation and rage.

Now when Mrs. Willis talked about her life, I understood in a way I never could have before. Unlike me, she had no one to lean on. She was all alone with three children. I was worried. The pressures she was forced to live with were mounting, and they could cause her to explode at any time. Time was passing, and I had to step up my efforts to get to the bottom of this business about Sharita and her father. More and more, I suspected that this information would give me the answers I was looking for.

It was a Thursday. I had just finished an afternoon session with Mr. Glass and had had my usual conference with Dr. Rosen. As I walked toward the outpatient clinic, I began thinking about Evie. I hoped she was not picking up on the gloom Eddie and I were feeling. I wondered if the pressures we were experiencing might be affecting her. Then I was reminded that perhaps Mrs. Willis might have transferred her rage, her confusion, onto Sharita. I decided that today was as good a time as any to attack her resistance again.

She was wearing a colorful print dress and smiling. Despite the dreary weather, she was feeling "up."

"There's a chance I might get an apartment in a new building, a new project in another borough, Dr. Greenbaum," she said. Then she leaned forward. "But there's only one problem. If I do move, I won't be able to come here anymore. It will be too far away."

I knew this was my chance. If Mrs. Willis did move, she would leave without ever revealing the source of her problems with Sharita.

I began slowly. I asked about all the children. She told me that her little boy and girl were doing well in school and they had received good marks on their report cards. Then she was silent.

"What about Sharita?" I asked.

"I knew you'd start that again!" she shot back. "The girl is still acting up, misbehaving, shaming me every chance she gets."

"Who does she remind you of?" I asked.

Mrs. Willis stared at the ceiling. She had the answer, but she wasn't talking.

"A child often reminds her mother of someone else," I continued. "Why don't you tell me about Sharita's father?"

Mrs. Willis began to sweat. She balled her large hands into tight fists. Her foot tapped uncontrollably against the rung of the metal chair.

"Her father, her father," she repeated as she shook her head from side to side.

Then she turned to me. "You want to know about her father?" she challenged. Then, without waiting for an answer, she continued, "Ask me about *my* father."

"I don't understand," I said, stumbling. But deep inside I did understand. Perhaps I had known unconsciously all along.

The words were clear and hard. They sliced through the air like razors.

"Sharita's father is my father. That bastard raped me when I was fifteen. That girl is not only my daughter, she's my sister."

The treatment room took on an eerie, dreamlike quality. Mrs. Willis's confession clung to my chair, crawled into my lap. I felt my chest rise and fall with the beat of my own heart. I thought I could see my pulse throb in my wrists. Mrs. Willis stared at the floor.

"I'm glad you told me this," I said. "It's important." I hoped I sounded professional, and for a second I thought my voice sounded like Dr. Rosen's voice. Inside I was filled with horror, rage and fear. But I sat riveted to the chair.

"What's so important about it?" Mrs. Willis challenged.

"I think it's something you need to talk about, something that was very painful for you and still is."

I didn't say anything about Sharita just then. I knew that having shared her secret with me, Mrs. Willis wanted only to be washed clean, to be free of the burden. Telling her my thoughts now would only be destructive.

The session was over. Mrs. Willis gathered up her purse and her books. The bright print dress, which had seemed so cheerful at the beginning of the hour, now seemed sadly faded. She walked from the clinic like a tragic, broken bird.

As I waited for Eddie to pick me up, I began to shiver. For the first time, I understood Mrs. Willis's anger at Sharita, knew why she thought the girl was out to "shame" her and why she believed she was "evil." But how would knowing all this change things?

I needed to talk with Eddie. But when he pulled up, I saw that Evie was sitting beside him. My news could wait.

"We're going to the grocery store before we head home," Eddie said. "Let's stop and get some gas first."

I nodded as Evie crawled into my lap and put her arms around my neck.

Eddie drove silently. Evie began to talk.

"Mommy, I have a problem," she said.

I stopped myself from sighing.

"What is it, honey?"

"Michele is eating my cookies, the ones you pack in my lunch bag for dessert."

"Why don't you tell her *you* want the cookies?" I suggested.

"Because she says if I was really her friend, I would let her eat my cookies. Her mother gives her carrots. She said I can eat her carrots."

I suppressed a laugh. Evie hated carrots. But I was exhausted and tired of playing psychiatrist. I assumed Evie's problem could be easily solved.

"I'll call Michele's mother and make sure she doesn't do that anymore," I said.

Evie's face twisted into an unhappy grimace.

"Oh, no, don't do that!" she begged. "Promise you won't. Michele won't be my friend if I tell on her."

I was beginning to feel helpless. Some psychiatrist. I couldn't even solve this simple problem.

"What would you like me to do, Evie?" I asked.

"Nothing," she said. "I'll think about it."

Eddie shot me a surprised look. We both eased into our seats and smiled.

We drove up to our usual gas station. The meter read "empty."

"Not a minute too soon," Eddie said.

We pulled the car up to the pump. The attendant looked at us and then walked around the back of the car. He leaned over and motioned for Eddie to roll down the window.

"Looks like that back tire is a little low," he said. "Why don't you folks pull into the garage here for a minute?"

Eddie looked puzzled. "I just checked the tires yesterday," he whispered to me.

"Well, let them take a look," I answered as Evie and I stepped out of the car.

Eddie drove toward the open garage. The attendant and the mechanic huddled together in the glass-enclosed office.

A moment later, the mechanic stepped out of the office and told Eddie he'd take the car up on the lift. Eddie handed him the keys. In an instant the garage door slammed closed with a thud.

"What the hell's going on here?" Eddie asked indignantly.

"Sorry, folks," the mechanic said, "but we're impounding this car. Your gas credit card is in arrears, and we're keeping the car until you make things right."

At first I thought it was all a joke. People didn't do things like this, not really. I expected the mechanic to slap Eddie on the back and have a good belly laugh. But the punch line never came.

Evie stood behind me, holding her schoolbooks and looking frightened. Eddie and the mechanic were arguing. She heard the man call her father a "thief," and heard Eddie as he demanded to call a lawyer.

Then the police arrived. There were two of them, big red-faced men with guns and blue uniforms. I didn't want Evie to see this. I explained that the policemen were going to help us get our car. Evie, pale and quiet, clung to me. We watched as Eddie handed the mechanic our grocery money. The garage door was unlocked. We drove away with enough money for half a tank of gas and a dinner of bagels with cream cheese.

I was humiliated and enraged. As soon as Evie was tucked safely in bed, I broke down.

"How could this happen?" I shouted. "How much worse can things get?"

Eddie remained calm and controlled, his face a mask of composure. But I knew he too must be feeling the pain and the anger.

"He's got to let it out," I thought. "He can't keep holding things in."

I wanted him to blow up, to throw something, to shout, but he only stared silently at the evening paper. Images of Mr. Glass looking vacantly at the wall forced me to act.

"Maybe I can humor him out of it," I thought.

"What could they have done with a '67 Chevy, anyway?" I joked. "They'd probably have to pay someone to take it off their hands."

Eddie didn't move, didn't smile. "We've hit rock bottom," he said. "Do you realize we were treated like common criminals today?"

I nodded.

"Thank God we're both not teachers," he said as he ran his fingers through his hair. "At least we know we have a future. I don't think I could handle this if we were both out of work and we both had to worry about being rehired."

I hadn't thought of it that way, but Eddie had a point. Teachers were being laid off and fired all over the city. Policemen, fire fighters and other municipal workers were in similar situations. Although I wasn't bringing in any money, we both knew that as an intern I would at least earn a small salary. If only we could make it until then.

"We just need time to get back on our feet," I said as I curled up beside Eddie. "In a few years we'll look back on this and laugh."

"I doubt it," Eddie said. "Let's just hope that in a few years we'll be rid of that damned Chevy!"

The next morning Eddie dressed and showered as usual. At seven o'clock the phone call came. He was to report to substitute teach at a school in the Bronx. We both knew it was a tough school and it would be a tough day, but at least he would be away from the apartment and the bills and the feeling of being useless.

I was preoccupied with my worries when I arrived at the hospital. Mr. Glass was my first patient. "I can't bear it," I thought. "I can't bear talking to him, getting nowhere. It's like banging my head against a brick wall."

But I sat dutifully with my patient, talking, questioning, listening. His mood never seemed to change. He was flat and unanimated. I had, finally, ordered a series of tests for hypoglycemia and hyperthyroidism. Dr. Rosen had laughed, claiming I was too anxious to find a cure—a medical cure. The tests had all come back negative. "Maybe he *is* dead," I mused as he shuffled his feet and walked slowly from the treatment room.

Krissy was already in the cafeteria when I got there. I had brought my own lunch, as usual, a container of yogurt. She looked at me with concern. "Dorothy, is that all you're eating?" she asked.

"I guess I'm just not very hungry," I answered.

"Is Eddie still out of work?" she inquired.

"Nothing's changed," I answered, hoping we could avoid the entire subject.

"Why don't you come out to dinner with us this weekend?"

Out to dinner. Krissy had no idea how bad things were with us. I wondered what she would say if she had seen us yesterday at the garage.

"Well, Krissy," I said, "we're really kind of short on funds right now, and eating out can be pretty expensive."

Krissy put her hand on my arm. "Oh, I'm not thinking about anything extravagant or fancy. Ben and I know a little place in Chinatown. The food's great—and cheap! I promise you it will cost almost nothing."

I could definitely use a night out, some time off, but I had to make sure what "almost nothing" meant.

"What do you mean by cheap?" I asked Krissy.

"Listen, it will cost you less than eating at home, I promise. Come on, we'll be three couples. You'll have a terrific time. Give yourself a break."

It had been months since Eddie and I had been out anywhere. Maybe Krissy was right. A night with other people, away from the TV and the apartment, would distract us. I knew it would not be easy to convince Eddie, but I was sure a dinner in Chinatown would provide time off from our hard times.

I was thinking about how I was going to bring up the subject with Eddie as I walked toward the outpatient clinic. Mrs. Willis was not there. I waited for her in our usual room. As the minutes ticked away, I realized she was not coming. "Maybe she can't face me," I thought. "Maybe the confession was too painful." But when I checked at the desk, the nurse informed me that my patient had called and left a message. She was moving across town and was sorry she couldn't make it. She would be there for our next session. "I hope so," I thought as I gathered up my notes. "We don't have much more time to work together, and now every session counts."

It wasn't as difficult to convince Eddie to join Krissy for dinner as I had anticipated.

"Are you absolutely sure they understand our financial situation?" he asked.

"I'm telling you, she said it would cost us the same as eating at home. She knows you're out of work. You know Chinatown is cheap. Let's do it!"

Eddie agreed. He was too exhausted from chasing students out of the halls, the bathrooms and the wrong classrooms to put up a fight. He didn't say it, but I knew he wasn't doing any teaching. He was merely maintaining order.

The next few days melted into one another. I shared my observations with Dr. Rosen and my lunches with Krissy. I was counting the hours until my psychiatry rotation would be over.

"I think psychiatry is what I want to do," Krissy told me one afternoon. "It's such a mystery, such a challenge."

"Don't you find it frustrating?" I asked. "Don't you ever want to put your hands on a patient and heal him?"

"Don't be naive and impatient," Krissy answered. "Psychiatry is a cerebral process. It isn't a quick cure. Do you realize what would have happened to these patients twenty years ago? They would have been locked away with no hope of ever being part of society. I feel I'm *really* practicing medicine here. To tell you the truth, Dorothy, I'm surprised at your attitude. With your literature background, you should understand the character analysis and enjoy untangling all the plots."

"Maybe I just don't have the temperament for psychiatry," I answered.

Krissy nodded her head in agreement.

That night we were to meet Krissy and Ben and their friends for dinner.

The streets of Chinatown were narrow and winding. Eddie and I found the restaurant by stopping passersby and asking directions. It was a tiny "hole in the wall," a small, plain storefront decorated with red paper lanterns. I squeezed Eddie's hand. We had both feared something much more elegant.

Krissy and Ben and another couple were already seated.

"We've been waiting for you," Krissy said smiling. "We've already ordered drinks."

"And," added Ben, "I hope you don't mind, but I took the liberty of ordering appetizers. Two Peking Ducks."

Eddie and I froze. Peking Duck was an elaborately prepared and expensive dish. We slid into our seats. I scanned the menu. Peking Duck cost twenty-five dollars. Fifty dollars and we hadn't even ordered yet.

Eddie's face was ashen. Beads of sweat dotted his forehead. His mouth was set in a thin, angry line.

Krissy was talking nonstop. She was recommending dishes, ordering a second round of drinks. "I can't believe this is happening," I thought. She had promised me. She had said it would cost the same as eating at home. Eddie had eight dollars in his wallet. I knew before we ordered that we could not pay for the meal.

Ben leaned over and smiled at Eddie. He sipped his cocktail. "I hear you lost your job," he said. "What are you doing with all that free time?"

Eddie muttered something no one seemed to hear. But that hardly stopped the conversation. It had shifted to summer homes and vacations.

"Where are you planning to go this summer?" Krissy asked me.

Just a few days ago I had told her we couldn't afford to go out for dinner. Had she forgotten?

The room began to swim. Ben was bragging about his hourly fees. The other couple was laughing and telling stories about their previous summer in the Hamptons. My rage was building. I could feel it move in a dry lump past my throat. The room was now a blur of paper lanterns, smoke and clinking glasses. I blinked back the tears as I stood up.

"I can't believe any of this!" I shouted. "I can't believe you could all be so insensitive to Eddie and me!" The restaurant got very quiet. And then Eddie was standing. His hand was on my arm. He threw some money down on the table. As he guided me from the restaurant, I was trembling with rage.

Once we were out on the street, I turned to Eddie. "I'm so sorry," I cried. "This is all my fault. I put my needs above yours. I should have known. Krissy couldn't possibly have understood—or cared."

Eddie hugged me. "I felt defeated," he confessed. "I thought you were fed up with me. I only agreed to go because I wanted to do something that would help us feel close, that might make us laugh again."

All the tensions and pressures of the past weeks burst through the surface. We were both crying. The red-and-green pagoda phone booths, the brightly decorated restaurants, the crowds of people became a kaleidoscope of color and noise. It was just the two of us, and we were all that mattered.

On the drive home we began to talk. It was the first time in weeks that we had discussed anything other than our finances. Eddie explained how losing his job had stripped him of his self-esteem and his confidence. He was afraid he was losing my respect and my love. I had been so involved with my patients that I hadn't taken the time to give him the reassurance he needed. I promised Eddie I would make it up to him. But all he wanted was to get through these bad times and to keep the "core," as he called our love, intact.

"Is everything okay with us?" I asked as I held Eddie's hand. "Are we still a team?"

"Everything is more than okay," he answered. "We've been through some rough times, but we're still partners."

"Do you think we've survived all these setbacks because we're both so damned headstrong?" I asked.

"No, Dorothy," Eddie said. "We're not headstrong. We're love-strong."

That night Eddie and I made love. Krissy, Ben, Mr. Glass, Mrs. Weingarten and Mrs. Willis finally disappeared in the darkness.

Two days after the "Peking Duck Affair," as we now called it, Eddie was rehired. It was a different school in a different part of the city, but Eddie was too grateful to complain. Evie came to me that same afternoon and told me she had solved her problem with Michele. They would take turns sharing each other's desserts. I shook my head in disbelief. My six-year-old daughter had coped with her problems a lot better than I had been able to deal with mine or with my patients'.

My psychiatry rotation was almost over. Three days remained before I would move on to electives. These last days were long and lonely. Krissy and her friends ate at one end of the cafeteria and I sat alone with my yogurt and coffee at the other. She made no attempt to apologize or even to explain.

"Some psychiatrist she'll be," I muttered to myself. I was still furious about the night in Chinatown.

Mrs. Willis had moved and had canceled a few sessions. Today we were meeting for the last time. I walked wearily toward the outpatient clinic. I had no idea what I would say to her. I knew she needed to continue her therapy, but I wasn't sure if she would. Now that she had finally shared her secret with me, it would be that much more difficult to begin again in a new clinic, with someone else.

She was waiting when I arrived. "Dr. Greenbaum," she said, smiling, "it's good to see you."

We walked into the treatment room and took our seats automatically.

"I've moved to a new building, a subsidized project," she began. "Things are looking up."

Mrs. Willis was positive and enthusiastic. There was no mention of Sharita or her father. It was as if nothing had ever happened, no truths had been revealed.

"I won't be able to come here anymore," she said.

I nodded and explained that this, too, would be my last day. Mrs. Willis chatted enthusiastically about the future, yet she seemed reluctant to leave. She began to describe her new apartment.

"It's got two bedrooms and a living room," she said. Then she began to frown. "Only one problem," she added. "I've got mice."

"What are you doing about that?" I asked.

"Well," Mrs. Willis began thoughtfully, "I haven't actually seen 'em, but I've heard 'em. So I put rat poison down on the floor."

That seemed like a logical solution. I hardly gave it another thought.

I reminded Mrs. Willis that our session was already fifteen minutes past the hour. She smiled and thanked me for all the time I had spent with her. I wished her luck and watched as she left the clinic for the last time.

On the way back to the hospital, I sat on a wooden bench and mulled things over. A patch of sunlight washed across the lawn: spring had finally arrived. Something was nagging at me. I was sure something important had been left unsaid—undone. Then it hit me.

Rat poison on the floor. Sharita. She ate things on the floor.

I began running toward the hospital.

All the pieces fit tightly together. For the first time, it all made sense.

I pounded on the locked door until the nurse opened it. I was sweating and shaking.

"Where's Dr. Rosen?" I asked. "It's an emergency!" The nurse looked alarmed and pointed to the conference room.

Dr. Rosen was drinking coffee with his colleagues. His feet were propped up on the walnut table, and he was laughing aloud. When I walked in, he stopped and introduced me to another psychiatrist. "Mike," he said, "this is Dorothy Greenbaum. She's the one I was telling you about, the one who wants to cure everyone."

Dr. Rosen's words stung, but I pretended to ignore them. I told him about Sharita. He sighed.

"Dorothy, when are you going to learn? When are you going to stop acting out? It's not *your* problem. You can't go hounding people because of a hunch. You've got to work this out, discover why you need *to do something* about everything."

Ordinarily, I would have backed down, but today was different. I felt the old energy returning.

I ran to the nurses' station.

"You've got to help me find a phone number for a Mrs. Katherine Willis. It's a new number, but it's urgent—an emergency."

The nurse looked at me doubtfully but went to the files. She returned with a little white card. There were several numbers on it for Mrs. Willis. She had moved five or six times in the past year. I called the last number on the list. It rang several times. "Please be home," I prayed. Finally I heard a voice on the other end. I could hear a child crying in the background.

"Thank God I reached you," I gasped.

"Who is this?" she asked.

"It's Dr. Greenbaum. I'm calling to warn you."

And then I explained. The poison. Sharita.

Mrs. Willis was silent. "Thank you for calling, Dr. Greenbaum.

I'll take care of it," she said curtly. "I hadn't thought of it quite that way, but now that you mention it, maybe. Maybe."

The nurse smiles at me as she opens the door.

"Good-bye, Dorothy," she says. We shake hands. I have already said my good-byes to Mr. Glass, who merely nodded, and to Mrs. Weingarten, who is eagerly preparing to meet her new doctor. In all these weeks nothing has changed.

Then I hear the familiar sound. They key is turned in the lock. It is the last time.

Outside, a ribbon of ivory light streaks across the grass. I turn my face toward the sun and never look back.

13
Birth

Eddie, Evie and I walk hand in hand along the bay, watching as the sun dances on the water and the fishermen haul in their morning catch. I am wearing a blue-and-white T-shirt with the word DOC printed on it, a present from Eddie when I finally finished my psychiatry rotation. Evie is licking a chocolate ice cream cone and pointing at the tiny brown birds flying from tree to tree.

Today I feel I have everything—my husband, my child, my career. As we approach a small park with swings, Eddie and I exchange a special smile.

We watch as Evie swings back and forth, her blonde braids flying in the wind. We have made it through the worst of times. Eddie is happily back at work, and we have begun to pay off our debts. I have a single term of electives left before I graduate from medical school. There is only one thing missing. And today Eddie and I have decided we will have that, too—a second child.

When I first brought up the subject, Eddie was surprised. He had always planned on a larger family, but was this really a good time? Then we began to talk. Evie was six. I was twenty-eight. This term I would be taking electives; there would be no late nights, no double shifts. But next fall internship would begin. I knew that if I were pregnant, I would have difficulty standing on my feet and remaining attentive and careful for those thirty-six-hour shifts. Internship would be followed by two years of residency. I didn't want Evie to be ten years older than her brother or sister. I didn't want to wait three more years.

"Let's make a decision," I had urged Eddie. But he was cautious.

"Why don't you ask around? Speak to some of the women doctors at the hospital, see what they say," he answered.

I began by asking Dr. Kern, the head of obstetrics. She had two children herself. I made a special point to seek her out in the hospital cafeteria.

"When do you think it would be a good time to plan a second child?" I had asked.

Dr. Kern looked up from her lunch, took off her glasses and answered, "You're past all the good times. I suggest you have your baby when you want it."

Dr. Virginia Bartlett, the head of internal medicine, was very scientific.

"After you've finished medical school, take a year off. Do your internship later and make sure you have plenty of outside help," she cautioned.

But Dr. Bartlett's solution wouldn't work for me. With my first paycheck so close, there was no way I could take time off and delay internship. Then I talked to Fern. We were doing an elective in pediatrics in the same suburban hospital.

Fern had been married now for three years. She still planned to be a surgeon, but she, too, was mulling over the idea of motherhood.

"Dorothy," she said as we sat together in the cafeteria, "right now is a perfect time. We're in charge of our hours, there's no night call, and we finish up by six. Just think, if we time it right, we'll have a few months off between graduation and internship!"

Fern's eyes were glowing. Her enthusiasm was catching.

"Oh, I'm dying to try," she said as she grabbed my hand.

"I don't know," I answered. "What would the administration do if a med student got pregnant?"

"What *could* they do?" she answered. "Especially if we both got pregnant. They couldn't throw *two* students out!"

In an instant we both had our calendars on the table. We were planning our pregnancies as carefully as we had planned our careers. Then we threw our heads back and laughed.

"Fern," I said, "if everything goes according to schedule, our kids will grow up together!"

That evening Eddie and I discussed what Fern and I had figured out over lunch. He agreed it all made sense.

"But we have to act fast," I said with serious determination. Eddie broke into a wide grin. "Doc, that's the best advice I've heard all day!"

As the weeks passed, I busied myself with my work and tried not to concentrate too much on the calendar. Although I did not have to decide what specialty I would choose until residency, I seemed drawn to pediatrics.

Once again I was back in the wards, working in adolescent medicine, dealing with children and their families. It was a relief to be able to lose myself in the excitement of a busy hospital and to be caught up once again in the drama of medicine.

My first two patients were both suffering from the same illness, a form of self-induced starvation known as anorexia nervosa.

Susan was fourteen years old, five feet six inches and weighed ninety-two pounds when her mother brought her to the outpatient clinic. The worried woman confided to me that her daughter, who normally weighed one hundred twenty pounds, had begun using laxatives, throwing up her food and exercising constantly. "Look at her," she said. "She's nothing but a bag of bones, and can you believe she actually thinks she's fat?"

A preliminary examination showed that Susan had lost far too much weight. Already she was exhibiting symptoms of anorexia: extra hair growth on her face and belly, missed periods and a stubborn determination to grow thinner. When I talked with Susan, I immediately recognized that she was depressed. Her father was an alcoholic, and she felt that her two older brothers constantly picked on her. I tried to be sympathetic to Susan's situation, but I had to warn her that if she lost any more weight, she would have to be hospitalized. Susan seemed to respond. She listened intently when I told her how dangerous her dieting had become. Then she confessed that she had been forcing herself to throw up.

"I just hate the way I look," she told me. "When I see myself in the mirror I still think I'm fat."

When sixteen-year-old Debbie arrived at the clinic, she was five feet four inches and weighed just under eighty-two pounds. I tried to talk to her, but she only turned away and claimed that "no one understood her." But when I warned her that any further weight loss would result in hospitalization and force-feeding, she seemed genuinely alarmed. I knew how much anorectics feared weight gain. Debbie was gaunt and weak, and she had developed a painful and ugly eczema-like condition on her face. Both girls were to return to the clinic within the week to be reweighed and examined.

Now Eddie and I were back in the familiar routine of "big time" and "little time." I was practicing medicine but was still home early enough to eat dinner with my family. The long hours of internship loomed in the future, and all my loans would haunt me for at least ten years after I finished my residency, but right now I was content. Only the little red Xs on the calendar reminded me that I was waiting for something else to make my life complete.

By the end of the month I was on pins and needles. There was a chance, a good chance, that I was pregnant. But I kept my secret. I wanted to surprise Eddie and I didn't want to tell Fern until I was absolutely sure. When I had the time, I ran up to the third floor and handed in my urine sample. Toby, the nurse who supervised the abortion clinic, was a friend from County Hospital, and I wanted her to run the pregnancy test. She accepted my sample with a grim smile.

That afternoon Debbie arrived for her weigh-in. She stood on the scale and beamed. She showed a weight gain of five pounds. But something didn't seem right to me. Her face was gaunt, her rash even more noticeable, and her arms looked skeletal. Debbie wore only a hospital gown over her jeans.

"Do you have a belt on those pants?" I asked, wondering if perhaps a heavy belt and buckle would add extra pounds. Debbie looked away. I pushed aside the hospital gown and requested that she remove her belt. She refused. I immediately became suspicious and quickly unbuckled it myself. Her jeans fell to the floor with a loud thud. Debbie turned her face to the wall. I checked the pockets of the pants and discovered what had caused her impressive weight gain. Debbie had stuffed two 2½ pound weights in her pockets. She seemed embarrassed but remained sullen and withdrawn as I called her family and informed them that their daughter would have to be hospitalized.

I picked up the weights Debbie had concealed in her pants. I had read all about the obsessive and ritualistic behavior of anorectics, but this was the first time I had ever had to deal with it. I was grateful that Debbie would soon be in the hospital, where she could be fed and observed until she proved that she would begin to nourish herself voluntarily. But as I put the weights with her other possessions, I had a sneaking suspicion that this seemingly simple goal would not be easily achieved.

Although Debbie objected, she was admitted and began the horrible ordeal of NG (nasal-gastric) feedings through a tube in her nose. I felt sorry for the teenager, but I knew the feedings were necessary. She was bent on a course of self-destruction. Along with the dangerous weight loss, CAT scans had disclosed that continued anorexia resulted in changes in the size and structure of the brain. Extreme starvation caused the white matter to shrink and the ventricles to enlarge. Although no one was sure exactly what these changes meant, or what their long-term effects were, we did know that hospitalizing anorectics was the only way to save them from further damage and eventual death. A simple test done with a strand of Debbie's hair revealed that she had very low zinc levels in her system. It also dated her anorexia for us. Debbie had been starving herself for over three months.

As I walked down the busy ward, I stopped at the room at the end of the hall. In this room, a thirteen-year-old patient named Michael had been hospitalized for six weeks. He was dying of leukemia. Today was his bar mitzvah. I peeked inside as the boy, dressed in a yarmulke and tallith, sat in his bed and sang from the Torah. His frail voice trailed after me as I ran up to the clinic to get the results of my pregnancy test.

Toby nodded when she saw me. She asked me to step into the private office. She stared glumly from behind the desk. Her hands were clasped tightly in front of her.

"It's bad news," I thought to myself as I watched my friend lean forward and begin to speak.

"Dorothy," she said, "what do you want this test to say?"

I sat very still as Toby asked me this question. Was there any doubt? More than anything I wanted to be pregnant. But now I was sure something had to be wrong.

"I want it to be positive," I answered.

Toby's face relaxed. "Thank God!" she shouted. "It is! You're pregnant!"

The words hadn't completely sunk in when Toby began to explain.

"I thought you brought your test here because you wanted to have an abortion. I'm so relieved it turned out this way. Congratulations!"

She hugged me as we both laughed for joy.

I knew just how I was going to break the news to Eddie.

For seven years I had saved the homemade sign I had hung over the door when I discovered I was pregnant with Evie. It was still there in my drawer, neatly folded, with the words "The champagne is in the refrigerator" written in red crayon. When I got home, I quickly taped it up again so it would be the first thing Eddie saw when he arrived.

That evening, after our champagne celebration, we began to plan.

"I know it's going to be a girl," Eddie said.

I agreed. There hadn't been a boy in either of our families for a whole generation.

"I know," I added. "But Evie will be such a tough act to follow. She's like a beautiful swan."

"So her sister will be a duck!" Eddie joked as he took me in his arms.

Then we talked about what we both knew would come next: amniocentesis. I was painfully aware that there was a chance my child might be born with the same fatal heart ailment that had afflicted my twin brother.

"I have to know," I explained to Eddie. "After what we've been through this past year, I can't handle the pressure of not knowing if the baby will be healthy. The test will give us the information we need."

Eddie nodded. Amniocentesis is a simple procedure in which a small sample of amniotic fluid from the uterus is extracted and tested. It reveals various birth defects as well as the sex of the fetus. But the test could not be performed before the pregnancy was in its fourth month.

"More waiting," Eddie sighed as I cuddled next to him and fell into a deep sleep.

That week I made an appointment with my gynecologist. He confirmed the results of the initial test and told me the baby was due in February.

"I'd like to arrange for an amnio," I stated as I sat across from him in his office.

"Dorothy, you're only twenty-eight; there's no need to—"

I didn't let him finish his sentence. I told him about Albie and explained that my parents had never told me how my twin brother had died, and if they had, I would have had an amnio with Evie as well. He shook his head. "This is the way many parents think they are protecting their children," he said. Then we scheduled the test.

The next day at lunch I told Fern the news. She congratulated me and said she was almost two weeks late herself.

"Keep your fingers crossed," she said. "Let's hope our kids can be in the same kindergarten class."

Fern and I talked about pregnancy and speculated on the sex of our children. But the nagging fear that my child might not be healthy wouldn't disappear. It was a fear I would have to live with for the next three months.

I returned to the adolescent unit, taking care to avoid Michael's room. He was not my patient. But I couldn't forget he was there. He had grown weaker and more jaundiced. A resident had told me he was showing signs of liver failure. I resisted the urge to look in on him, reminding myself that Susan was waiting for me in the clinic.

She looked a bit better than she had the last time I had seen her. When she stepped on the scale, she showed a weight gain of three pounds. But my experience with Debbie had made me wary. I checked to make sure Susan wasn't playing any tricks. A quick look proved that her weight gain was genuine. I was delighted. Then I noticed an obvious bandage on her wrist.

"What's this?" I asked as I peeled the bandage back.

"I accidentally cut myself," Susan said as she looked into my eyes.

Since she had begun to gain weight, Susan was aware that her clinic visits would be less frequent. "I'll miss talking to you," she said. Then she confessed. "It really wasn't an accident, Dr. Greenbaum. I took a razor and cut my wrist. I just wanted to see how it felt."

I examined the wound and reassured myself that it was superficial, but I knew that Susan had made a suicidal gesture. I gave her my home phone number.

"Here," I said. "Call me anytime you need to talk."

During rounds I told the clinic director, Dr. Stern, about the incident with Susan. She was angry.

"Dorothy, are you completely naive?" she asked. "It's not good .medicine to give a patient your phone number. You can't adopt these children. Many of these anorectic girls are controlling and manipulative. All we can do is give them the tools to get well. We can't help them live their lives."

I had a feeling Dr. Stern was right, but I wasn't ready to admit my mistake—not yet, anyway.

When I looked in on Debbie, I was pleased to see that the NG feedings had been discontinued. She was maintaining her weight and would now be allowed to eat regular meals. I sat down to talk with her, but she remained withdrawn. She glared at me from her bed. "I'm getting fat," she said. "You're all trying to make me fat." I knew it was no use explaining that at eighty-three pounds she was hardly fat. As I got up to leave, I noticed her shoes resting neatly on a damp paper towel. I stopped a nurse in the hall and asked her if she had seen the shoes.

"Oh," she said, nodding, "that girl is so obsessive, she's been washing the soles of her shoes and putting them on that paper towel to dry. And by the way, we're going to begin watching her. The other night an orderly caught her jogging in the stairwell."

I shook my head. Debbie was intent upon destroying any progress she might make in the hospital.

As the weeks flew by, I busied myself with my work, trying to push away thoughts about the upcoming amniocentesis. Six weeks before the test, Fern gave me her own happy news. She, too, was pregnant. We went out for a special lunch and chatted hopefully about our futures. She was still determined to become a surgeon. More and more I was considering pediatrics.

When I returned from lunch, I was called to an emergency in admitting. A thirteen-year-old girl, the daughter of one of the nurses in the hospital, lay writhing on a stretcher. She was obviously in agony. When I asked her to sit up, she complained of a sharp pain that ran from her abdomen to her shoulder. I examined her and could hear normal bowel sounds, but the muscles across her belly tightened at my touch. This is an involuntary reaction, a way for the body to protect a damaged area. The young girl's face was twisted in fear and pain.

The diagnosis seemed clear. The sharp pain in her shoulder was probably caused by gas coming through a perforation in her fallopian tube. I was sure this teenager's pain was the result of an ectopic pregnancy, which occurs when a fertilized egg implants in a fallopian tube instead of in the uterus. It can result in a rupture, hemorrhage, shock, infection or even death. "But she's so young," I thought as I wiped her brow. Still, it was very possible.

There was no time to lose. I leaned over the girl's stretcher, held her shaking hand and told her I would have to do a vaginal exam.

She became hysterical. "Oh, no, that's impossible!" she cried. "I'm a virgin!"

I was aware that since Sandra's mother worked in the hospital, she would be reluctant to admit her condition to me.

"It's all right," I said as I continued to hold her hand. "I won't tell your mother, but it's important. I must know. When was the last time you had sex?"

Sandra looked genuinely confused. She stared up at me as beads of sweat broke out on her forehead.

"Sex, I'm not sure. I don't know what you mean," she answered.

"Sexual intercourse—with a boy," I said, assuming I had made myself perfectly clear.

Sandra shook her head. "I . . . I don't understand what you're saying," she countered.

Could this be true? Could a thirteen-year-old girl, the daughter of a nurse, have absolutely no knowledge of what sexual intercourse was?

"Maybe," I thought, "she doesn't call it by that name." I wiped Sandra's forehead and began to explain graphically.

"Has a boy ever put his penis in your vagina?" I asked.

Sandra looked shocked. "That's disgusting!" she said, her face wrinkling into a combination of surprise and disgust. "Why would I ever do anything like that?"

Now I was the one who was confused. I had ruled out almost every other cause for Sandra's intense pain, and I knew if I waited too long she would rupture.

I spoke with the attending physician. "Let's give her a vaginal examination," he said gruffly. "It sounds like an ectopic to me."

Sandra was rushed into the examining room. Now she was crying and begging to be released. Minutes later we had her diagnosis. There was no doubt; Sandra was suffering from an ectopic pregnancy. We had to operate, and for that we needed parental consent. We called her mother immediately.

I watched from the examining room as the nurse was told of her daughter's condition. She stiffened and carefully adjusted her glasses. Her posture was rigid, her lips pursed.

"I don't want the word *pregnancy* written on my daughter's chart," she stated matter-of-factly. The attending physician turned and looked her straight in the face.

"That's ridiculous!" he shouted. "Her chart is privileged information. We can't alter it to suit you!"

The nurse swallowed hard. She knew hospital policy.

"All right," she answered, "but I intend to tell the family that my daughter had a ruptured ovarian cyst, and I request that no one involved with the case say anything to the contrary."

The attending physician nodded reluctantly. I was surprised that the girl's mother had not yet gone in to comfort her child. I watched as she carefully smoothed her uniform, adjusted her cap and walked very slowly toward her daughter's room.

I stopped abruptly at the door. The nurse was standing over her daughter's bed shaking her finger and angrily accusing her of being "evil and bad." Minutes later, the furious nurse turned on her heel and walked briskly down the corridor. She had never asked her daughter how she felt, never held her hand or wiped away the tears.

I scurried back down the hall to look in on Debbie.

Sitting up in her bed, looking gaunt and skeletal, she was as reluctant as ever to talk with me. After her examination, a nurse called me over and began to complain: "Your patient has not been cooperating," she said. "One of the orderlies heard her vomiting in the bathroom yesterday, and today I found bits of her breakfast hidden beneath her mattress."

I thanked the nurse for her information, and after I had a brief discussion with the head of the clinic, we decided that Debbie would be denied use of the bathroom. She would have to use a bedpan, and she would once more have to suffer the humiliation of NG feedings. When Debbie did return to solid foods, she would be watched every minute. It saddened me that she was resisting treatment, but I was becoming more and more aware that anorexia was a disease of both mind and body. The restoration of Debbie's physical health would constitute only a partial recovery. She would require psychiatric help as well.

As I proceeded down the corridor, I inadvertently stopped at Michael's door and peeked inside. The boy was propped up against his pillows. I smiled weakly at him when he acknowledged my presence. Then without thinking, I nervously patted my stomach and left the hospital for the night.

I was now in my eighth week of pregnancy, and already I had gained fifteen pounds. It was becoming increasingly evident that I was expecting, and I decided that I was ready to begin wearing maternity clothes. Eddie and I realized that it was only a matter of time until Evie began to notice. Originally, we hadn't planned to tell her about the pregnancy until after the amniocentesis, but now it seemed wise to explain what she would soon be asking about herself. I had made up my mind to enjoy this pregnancy and to deal with the results of the test when the time came. Telling Evie that she would have a little brother or sister would make everything more real and more exciting.

"Evie," Eddie began, "we have some wonderful news. You're going to be a big sister!"

For a moment Evie's face was clouded in confusion. Then the questions tumbled out one after another. Eddie and I suppressed a laugh when our daughter asked us if the baby was inside me right now, if it was dressed and what it was wearing. Then she asked me if it was a boy or a girl, how big it was and if that was why I had gotten so fat.

We all sat on the floor while Evie opened a picture book about fetal development we had given her a year before. She asked us to point out the pictures that showed her new baby brother or sister.

"When will we know if it's a boy or a girl?" she asked.

"Soon," I said as I looked into her sparkling blue eyes. "Very soon."

After we put Evie to bed, Eddie told me he had been thinking. He had the perfect name for our child.

"I know it's probably going to be a girl," he explained, "but just in case, I have a great idea. Since you want to name the baby after your grandfather, Mordecai, why not call him Michael? Mike Greenbaum," Eddie said, smiling. "I like the sound of that. It's a strong name." Then he turned to me. "What do you think?"

What could I think? Michael was the name of the teenager who was slowly dying from leukemia. I couldn't erase the memory of him chanting his Torah portion in the bleak hospital room. If my baby was named Michael, I would always be reminded of another Michael when I looked at him. Rather than burden Eddie now, when he was so hopeful, I just laughed and said, "Mike's a strange name for a girl."

When the day of the amniocentesis finally arrived, I awoke bathed in sweat. Eddie was nervous, too. The procedure was simple and quick, but then there would be three long weeks between the day the test was taken and the day we would discover if our child was healthy.

Eddie took the morning off from work. He kissed me gently on the cheek and helped me into the gold Chevy. As we drove toward the hospital, I thought about how much I wanted the child I was carrying. If it were damaged, I wasn't at all sure I could discontinue the pregnancy. Perhaps as a doctor I was destined to give birth to, and care for, a sick child. "If not a doctor, who else?" I thought. That's when I felt it. A tiny flutter, almost like a gas pain in my belly. "It can't be," I thought. "It's too soon." But I felt the flutter again, and I knew I was feeling life. I touched my stomach and smiled, then I remembered I was on my way to the amniocentesis. If my baby weren't healthy, Eddie and I would be faced with a horrible choice. And what if I were carrying twins? What if one were healthy and the other sick? Images of my twin brother filtered through my mind. In some mysterious way, we were still tied to one another. At that moment Eddie grasped my hand, and we drove the rest of the way to the hospital in silence. It was a silence that would persist for the next three weeks.

Those weeks were the longest and most difficult of my life. I was so worried, so distraught, that I closed up. "Pass the salt," was the extent of my dinnertime chatter.

I didn't want to talk, but at two A.M., when my patient Susan called, I spoke with her.

"Dr. Greenbaum," she said in a breathless voice. "I'm in trouble. I feel depressed again. I forced myself to vomit today. I'm worried that it's all starting up again."

Susan had been doing so well. She had been gaining weight steadily. But now she was calling and asking for help. I wasn't sure what aid I could give her. I recalled her former suicidal gesture, and I tried offering her words of support and encouragement.

The next morning at the hospital, my lack of sleep clearly showed. I told Dr. Stern that Susan had called me.

"I told you giving her your home phone number was a mistake," she said. "You're going to regret it—mark my words."

I rubbed my tired eyes. I was already beginning to regret what I had done.

Although it was still early in my pregnancy, I had gained so much weight, the hospital staff began to joke that I was carrying twins. I prayed they were wrong. Thinking about twins had become a constant worry. I had a nagging premonition that because I had been the twin who survived, I would have to pay a terrible price for my success and my happiness.

My colleagues were not the only ones who noticed my weight gain. Patients were beginning to make comments as well. Most reactions were positive and encouraging. But Debbie, who was beginning to gain weight herself, found my pregnancy repulsive. More and more, she turned away from me when I made morning rounds. I was growing heavier. She was obsessed with remaining thin, and here I was, forcing her to eat and to nourish her body.

I asked Dr. Stern to take me off the case. I told her that I felt my pregnancy was impeding Debbie's progress. "Nonsense," she said. "You're her doctor. You'll stay on the case, and the patient will adjust."

And Debbie *did* adjust. In spite of herself, she had soon gained twelve pounds. Although she still looked quite thin by normal standards, she was strong enough and had put on enough weight to be released from the hospital. When I stopped by her room to wish her well, she only looked at me with the same hostile and rejecting expression she had maintained for the length of her hospitalization.

"Well, at least she's going, and it's all over," I said to the nurse who had reported her incidents of hiding food and forced vomiting.

"Don't be so sure," the nurse said as we watched Debbie walk down the corridor. "These anorectics have a way about them. I can't explain it, but they hate to relinquish control. You'll see."

That evening when Susan called me again, this time at eleven P.M., I began to understand.

"I'm starting to lose weight again, Dr. Greenbaum," she sighed, "and I feel bad about myself. My father is drinking, and I think I might do something destructive," she added.

I talked to Susan until almost midnight, and then fell wearily into bed. Only two weeks to go until I had the results of the amniocentesis.

The days faded into one another. Eddie and I barely talked. The pressure and the tension had forced us into our own private silences. Fern had the patience to sit with me in the cafeteria and to listen as I agonized about the outcome of the test. Whenever she saw that the stress was mounting, she suggested we go out for lunch. Soon the local Szechuan restaurant became a favorite eating spot. I began to develop a craving for this hot, spicy Chinese food.

"I don't think you'll have to worry about the baby, Dorothy," Fern joked. "He'll probably be born speaking fluent Chinese!"

Three weeks to the day after the amnio, I called the doctor's office.

"Hello, this is Dorothy Greenbaum," I said. "I'm calling about the results of my—"

The receptionist interrupted me. "Just one minute," she said.

I waited anxiously, and in those few seconds, I made a thousand bargains with God.

Then I heard the doctor's voice on the other end.

"Mrs. Greenbaum?" she asked.

"Yes," I answered. I knew there was nothing else to say.

"The results of your amniocentesis are in," she began. Then she spoke, but the only words I heard were that the baby was normal.

Just before I hung up, I thought to ask, "Is it a boy or a girl?"

"It's a boy," she answered.

For the first time in weeks I felt the grayness disappear. Everything came into sharp focus. Even the dim corridor seemed to be glowing.

"It's a boy!" I screamed. "And he's beautiful!" Nurses, residents, interns and orderlies came running. Everyone was congratulating me and pumping my hand. Someone pressed a dime in my palm and I dialed Eddie.

"It's a boy!" I shouted into the receiver, "and he's perfect!"

"My boy," Eddie shouted back. "My boy Mike!"

I took a few minutes off and went downstairs to the hospital gift shop. I had had my eye on a stuffed toy, a blue camel with wrinkled knees, for weeks. I promised myself the minute I got the news, the minute I knew my child was well, I wouldn't waste any time. That afternoon, after I shared my good news with my friends and colleagues, I bought my son his first toy.

Eddie and I were beside ourselves with joy. Now that I was free of the worry, I talked to him about some other feelings I had been having.

"These last weeks have been such a strain," I said. "I've never felt so vulnerable and helpless. Now I'm concerned that two children and a career are more than I can handle."

"All that *is* more than any one person can handle," Eddie said, "but remember, we're a team. We're in this together. Together, we're one hell of a parent!"

"You're right!" I said, laughing. "We can do it!" ˙

We knew it was time to tell Evie. She had been curious and interested when we had told her I was pregnant. But now we had even better news. She was going to have a brother.

"I don't want a brother," Evie said as she bit her lip and looked down at the floor. She twisted from side to side, trying to hold back the tears.

"But just think, honey," I said. "Now you'll always be my best girl."

Evie could tell we wanted her to be happy.

"Okay, Mommy," she said as she ran to her room.

"I think we're going to have some sibling rivalry on our hands," I said to Eddie.

"She's always been the center of our attention," Eddie said. "Now that Mike's coming, things will be different for her. But she'll adjust. We'll make sure she feels special and important, too."

Eddie was already calling him Mike. How was I going to tell him that I couldn't possibly name our son Michael when I was watching another Michael lose ground every day?

When I went to tuck Evie in for the night, she was crying.

"What's the matter, honey?" I asked as I kneeled down beside her. "Don't you want a little brother?"

Evie reached beneath her pillow. She showed me two shiny pink ribbons.

"I was saving them to give to my baby sister."

I smiled as I hugged Evie. "Maybe the next one will be a girl," I assured her as she fell asleep in my arms.

The next morning the hospital was bustling. As soon as I arrived, I rushed down to admitting, where an eight-year-old boy was complaining of severe abdominal pains. I suspected appendicitis, but his belly seemed soft to the touch—no tightened muscles—and he had normal bowel sounds. Still, he fought back the tears as he moaned and grasped his mother's hand.

"We'll have to send him up to X ray," I told his anxious mother. She looked at me suspiciously. Perhaps she was surprised to see a woman doctor, and a pregnant one at that. But she nodded her approval and the boy was whisked upstairs.

A few moments later, the resident called me to look at the pictures.

"Okay, doc, what's your diagnosis?" he asked with a serious expression as he handed me the X rays. I looked curiously at the picture. I saw an eight-inch chain of strangely familiar objects in the child's abdomen.

"What *are* they?" I asked.

"What do they look like?" the resident asked.

I examined the X ray a second time.

"They look like . . . paper clips," I said.

The resident smiled. "Yep, that's just what they are. The kid's been swallowing the things, and we'd better keep him here until he passes them. Why don't you explain this to the mother?"

I carried the X rays with me. Mother and child were still clinging to each other in the examining room. I leaned over and touched the little boy on the shoulder.

"Have you been swallowing anything unusual?" I asked. He looked up at me with sad brown eyes.

"No," he said as he shook his head from side to side.

I asked his mother to step outside.

"Your son's fine," I assured her, "but I think you should take a look at this."

I lifted the X ray toward the light. "This is a picture of your son's stomach," I said. "Do you notice anything unusual?"

The mother's look became indignant.

"I'm no doctor," she said. "How would I know if something is unusual or not?"

"Well, why don't you just take a look?" I urged.

She reached into her bag and put on her eyeglasses.

"What are those *things?*" she said as she pointed to the strange oblong shapes linked together in a long chain.

"Well, what do they look like to you?" I asked.

"I know you'll probably laugh," she said, "but they sure do look like paper clips."

Now it was my turn to smile. What wasn't so funny, I reminded myself, was that the paper clips might have perforated the child's stomach. His mother agreed when I told her we'd like to keep her son under close observation until the objects he still vehemently denied swallowing were safely expelled.

I returned to the ward, hoping to find Fern so I could tell her about my latest patient. But no one seemed to be around. One glance down the long corridor, and I knew instinctively what had happened. A group of doctors and nurses were standing outside Michael's room. He had died. I closed my eyes and remembered what Dr. Goldman had told me months ago: "No one ever gets used to the death of a child. No one. Not ever."

That afternoon I decided I would try to convince Eddie to name the baby something other than Michael. Something with an *M* in honor of my grandfather. Something strong and beautiful. "Matthew," I thought to myself. After the poet Matthew Arnold.

As the weeks progressed, Fern and I became increasingly involved with our pregnancies. As women, we were naturally a bit nervous, but as women doctors, we saw danger and problems everywhere. We were constantly reassuring each other that every little symptom was normal, but of course, we just couldn't be sure. Fern, who had noticed periods of hypertension, was taking her blood pressure several times a day. She decided to pass up her opportunity for a surgical rotation in order to minimize stress and maximize the chance that her baby would be healthy. As I grew bigger and heavier, I began to think that I might have diabetes. Fern suggested I test my urine. I used a urine strip from the lab, and found that although I did not have diabetes, I was releasing ketones, which are a breakdown product of fat, in my urine. Ketones are usually found in patients who are dieting or losing weight involuntarily. But I was eating *more* than usual. Fern couldn't figure it out either. She suggested I make up some high-energy snacks of raisins and nuts to nibble while I was on duty. "Maybe I'm not getting enough nutritional supplements," I mused as I filled my pockets with tiny boxes of raisins and bags of nuts.

More and more I became obsessed with my body chemistry. While other women might depend upon a monthly checkup at their obstetrician, I began to examine myself.

"You're becoming your own lab rat," Fern cautioned as I showed her an intricate graph I had plotted, which reflected the rise and fall of ketones in my blood. My own doctor had rejected the idea that it was anything serious.

"Stop being such a doctor," he had said. "Let me worry about it."

In my seventh month of pregnancy, Susan called at the clinic. I had not heard from her for weeks, and I was hoping she was all right. But the tone in her voice told me something was very wrong.

"I'm out of control," she said. "I have a bottle of pills, and I think I'm going to swallow them."

I knew her call was a last plea for help.

"Where are you, Susan?" I asked. She gave me a phone number and hung up. I had just enough time to copy the number before I heard the dial tone. I called her back. There was a busy signal.

"Oh, my God," I thought. "She's taken the phone off the hook. She's really going to hurt herself."

In desperation I called 911. An operator put me in touch with someone from the phone company. They quickly checked the number Susan had given me. It was a public phone booth, one that could not accept incoming phone calls.

I ran to the director of the clinic. "What can we do?" I asked.

"I've seen this sort of acting out again and again with anorexia," Dr. Stern said. "I doubt if the girl would really kill herself, but the gesture mandates hospitalization. I think we should have her placed in the psychiatry unit. This just can't continue."

I knew Dr. Stern was right—she had been right all along—but I still worried. An hour later Susan called back. She was feeling better. She hadn't taken any pills after all. I wanted to tell her how much she had put me through and how angry I was, but I remembered what Dr. Stern had said. Susan's problem could no longer be treated with nutritional supplements and medical supervision. It took some convincing, but after a while, Susan agreed to return to the hospital, to the psychiatry unit, where she would get the care she needed.

That afternoon as I left the hospital, I noticed that the sky was filled with large gray clouds. The air smelled moist and cold. Matthew was due in eight more weeks. The timing was perfect. I had doubled up on my course work, and if Matt arrived as scheduled, I would be through with this rotation just before my due date, and would have some time to be with the baby. Then I would graduate in June. "I just hope it doesn't snow on his birthday," I said aloud as the first wet flakes fell on my shoulders.

Four weeks before my due date, Dr. Stern called me into admitting.

"There's someone here I think you should see," she said.

By now I had gained almost forty pounds, and standing on my feet was beginning to take its toll. But I forgot all about my own discomfort when I saw the patient. It was Debbie. When she had been released she was thin but clearly on the road to recovery. The girl I saw before me was positively skeletal. Her eyes bulged; her hair hung in greasy strands. I could almost see her ribs pushing through her skin.

"God," I thought, "she's totally relapsed."

Dr. Stern looked over her chart. "The patient shows a weight loss of fifteen pounds in two weeks," she said. Debbie averted her eyes. I could tell she was even more repulsed at my weight gain than I was at her dramatic weight loss.

"I think that it's best for Debbie to report to our psychiatric unit," Dr. Stern said. "It seems she needs the kind of help they can provide."

Debbie bit her lower lip as she stared down at the floor. I walked toward her to wish her luck, but she only turned away.

On February 6, I awoke with a start. Something was wrong. Eddie, too, was sitting up in bed. "What's wrong?" he asked. Then he looked at me. "Are you all right?"

"Yes," I said, "but something is missing. Something is different."

Eddie nodded. He went to the window and let out a low whistle.

"You're not going to believe *this*," he said.

I ran to his side. The streets were deserted and silent. The window of our apartment that overlooked the parkway told it all. Not a car was moving. A thick white blanket of snow covered the streets and the highway.

"It's a blizzard!" Eddie said, laughing. "No school. No hospital. Hooray!" Then his face grew tense. "Oh, no," he said, "what if you go into labor?"

"The baby's not due until the end of the month," I assured him. "Relax."

By the afternoon, Eddie had become obviously worried. The blizzard had shut down the entire city. There was virtually no transportation. It would be days before we could dig out.

"Don't move," Eddie cautioned when he saw me get up for a glass of milk. "Promise you'll sit very still until the roads are clear. I'll get you anything you want."

"Are you forgetting that I'm a doctor?" I laughed. "If worse comes to worst, you can deliver the baby yourself. I'll guide you every step of the way."

Eddie blanched. "You've got to be kidding!" he said. "I'll call a police helicopter and have you flown out of here before I try *that!*"

Despite Eddie's concern, the snow was cleared and the roads were passable when my obstetrician called. It was the morning of February 11.

"Dorothy," he said, "I think we should induce labor. I've been a little worried about this ketosis thing myself. I think it would be better if we didn't wait another two weeks."

Eddie drove me to the hospital. Evie waited upstairs with my parents. As I looked at the snow-covered streets and the stark winter landscape, I said one last, silent prayer for my unborn son. "Just let him be healthy," I prayed.

At six-ten P.M., on February 11, Matthew was born. He weighed nine pounds. He was alert, beautiful and perfectly formed.

Eddie and I sat with our son in the recovery room for three hours.

"He's so peaceful and quiet," Eddie said. Matthew wrinkled his tiny forehead. Then he opened his eyes and looked up at us.

"Hello, sweetheart," I whispered.

Eddie moved closer. He placed his hand in mine, and we kissed. The warmth of our love wrapped around us like a new baby blanket.

14

Graduation

It is the day I have been waiting for. I am nursing my baby as I look at the gift my husband has given me. It is a large gold pin. In the center is a caduceus and the letters M.D. I turn the pin over. Engraved on the back are the words "WE DID IT!"

I smile as Matthew makes a cooing sound. Now I really do have everything.

When I arrive at the university, the graduates are a sea of black and purple amidst the flowers. I look for a familiar face. I see Simon from my anatomy class, Dr. Goldman from pediatrics, Dr. Gross from obstetrics. Then I see Fern. She kisses me on the cheek and tells me that her son, Kevin, smiled for the first time today. I squeeze her hand as we take our seats.

The sun is high in a cloudless sky. The air is warm. I smile out at the audience. The dean is calling out each name. I strain to hear my own.

"Doctor Dorothy Greenbaum," he announces. I walk slowly up to the podium, wanting to savor every second. He congratulates me and places the diploma in my outstretched hand. I turn to the audience. My whole family is standing. Evie is perched on Eddie's shoulders. My sister-in-law holds up Matthew. They are all applauding wildly.

I don't even try to hold back my tears.

I wave the diploma and smile.

This is real. We *really* did it!

PART III

15

Major Medical Center

The July sun is hot on my back as I walk up the steps of the medical center. It is my first day as an intern. My first day as a real doctor. For the next year I will be required to be on call thirty-six hours at a time every third night and to work from seven A.M. to seven P.M. all the other days.

I am wearing slacks and a short-sleeve cotton blouse. I touch my pocket and feel the gold pen in the felt case, a graduation present from my old friends Suzie and Jack. I think of them now as I walk through the revolving doors and take the elevator up to the sixth floor.

I am greeted by the pediatric resident, Jonathan Stein. He is small with brown hair, a mustache and a goatee. He smiles at me as I hold out my hand.

"Welcome aboard, Doctor Greenbaum," he says as he motions for me to join the small group of nervous interns.

There is only one other woman standing in the hallway with Dr. Stein, and I am immediately drawn to her. She is tall with short, dark hair. Although she is younger than I am, we do look alike. Her name is Denise, and she nods to me as I take my place beside her.

Major Medical Center is a tertiary care center. Patients are referred here from several other hospitals. The pediatric unit in which I will be doing my internship is well equipped to handle long-term illnesses such as leukemia. It is an excellent place to do an internship, and Jonathan Stein seems gentle, casual and eager to help us all learn the ropes as quickly as possible.

Denise and I have been assigned a block of patients, and we have decided to split them up between us. Elizabeth, my very first patient, is fifteen years old. The walls of her room are covered with posters of rock stars, and her bed is littered with stuffed animals and satin pillows. She wears a colorful bandanna around her head. I am smiling at Elizabeth when Dr. Stein takes me aside. We stand together in the yellow corridor.

"She doesn't understand the significance of her diagnosis," Dr. Stein explains. "She has a very malignant form of leukemia."

"Is it fatal?" I ask.

Dr. Stein looks at the door to Elizabeth's room. He bites his lip. "There's always hope," he says.

For an instant I think I detect something in Dr. Stein's voice, something more than a doctor discussing his patient, but when I look at him again, he is adjusting his jacket and scurrying down the hall.

I walk eagerly into each of the ten rooms to which I have been assigned. Some hold four beds, others only two. I read the charts of children who are here for simple broken legs, appendicitis operations, and some who are close to death. I am responsible for fifteen patients, and as I touch the pen still neatly clipped to my pocket, I begin to comprehend the enormity of my responsibility.

After the interns have become acquainted and Dr. Stein urges us all to be on a first-name basis, we meet with the chief resident. He is a large, stocky man with huge hands. Standing beside him, Jonathan looks like a sprightly elf. Dr. Baker tells us we will now decide who will be on call until seven P.M. tomorrow night. I look down at my shoes as he moves his pen over the list of names. I am thinking of my baby. This is the first day I have been away from him since he was born only four months ago. Eddie has taken the summer off to be with the children. We agreed he should be there full-time to make this transition less difficult. He has stocked up on books to read, signed Evie up for day camp and is enjoying spending his time alone with his son. I am looking forward to leaving the hospital at seven P.M. I ache to hold Matthew in my arms.

"Greenbaum, you're on tonight with Dr. Stein."

The words interrupt my reverie. For an instant, I feel like declining—explaining that I have an infant waiting for me, that I'm not ready. I don't have a change of clothes or a toothbrush, and my husband is expecting to pick me up at seven. But instead I only nod. "I'll call Eddie at lunch," I think to myself as I follow Denise back to our section of the ward.

The next time I look at my watch it is four-thirty. I'm sure something is wrong. I only just got here. Then I feel the hunger pangs and I realize that I have not eaten—not stopped—since I arrived here at seven in the morning. I reach into my pocket and find a dime to call Eddie.

"How is it going?" he asks.

"I'll never catch up," I say. "There's so much to do, so much to know." Then I explain about being on call until tomorrow evening.

"Tomorrow night when I pick you up, you'll tell me everything," Eddie says.

When I ask about the children, Eddie hands the phone to Evie, who tells me her little brother made happy cooing sounds when she stood by his crib and said, "Hi ya! Hi ya!" I get a sinking feeling just thinking about missing any part of Matt's growing up.

I tell Evie to kiss the baby for me and remind Eddie that I will be here a whole day and night.

"Everything's under control at home," he assures me as I hang up the phone and rush back to the sixth floor.

Jonathan stops me as I am rushing down the corridor. He reminds me that tomorrow morning at seven A.M. sharp we will have grand rounds. I must be prepared with background information, prognosis and course of treatment for all fifteen patients. I smile politely. As soon as things quiet down, I'll be able to write.

I am called to a room at the end of the corridor. A fifteen-year-old boy who was hit by a car has his broken leg in a temporary cast to prepare him for traction. The boy is obviously in pain. I see at once that the cast is too tight. The teenager's toes are purple. I call the orthopedic resident, but the orthopedic intern answers the phone. This is his first night, too. He is tired and impatient. "I have a feeling you're overreacting," he snaps when I describe the patient's discolored toes. "They had better be purple!" he shouts as he hangs up the receiver. I sit with the teenager and his family until the intern shows up. I am too exhausted to smile when he begins to cut the cast open.

By four A.M. I still have not eaten. There is a steady stream of children and parents plus the fifteen patients who have been assigned to my care.

I finish with my last admission at six-thirty A.M. Having only thirty minutes before grand rounds begin, I gather up the charts and frantically begin to review each case. My ankles are bulging over my shoes. My mouth has a dry, sour taste, and hunger continues to gnaw away at my concentration. I am not sure I can last twelve more hours.

At seven A.M. Dr. Baker leads the interns down the long corridor. When we pass Elizabeth's room, he points to the closed door, and I begin my presentation.

"This is the first admission for a fifteen-year-old white female, diagnosed three months ago with AML, acute myelogenous leukemia—"

Dr. Baker waves his hand in the air: "Next case, please."

"But I haven't finished," I stammer.

"It's hopeless. There's no point going any further," Dr. Baker says curtly.

His words fall with a finality I cannot accept. As we continue down the corridor, I see Elizabeth's mother open the door to her daughter's room. I catch a glimpse of the girl tapping her feet to the music of her radio. I feel the horror and disbelief of Dr. Baker's diagnosis. How can he be so sure?

As grand rounds continue, I present my cases. I nod to Jonathan as he stands behind Dr. Baker and mouths the answers to many of the questions. He holds up his fingers to help an intern who is unsure of a white count. "At least we have a friend here," I whisper to Denise as we move in a group toward the end of the corridor.

By mid-afternoon, I manage to sneak a quick cup of coffee. Then I am notified that one of the attending physicians has ordered more chemotherapy for Elizabeth. When I enter the girl's room, I remember Dr. Baker's words. Elizabeth is leafing through a teen magazine. When she greets me, I notice the black-and-blue sores on her lips. Otherwise, she looks like any normal teenager, except for her bright bandanna, which I suspect hides the baldness that is often a side effect of chemotherapy.

When I look for a vein in Elizabeth's arm, I am disturbed to discover that most of her veins are collapsed. She has been hospitalized for three months, and the constant chemotherapy has taken its toll. I examine both arms and both hands. There is not one vein that looks as though it will yield blood. A nurse opens the door and watches me carefully. "I suggest you try her feet," she says.

Elizabeth, obviously used to this ritual, props her foot up on the bed. I tie a tourniquet around her ankle, and as I do so, she begins to tie a band tightly around her head. I look questioningly at the nurse, who has seen all this before. Assuming that Elizabeth is tying the band to distract herself from this painful procedure, I touch her shoulder and say I will try to be as gentle as possible. Elizabeth says nothing. She twirls the band tighter and tighter.

The veins on Elizabeth's foot are a web of thin, blue lines. My confidence is shaken. I ask the nurse to call Jonathan. She looks at me quizzically and motions for me to follow her outside into the corridor.

I stare at the chipped yellow paint as she talks in a whisper.

"Dr. Stein is losing sensation in his fingertips from the chemotherapy," she explains.

For a moment I am petrified. Does this mean I, too, will lose sensation in my fingertips from administering chemotherapy? I think how it will be if I am unable to examine a patient or to feel my baby's skin.

"Maybe I should wear gloves," I say.

The nurse looks at me as if I am an idiot. She shakes her head and clicks her tongue.

"You don't understand," she whispers. "Dr. Stein *takes* chemotherapy. Don't you know? He has lymphoma."

I look up to make sure the nurse is telling the truth. I can see from her expression that she is not joking.

I picture the smiling, elfin Dr. Stein. How can he do this? How can he work with leukemic patients when he has cancer himself?

Just then he walks by.

"What's the problem?" he asks.

Avoiding his eyes, I explain the difficulty I am having with the thin veins in Elizabeth's feet. Jonathan smiles and leads me back into the room with the stuffed animals, the posters and the fifteen-year-old girl with leukemia. Deftly he slips the needle into a hair-like vein in Elizabeth's ankle and administers the chemotherapy. I am in awe of him.

As we leave the room together, he asks me if I noticed Elizabeth tying that band around her forehead.

"How could I miss it?" I answer. "Do you think it really works? I mean, do you think it distracts her from the pain?"

Jonathan does not smile. "Dorothy, that band has nothing to do with pain. Somehow word has gotten around on this floor that if the kids tie bands around their heads during chemo, they can prevent hair loss. It's really very sad, but I think it's best not to discourage them. In this sort of case, whatever makes things easier for the patient is good medicine."

I walk slowly down the corridor. It is six P.M. I have a little over an hour to finish up, take the last blood tests, leave detailed notes for the interns on the next shift and, finally, sign out.

At seven-thirty P.M., I am standing in the hospital lobby. My clothes are rumpled and stained. My eyes are rimmed in red. In the past twenty-four hours I have not been off my feet for a minute. I have had only a quick cup of coffee and a few swallows of soda. My new pen has left ink marks on my pocket, and when I look down at my swollen ankles, I shudder.

Eddie greets me with the first real smile I have seen all day. Then he sweeps me through the revolving doors into our own private world.

"I can't do this," I say as I wipe away the tears. "I miss the kids. These children are all dying. This is no way to spend my life."

Eddie silently hands me a cup of coffee and a Danish.

"How are my babies?" I ask as I gulp the coffee.

"Everything is fine. The kids are in your parents' apartment. When we get home, you'll take a long shower, you'll eat, you'll relax, and we'll be a family."

I'm surprised the apartment is still there when Eddie opens the door for me. It seems like another century when I dressed, showered and left for my first day as an intern. I'm glad the children aren't here now. I have something I must do. I walk into my bedroom, take off my clothes and slip them into a brown paper bag. Then I push the bag way back into the darkness of our closet. In my head I know cancer is not catching, but in my heart, I am still not sure.

As I wash away the sounds and smells of the hospital, I make a thousand secret bargains with God. "I'll do anything," I say as I look up at the bathroom ceiling. "Just please promise that my kids will never get that sick."

When I have showered and changed, I go upstairs to my parents' apartment. Evie comes rushing toward me, Matt is cooing in his playpen. My mother looks at me very carefully. Just before Evie tumbles into my embrace, she holds up her arm.

"Dorothy, did you wash your hands?" she asks.

As the first few days of my internship passed, I became more accustomed to the routine; to the sights, the sounds, the constant drama of pediatrics at Major Medical Center. But nothing could have prepared me for the Rizzo family and their two-and-a-half-year-old son, Billy. Billy had already been diagnosed as having leukemia. Since our hospital was a referral center for leukemia, I had already seen and heard of so many cases that I was beginning to view this cancer as a common childhood disease.

Right from the start, I saw that Billy was special. He had soft blond ringlets framing his sweet round face. His gentle voice was especially endearing. It was impossible not to like Billy, and even more impossible not to befriend his family. His parents, Marie and Tony, were accompanied by Marie's mother. The family was close-knit and loving. They fondly called Billy their "little man."

Once the child was settled in and had been assigned to my care, it was time to begin his chemotherapy. Marie and her mother asked if they could be present in the treatment room. Billy had been through this procedure many times before, and they knew he would need their support. I believed that in cases like these, a doctor should adjust to what is best for the child. I smiled warmly at the two women and watched helplessly as they led their brave "little man" into the small room.

As I struggled to find an adequate vein on the patient's arm, Marie stroked her son's hair and the elderly grandmother talked softly in Italian. For a moment, Billy looked up and saw me poised over him, needle in hand. His big brown eyes widened, and he bit his lip as the tears streamed slowly down his cheeks.

"No more pins, please, no more pins," he said in a pleading voice.

I wanted to gather his tiny, sick body up in my arms and make him better with kisses and hugs. I couldn't stand the thought of bringing him any more pain. Instead I turned off the volume and the picture. I blotted out the tiny body, the big round eyes, the mother and the grandmother. All I permitted myself to see was his hand and my needle. Then, as I concentrated on threading it through the skin and into his vein, I whispered a silent prayer. "Please God, make this a good IV."

When the chemo was finally over and Billy was back in his bed clutching his Batman and Robin dolls, Marie and her mother took my hands in theirs and thanked me for being so gentle. But in truth, I felt like a torturer. Billy's words, his pleading eyes, haunted me. The fact that he looked like my own baby made it even more painful. And somehow I sensed that Marie Rizzo knew just how I felt.

That afternoon, as I walked through the lobby on my way to meet Eddie, I was surprised by a flashing ball of blonde curls and energy. Evie. She put her arms around my legs and shouted, "Mommy! Mommy!" As I bent down to hug her, I sensed that someone was watching. It was Elizabeth's mother. When our eyes met, I was at once a doctor and a mother. My child was the picture of health; upstairs, her child was waging a losing battle against cancer.

Elizabeth's mother looked down at Evie. At that moment, I wanted to blot out the vision of my daughter's health and beauty. I remembered an old superstition my mother had told me about. Envy. The "evil eye." I knew I'd bargain my soul for the safety of my child. When I looked up at Elizabeth's mother, it was as if she could read my mind. She smiled weakly and nodded as she clutched the giant stuffed panda bear she had bought for her daughter.

That evening, after the children were tucked safely in bed, I told Eddie about Billy.

"It's so hard," I said. "I don't know if this is for me. All these terribly sick children. Maybe I should reconsider and choose OB."

That's when Eddie explained about the "hold button."

"Whenever things get too tough," he said, "just picture a telephone switch in your mind. Then flick it on hold. Take each day, each hour, each minute as it comes."

Eddie's idea was a good one. I didn't know it then, but I would be putting myself on "hold" almost every day of my internship.

The next morning during grand rounds I presented the case of a two-and-a-half-year-old white male with leukemia. Everything about Billy's case pointed to a positive prognosis. All the facts, including his age, were encouraging. There was a good chance that Billy Rizzo would survive.

As I walked down the hall with the rest of the interns, we stopped at each room and peered inside. When I opened Elizabeth's door, I noticed that her small stuffed animals were being replaced by larger, fluffier ones. Elizabeth was slowly being ravished by her illness, and in contrast, her toys became more hearty, more life-size. And so it was with many of the other critically ill children. Eventually, even the infants lay beside enormous toy bunnies, teddy bears or ducks. Purchasing the toys and arranging them on their childrens' beds was the only way distraught and helpless parents could provide joy for their dying children. But eventually, the toys became an eerie presence. They dwarfed the frail, sickly bodies, casting foreboding shadows across the narrow hospital beds.

One morning I watched silently as a young mother, bending over a crib to kiss her child, stroked the large stuffed dog she clutched in her arm. It was as if the toy had become a substitute, a "transitional object," for the parent who knew she must slowly distance herself from the child she would soon lose.

In the evenings when I made rounds, I found myself moving gigantic stuffed animals to the corner of a crib or the edge of a bed so I could adjust an IV or check the pulse of a sleeping child. After a while I came to call this phenomenon "the hyperplastic bunny syndrome," hyperplastic being the medical term for an overgrowth of tissue.

One morning during grand rounds, I shared my insights with Jonathan, Dr. Baker and the other interns. Dr. Baker nodded his head. "That's quite true, Dr. Greenbaum," he said sadly. "And if you observe carefully, the next thing grieving parents will tell you is that they are planning to take their child to Disneyland."

That afternoon, Marie and Tony Rizzo stopped me in the hall. They were anxiously waiting for the chemotherapy to put Billy's leukemia into remission. I joined them as they opened the door to his room.

"How's my little man today?" Tony asked as he reached down and brushed the now thinning hair from his son's forehead. Billy smiled weakly.

"Dr. Greenbaum is here, Billy," Marie said. "Why don't you tell her what we're going to do as soon as you get well."

Billy looked up at me with his sad brown eyes. "We're going to Disneyland," he said in his special little voice.

The following Sunday I was off. The weather was warm and the sky was clear. Eddie and I decided to take the children to a neighborhood park. Eddie pushed Matthew in his stroller, and Evie ran around the three of us in excited circles. The clouds floated like bits of white cotton above our heads.

Evie and I sat on the swings and began pushing up toward the white fluff. I could feel the rush of warm air against my face. I was healthy and alive. "Come on, Mommy," Evie cried. "Let's see how high you can pump!" I began to push the swing higher, higher into the blue. Evie was right beside me, her yellow braids flying wildly in the wind. Just then, for a split second, I knew what I wanted for my daughter. I wanted her to grab every joyful minute of life. I wanted her to taste life like a navel orange, biting hungrily until the sweet, rich juices streamed down her chin. Because I was buried in the suffering of so many families, I wanted my children to experience the beauty of a life brimming with health and pleasure.

Later, as the sun glowed copper in the darkening sky, Eddie and I talked quietly as we walked home.

"I feel so guilty," I explained. "We have so much, there's no way anyone can know why some families have such pain and others don't. It just seems to be the luck of the draw."

Eddie nodded. Then he cautioned, "Guilt is destructive. We should luxuriate in what we have. Any one of those parents you see at the hospital would tell you that. We should enjoy what we have right now because no one knows what tomorrow may bring."

The tomorrow Eddie talked of came all too soon. At eight A.M. Patrick was admitted. He reminded me of a young Huck Finn. Five years old with bright red hair and freckles, Patrick was the stereotypical "boy next door." That night his sleep had been disturbed by a headache and a bout of vomiting. By the time his mother brought him to the ER, his fever was 104°. Patrick's neck was stiff, and his face was covered with purple dots. On close inspection, I could see that some of the dots contained black marks in the middle. I ordered a spinal tap immediately, hoping my suspicions were wrong.

Within the hour we had Patrick's diagnosis. My worst fears had been confirmed. He had meningococcal meningitis—a highly infectious disease that rapidly devastates its victims.

I knew we didn't have a minute to spare. With this particular form of meningitis, timing was everything. If Patrick was to survive, we had to begin administering antibiotics and get him into isolation in the ICU immediately.

When word spread that we had a case of meningococcal meningitis, the entire staff went into high gear. Everyone who might come into contact with the patient had to wear masks, gowns and gloves. There was an air of urgency on the ward. Nurses and doctors worked together quickly and efficiently. When Patrick was settled in and the antibiotics had been administered, Jonathan took me aside.

"Get ready to go out on an emergency transport," he said.

I had never ridden in an ambulance before, and I was nervous. Jonathan tried to calm my fears.

"It's nothing too serious," he explained. "It's a call from an outlying hospital. It seems to be a case of cardiac infection, but the child appears to be stable. I don't think you'll have any problems."

I knew that in the ambulance there would be no backup. I would be alone except for a nurse and the driver. Jonathan would not be there if I needed him.

"I'll take my emergency drug sheet, just in case," I said.

Jonathan nodded. "I even take mine to the beach!" he laughed as he shooed me toward the waiting ambulance.

Jane was waiting for me. She was an experienced nurse with a reputation for being tough. She nodded curtly to me as we took our seats in the back of the ambulance.

We moved quickly through the city streets. In no time at all we reached the small hospital. The patient was a twelve-year-old girl. She looked sicker than I had expected. When I turned around, I caught an expression of concern on Jane's face. The staff at the hospital seemed eager to get the child into the ambulance. A bit too eager. They already knew what I didn't.

When I hooked the patient onto the monitor in the ambulance, the EKG showed she was in V Tach (ventricular tachycardia). The child's heart was beating so fast that it didn't have time to fill with blood and be an efficient pump. V Tach is serious, one step away from V Fib (ventricular fibrillation). In this condition, the contractions of the heart are so erratic that the only way to save the patient is to electrically shock the heart back to a normal rhythm.

I watched the monitor closely. The waves on the small screen indicated that the child might go into V Fib any moment. I had never cardioverted a patient before, I had never even handled the paddles. I turned to Jane.

"Where are the paddles? I think we're going to need them."

Jane began to sweat. "Oh, shit!" she said as she wiped her brow. "Is the kid really in that much trouble?"

She looked at the monitor and didn't bother to ask a second time.

While Jane set up the paddles I shouted to the driver: "Go as fast as you can. Don't drive. *Fly!*"

I heard the screaming siren. The ambulance lights were flashing. I glanced up from my patient and saw the traffic separate as we approached. I thought of all the times I had been out there in a car watching an ambulance, straining to catch a glimmer of a white coat in the corner of the window, thinking how brilliant and how skilled doctors were. Now I was the one in the white coat. I was alone except for Jane and a child whose heart was failing.

Jane handed me the paddles. I prepared to test them. I waited as she turned on the machine.

Nothing happened.

Jane looked up at me. The perspiration was pouring from her forehead.

"The machine's dead," she said.

I began to administer drugs. The child did not respond. She seemed to be going into V Tach again. I reached for the two-way radio. If I could only hear Jonathan's voice, if I could only feel I wasn't totally responsible.

The radio was dead.

Jane looked up at me questioningly. Her mascara was running in black streams down her cheeks. I sat on the floor beside the child and checked her pulse. I stroked her hair. It was all I *could* do.

When we arrived at the hospital, we raced up the ramp and screamed for security. As the patient was rushed inside, Jonathan came out to meet me.

"How did it go?" he asked.

"It was a complete disaster. Everything went wrong. This little girl is in a lot of trouble."

Jonathan nodded. "Welcome to the real world," he said.

I followed the patient into X ray. Her heart was enlarging rapidly. The sac that protects the heart was filling with fluid. The chief of thoracic surgery and the cardiologists were called. We knew she would need a procedure called pericardiocentesis, in which the fluid between the heart and its protective sac, the pericardium, is removed by a needle.

Within minutes, everyone gathered around the child's bed. The chief of thoracic surgery decided to conduct the procedure himself in the ICU. He wanted the entire staff to observe.

I was relieved to know that the child was in the best possible hands. I watched intently as the needle was deftly inserted through the girl's chest. The fluid was slowly draining. Then, before everyone's astonished eyes, the child thrust her head back, and we heard a cry. She arrested on the table. Instantly, Jane jumped on the patient's chest. The thoracic surgeon thrust a hard board under the child's back for support. Jane administered CPR. A resident hooked the patient up to a respirator, and I drew up drugs. Nurses handed syringes back and forth. Everything was orderly and efficient, but still the child lay there—pale and dead.

I was shaking, but I had no doubts. We had done our best. Jonathan motioned to me. "Go out there and tell the mother," he said.

I walked into the waiting room. A young woman grasping a leather handbag and nervously pacing the floor looked up at me. My words came out slowly, carefully.

The patient's mother stared at me calmly. "This will take a while to sink in," I thought.

"Can I see my child now?" she asked. Her voice was clipped— controlled.

I led her into the ICU. She looked down at her little girl.

Then it hit her, a sharp bullet of pain shooting violently through her body. She jerked back.

"Oh, my baby! My baby!" she moaned as she grasped the railing of the bed for support.

I wanted to close my eyes, to make it all go away, to bring the child back to life. I began to sway. The floor seemed to be moving toward me. I felt an arm firmly grasp my elbow. Jane. She led me to an empty conference room where I began to cry. I could still hear the grieving mother, could still see the dead child. Jane sat beside me, holding my hand.

"Please cover for Dr. Greenbaum. She'll need a little time alone," Jane said to two of the nurses on the floor.

I sat alone in the conference room for a few minutes and remembered what Eddie had told me. I switched the imaginary button to "hold," adjusted my clothes, wiped my eyes and walked back out on the ward.

Patrick was sleeping in the ICU. I could see at once that the disease was worsening. He had developed *purpura fulminans,* a gangrene that often accompanies meningitis. There were blackened areas on his fingers, toes, lips, buttocks and the tip of his penis. But he was not in a coma. He was breathing. There was still hope.

This was an endless night. I checked my watch. I still had twelve more hours to go. I peeked into Elizabeth's room. She, too, was fast asleep. The giant stuffed animals guarded her as she tossed restlessly in her bed.

Someone called to me from an open doorway. "Dorothy, let's talk."

It was Marie Rizzo. We had become friends. She was a constant presence in the hospital, a friend to many of the other mothers and to the staff as well. Billy had not improved. His most recent bone-marrow test had been a disappointment: he was not in remission. The cancer cells had not decreased. Maybe this was a tougher case than we had anticipated.

"I hear you've had a bad day," Marie said.

"Bad isn't the word for it. How's Billy?" I asked.

Marie shook her head. "He's losing that beautiful blond hair," she said. "I know it will grow back, but Carol is taking it badly. She doesn't understand. She can't comprehend what's happening to her little brother."

Carol was the Rizzos' older child, a perky six-year-old. She visited the hospital often, and increasingly she was becoming aware that Billy was very sick.

"Dorothy, how do you do it? Day after day, all these sick kids. Doesn't it get to you?"

"Sometimes I wonder if I'll stay here in pediatrics," I confessed to Marie. "If I could just see someone cured." Then, remembering that Billy lay in the other room, I added, "When we see Billy getting better, then we'll know this is all worth it."

Marie smiled and patted my shoulder. I waved as I walked down the hall to call Eddie.

"Can you come by the hospital for dinner?" I asked. "Can you bring the kids?" Lately Eddie and I had been meeting in the hospital cafeteria for dinner. He brought the children and whatever food was left over from the family dinner. Then we shared some "big time" together. Often our "big time" lasted only fifteen minutes before I was paged, but it was enough to keep me going through the long night.

Within the hour, Eddie, Evie and Matthew were huddled together in a corner of the hospital cafeteria. I changed my blouse and scrubbed before I went downstairs to meet them. I kissed the children. When Matthew crawled into my lap, I smiled my first smile in almost twenty-four hours.

I told Eddie about the emergency transport and the child who had died. I talked about Patrick and Billy. Eddie listened. Then he leaned over and took my hand.

"But *we're* here now, Dorothy. The children are well and happy. Let's enjoy our time together."

I nodded, trying desperately to push the events of the day out of my mind, to shut out the haunting visions of the children on the sixth floor.

That week Billy went home to spend a few days with his family. Now I was able to concentrate on Patrick, Elizabeth and the rest of my patients. But I knew Billy would return soon. His illness made him extremely susceptible to infection. I also knew that by extending my love to him I had broken all the rules. I thought about Billy as I walked down the busy corridors. I saw his sweet face looking up at me when I bent down to kiss my own little boy good night. "Please let him live," were the words I whispered when the Rizzo family returned to the hospital. Billy had a temperature of 104°. That night, as he lay quietly in his bed, Marie's mother brought me a cup of coffee.

"Have you seen my little man tonight?" she asked. "He looks so sick. You should have seen him in his baseball cap with his chubby little thighs. You should have seen him when his hair was all golden ringlets."

I grasped the woman's hand and smiled into her eyes. Nothing I could say could ease her pain. No medicine could help her forget that the Billy who had once played ball, whose hair had been thick and curly, whose flesh had been pink and dimpled, now lay emaciated and nearly bald in the room at the end of the hall.

A few doors away in ICU, Patrick was slowly and miraculously improving. He was becoming more alert and was able to wiggle his fingers and toes. The blackened, gangrenous areas began to slough off. His shock of red hair and his freckled face looked startlingly out of place in the bleak isolation unit. Like Billy, he belonged out there, running, laughing, drinking life in, instead of having it slowly drain away through tubes and catheters.

I realized as I stood in Elizabeth's room and looked at the posters, the get-well cards, the plants and the stuffed animals that many of my patients would never leave this place. Many would never survive. When they took a turn for the worse, I became despondent. I knew I was bonding with Billy, and I was sure that any day there would be another admission, another child for whom I would feel the same love. I went to Dr. Baker.

"I'm not staying in pediatrics for my residency," I said. "I can't take the sadness."

"You'll adjust," he said with confidence. "You'll get used to it."

I looked at Dr. Baker, and holding back the tears, I explained, "I never *want* to adjust. I don't know how you do it."

Dr. Baker looked away. "Give yourself a few more months. Let's wait and see."

As I walked toward the lounge, I felt better. "I have an escape," I told myself. "Only eleven more months to go."

When Eddie picked me up that evening, I breathed in the first golden breaths of autumn. The seasons were changing; my children were growing up. Not everything was sickness and death.

I began to talk to Eddie about my patients.

"Damn it, Dorothy!" he shouted. "I don't want to hear about

Billy and Patrick and Elizabeth. What about *our* kids? What about
me?"

"You're absolutely right," I answered. "I'm sorry. I'm going to
have to learn how to leave the hospital behind when I walk into
our home."

"I have to shut them out," I said to myself. "I have to forget."

But forgetting wasn't easy. Even while I was bathing Matthew
and Evie, or playing with them in the park, I'd think of the children in the hospital and know how much an hour, a day of vibrant
health would mean to them.

As the weeks passed, Patrick continued to improve. "He's my
ray of hope," I said to myself one afternoon when the freckle-faced
child opened his eyes and said hello to me for the first time. That
same afternoon, Elizabeth asked if we could talk. I nodded and sat
on the edge of her bed.

"Dr. Greenbaum, I'd like to go home," she said. "The drugs
aren't helping anymore. Why can't I get out of here?"

"You know you'll be susceptible to all sorts of infections," I
explained.

But Elizabeth had been in the hospital long enough to know
that she could return at any time for antibiotics if she needed to.

"I'll talk to Dr. Stein about it this afternoon," I said.

"Please do it soon," she pleaded. "I've got to get out of this
place!"

Jonathan was in the resident's lounge. He sat quietly stroking
his beard and staring into space.

"Elizabeth wants to go home," I said.

"There's nothing more we can do for her here. Let's release her,"
he said with a sigh.

Then, since we were alone, I decided to really talk to Jonathan,
to ask him the questions I had been mulling over since I first
learned he had cancer.

"How can you do this?" I asked.

He turned and smiled grimly. "So you know," he said. "I guess there just aren't any secrets from the hospital grapevine."

I waited for him to continue.

"I know what these kids are feeling on the inside. That's why I stay, and that's how I do it. The most important thing we can give a child, along with excellent medical care, is hope. Take Elizabeth, for example. Keeping her here now that her condition is so acute would be a punishment. Let her go home. Let her be with her friends and her family—in her own room. Who knows? She could make it. We can't take that last little bit of hope from her."

"What about you?" I asked.

Jonathan sighed. "I never let myself think that my illness is terminal. My prognosis is good. I have too much to live for—my wife, my son, my work. I'm a big one for denial. When I felt that lump on my leg, I waited almost a year before I did anything about it. That was a mistake. But you know, I still believe in hope and miracles, and all sorts of happy endings."

"Happy endings," I thought to myself the next morning as Elizabeth excitedly packed her suitcase. Her room was sadly bare. The posters were neatly rolled up and fastened with rubber bands. The cards and the stuffed animals were arranged in cardboard cartons. A pale, thin girl with a red bandanna on her head smiled at me.

I kissed her good-bye. "Get out of here and have a good time," I said.

She blew me a kiss and walked down the yellow corridor. I closed my eyes as I wished her a happy ending.

Something was different in the ICU. It was Patrick. His blue eyes were wide open. He was sitting up.

"Hi," I said. "How are you feeling today?"

"Okay," Patrick said, "but I miss my dog. When can I go home?"

"You'll be home soon enough," I answered.

"When?" Patrick asked again.

I looked at his chart. His recovery had surprised everyone. But it was not yet complete. His kidneys still weren't functioning. If Patrick couldn't urinate by himself, he would have to be put on dialysis. I didn't want that to happen to this freckle-faced five-year-old.

"Did he urinate today?" I asked the nurse. She shook her head sadly. Everyone was rooting for this kid.

"Patrick," I said, "it looks like you'll be here a little while longer."

"But what about school?" he asked.

"What grade are you in?"

"Kindergarten," Patrick answered proudly.

"Well, I think you can miss a few more days, don't you?"

Patrick nodded sadly.

That afternoon Marie and Tony Rizzo took Billy home. There was still no improvement in his bone-marrow tests, but the weather was warm and the Rizzos wanted to be a family again for a little while. In the past few days, Billy had become strangely quiet, smiling only when he was with his mother or when I came in for a visit, reassuring him there would be "no more pins."

Tony put his arm on my shoulder.

"Have a good weekend, Doc," he said with a smile. I looked down at Billy. He was wearing a blue baseball cap. I touched his face. "Take care of our little man," I said. I watched as the Rizzo family carried their son to the elevator. I knew they would be back—very soon.

My weekend began as soon as the Rizzos disappeared into the elevator. I had been on call for twenty-four hours. But tonight, Eddie and I were going out. He had finally had enough of the sadness that followed me when I left the hospital.

"I got tickets for a Broadway show," he had informed me a few days before. "It's one of those whodunits. We need a night out, away from everything." Eddie's idea was perfect. The play, *Deathtrap,* was supposed to be terrific. I was looking forward to the evening.

The exhaustion of twenty-four hours on call melted away when Eddie pulled up in the gold Chevy.

The children were upstairs with my parents. I took a warm bath, did my hair, polished my nails, and scrubbed away the smells and the memories of the hospital. "It feels good to feel attractive again," I thought as I looked in the mirror.

It was good to wear something other than my greens, to slip into high heels and a dress. "I had forgotten how this feels," I said to Eddie as he fastened my zipper.

"You're telling me!" he said. "I got news for you—we *both* need this night."

The theater was cool and dark. As I eased into my seat, I felt myself relax for the first time in weeks. I slipped my shoes off and prepared myself for an evening of entertainment.

Eddie was right about one thing—the play was definitely a whodunit. And just when I, like everyone else in the audience, was sure of the identity of both the murderer and the victim, the shocker came. The mutilated body of someone who was supposed to have been killed burst through a window. In that moment I forgot I was in a theater, forgot that this was "only a play." I jolted in my seat and shrieked. Eddie tried to calm me. I was still shaking as the rest of the audience settled down to watch the performance. "This is where you take me *to relax?*" I whispered to Eddie, and I watched the rest of the play gripping his arm.

Eddie laughed and whispered back, "You're too tense. It's only a play. It's not real life."

But as the days passed, real life was becoming more frightening and more unpredictable than anything I had ever seen on the stage.

That week Patrick was put on dialysis. His kidneys still stubbornly refused to function.

"Let's give it time," I said to his worried mother. "His kidney functions could return any day now."

"Any day, any day. But what if they don't?" she asked.

"Let's not worry about that now," I said.

But I was worried.

I was taking a break, drinking a cup of coffee and thinking about Matthew, when Denise touched me on the shoulder.

"Long time, no see." I smiled. Since our first day of internship, Denise and I had seen each other only for a few minutes at a time. Our case loads were heavy, and we were both involved with our patients. Denise knew about my feelings for Billy and the Rizzo family. She had seen all of us sitting together, sharing our midnight coffee, comforting one another. And she had seen me with Billy. She knew how captivated I was by the little boy. "He has such a gentle way about him," I had told her. "He never kicks or fights me when I give him chemo. You should see him when he's finally asleep. He clutches those Batman and Robin dolls and looks like an angel."

Denise cleared her throat. "Dorothy," she said, "Billy's just come in. Do you want me to switch services with you so that he can be your patient again?"

"Of course," I answered. Then I saw the look in Denise's eyes.

"How is he?"

"I want you to prepare yourself, Dorothy. He's bad. Really bad."

I rushed to Billy's room, but I was not prepared. Billy weighed twenty-four pounds. He was in agony. He whimpered and moaned when I tried to examine him. Now he didn't talk at all. He only whispered to his mother. The sheets were stained with his blood. He was suffering from severe intestinal bleeding.

Marie looked up at me.

"Thank God you're here. With you I can be irrational. You understand what we're going through."

I hugged her. "I'm here, and I'll be here for you and for Billy," I promised.

That night there was no chemotherapy. There was no need. I held Billy's hand and gave him painkillers. Then we waited.

When my beeper went off, I gripped Marie's hand and told her I'd be back as soon as I could. It was not a busy night on the sixth floor, but even that didn't make it any easier.

Billy's pain must have been unbearable. When I came to check on him, he didn't even look up.

"He told me to say hello," Marie said. "He knows you're here."

I was in ICU with Patrick when Jane came in. "Dorothy, I think you'd better get over to Billy right away."

The lights were dimmed. A small, frail body lay motionless on the stark white sheets. I watched as Marie and Tony held Billy in their arms. Blood poured from his rectum.

"We'll never let you go," Tony crooned over and over again.

I moved toward the child, quickly giving him something to ease the pain. Then I left the room.

I was pacing nervously outside the door when Marie and Tony came out.

"Dorothy, Billy told us to leave, to go out and have a cigarette." Marie was shaking. "He never asked me to leave the room before. Never. Do you think he knows? God, how can he understand? He's not even three years old."

"I think he's giving you permission," I said. "I think he knows."

Jane slipped into the boy's room. She opened the door and motioned for us to come back in.

Splinters of early morning sunlight curled along the sides of the window shades. It was seven A.M. Marie and Tony stood by my side. I gathered Billy's tiny body close to mine and put my stethoscope to his chest. I heard one beat. I wrapped my arms around him. There were no more beats.

My own voice seemed far away, muffled: "He's gone," I whispered.

Death was no longer a haunting and mysterious specter. It was no longer something that came just when you looked away, something that happened from a distance. Now it was close, real. I was holding it in my arms.

"Thank God. Thank God it's finally over," Marie moaned as I gently handed her her little boy.

Touching each other, we encircled the now peaceful body. I asked the Rizzos if they wanted to be alone. They nodded.

Billy had died quietly. He died as the beginning of a new day forced itself past our grief.

I stood in the hospital corridor and felt the different parts of myself begin to merge, to melt into each other. In one grief-stricken moment, I was a doctor, a mother and a surviving child. A little boy who now lay cold and still in the next room was my patient. He was my son. He was my brother.

I searched for the hold button in my mind, but this time it wasn't there.

I walked down the corridor. The noise did not stop after Billy died. People were moving, talking, laughing. Strange that they didn't know, didn't see the cold shadow that poured from the child's room.

I was in the resident's lounge. I dialed the telephone. I had to hear Eddie's voice. The phone rang many times. Finally someone answered, but it wasn't Eddie. It was my mother.

"It's Billy," I cried. "Mom, he died in my arms."

As my words took shape, I realized what I was saying. My mother had also held a dying baby in her arms.

"God," I said. "I'm so sorry. How can I ask you to comfort me? Now I know what it must have been like. I wish I could have been there for you. I wish I could have comforted you."

My mother's voice was soft. It was a voice that still bore the marks of an unspeakable loss.

"Dorothy, you *are* a constant comfort to me. You can't go back and take the pain away. God has his reasons. I don't know what they are. I'll never understand. No one can. I don't know what else I can say."

I knew, as I hung up the phone, that she had said it all. I dried my eyes and walked back through the dense fog that shielded me from patients, orderlies and nurses.

Marie and Tony were standing in the hallway. They looked suddenly smaller. A part of them had been taken. Their beautiful son was gone forever.

I embraced them, and we sat down together.

"How could this happen?" they asked. "How can we go on? What is there to live for?"

"I don't have the answers," I said. "But you *must* go on, you have your daughter."

"How will she take the news?" Tony asked. "How does a six-year-old cope when she's told that her brother has died?"

That's when I explained that I, too, had been a surviving child. "The most important thing I can say to you is not to let your daughter think she has to live two lives, that she has to make up for Billy's death."

Then I asked Marie about the funeral. She said I'd be called as soon as the arrangements were made. "You'll always be in our prayers," Tony said as he took his wife's arm. Bowed under the burden of their grief, they walked slowly to the elevator.

I watched until the doors closed behind them.

"Are you okay?" Denise asked as she put her hand on my shoulder. "Do you want to take off for a few minutes?"

I wiped my tears. The "hold" button floated up from the darkness. I pressed down hard. "That's all right," I said. "I only have twelve more hours to go."

When I stepped up to the gold Chevy, I crossed into another world. It was Friday. The gray clouds were shifting, the air was cold and clear.

"Your mother told me about Billy. I'm so sorry," Eddie said as he held me in his arms. We stood there in front of the hospital, in the cold morning air, for several minutes.

I needed to feel alive again.

"I want to go to synagogue today," I told Eddie as we drove home.

"It's Sukkoth," Eddie said, smiling as he drove through the crowded streets. "We can all go. They're building the hut today."

Sukkoth was the Jewish Thanksgiving, a holiday when families build huts of branches and leaves and celebrate the harvest and the renewal of life.

"I want to be in a room full of people, I want to be with families, and with children who take health and life for granted. I need it. I need answers."

Eddie spoke slowly. "Dorothy," he said, "you find the answers within yourself. Nothing can make sense of it. No one can tell you why."

That afternoon, as I sat beneath the roof of leaves and Matthew crawled along the ground with several other children, I began to see the renewal of life, to understand the changing of the seasons, to make sense of the truth the rabbi had spoken of during the service: "When leaves fall, new ones grow in the spring. Old generations pass, new ones take their place."

I threaded popcorn and cranberries with Evie and the other women. We talked of birthdays and celebrations.

I watched as Eddie stood on a ladder and helped construct a

frame of leaves. Families came with cartons filled with corn, squash and gourds. There was no sickness here, no talk of death, no cold shadows.

Afterward, as I sat drinking cider and eating doughnuts with the rest of the congregation, I looked around. The world was still going on. People were enjoying the fruit of their lives. The common cold was the most troublesome health problem most children had to face.

On Saturday, Eddie had an idea. "Let's drive out to Long Island with the kids. Let's go to the pumpkin farm." I bundled Matthew and Evie up in sweaters and scarves. I drank them in, touching them, singing to them, as we drove out to the pumpkin farm.

Autumn had turned the morning into a splash of red and brown; the leaves crunched under our feet. We looked out over acres of glowing orange, and with the air whipping against our faces, we ran out among the pumpkins. Biting back the cold, shouting and laughing, we filled our arms with the bright orange orbs.

We were still laughing when we brought our harvest home. Eddie searched through our closet and arranged hats and scarves. While I made hot chocolate, he sat with the children and carved happy faces into the thick, ripe fruit. Matthew crawled in excited circles, Evie giggled, and Eddie and I joked as we adorned our pumpkins with our own eye glasses and hats.

That night I held my babies very close as I whispered good night and fluffed the pillows beneath their sleepy heads. It had been a wonderful day, but I couldn't forget. The next day was Billy's funeral.

"I have to go," I explained to Eddie the next morning. "I want to pay my respects. You don't have to come if you don't want to. Believe me, I'll understand."

Eddie stirred his coffee. Our pumpkins sat smiling on the kitchen counter.

"Would you feel better if I was there?"

I looked up at the grinning jack-o'-lantern that rested on the counter. He wore my old glasses and my winter scarf.

"Yes, I would," I answered.

The room was crowded and still. People moved. They touched. They spoke in barely audible whispers. Marie and Tony walked through the crowd. It parted silently. "Thank you for coming. It means so much," Marie said. Tony shook Eddie's hand.

Friends and relatives sat and prayed. They made the sign of the cross as they filed past the tiny white coffin at the far end of the funeral parlor. A wreath of flowers hung over the casket. "Our Dear Little Man" were the words spelled out in roses.

Eddie was beside me. I moved as if through a dense fog of smoke—of faces—of grief.

Billy was dressed in a suit. His tiny body was nestled in blue satin. His brown eyes were closed. His blond ringlets would never grow back. Our little angel was peaceful at last. In his arms he still clutched his Batman and Robin dolls.

On Monday I was back in the ICU. Patrick was still on dialysis. I walked down the yellow corridors like a ghost.

Jonathan smiled sadly when he saw me look past the room where Billy had died. He took me aside.

"I know what you must be feeling, Dorothy," he explained, "but the survival rate for leukemia is better than fifty percent."

"I don't understand that at all," I answered.

"When you have the chance, you ought to go downstairs to the outpatient clinic. You'll see lots of kids there. Kids you won't recognize because they didn't have to be here on the sixth floor. The vast majority of leukemia patients only need outpatient care. They do get better. They go into remission. They live good lives."

"Happy endings, right?" I said.

"Right," Jonathan answered.

I went back to the ICU. Jane was checking Patrick's chart.

"Any new developments?" I asked. "Has he urinated yet?"

Jane shook her head.

I stood by Patrick's side as Jane pulled the sheet down. The sore on his penis was healing well. Just then, as Jane and I were examining him, Patrick released a full arc of urine.

It sprayed across the sheets, the wall and our clothes.

"He did it! He peed!" I shrieked as Jane and I jumped up and down hugging each other.

Patrick's beautiful little freckle face curled up in an embarrassed grimace. "I'm sorry, Dr. Greenbaum." He began to cry.

"Sorry—sorry?" I shrieked. "This is the best day of my life!"

"He peed! Isn't that terrific?" I shouted to no one in particular as I stuck my head out of the door.

I heard my own voice. It was loud and clear as it echoed down the halls of the sixth floor.

16

Bread-and-Butter Pediatrics

"You won't find any esoterica here," Jonathan said as he pointed to the emergency room in City Hospital. "This isn't like Major Medical Center. The kids here have appendicitis, sore throats, fevers. They've been involved in accidents, or as in this side of the ward"—he pointed to an area where tiny cribs were surrounded by glass partitions—"they've been victims of child abuse."

"This," he said, "is what I like to call plain old bread-and-butter pediatrics!"

I smiled at Jonathan. This meant there would be no more leukemics, no more chemotherapy and no more babies dying in my arms. I was ready for a simple diet of bread and butter, eager to treat a sore throat or a case of heat rash, or diagnose an attack of appendicitis.

I had just rotated to City Hospital with both Jonathan and Denise. I was glad I would have friends here, but as soon as I walked into the noisy, crowded, dirty ER, I knew I wouldn't be spending much time with them. Here, as in County Hospital, strings hung from bare light bulbs, patients were crammed into dark, under-staffed wards, and I knew at one glance that the conditions in the ER would make the waiting patients angry and hostile. Nights here would be long and hard.

When one of the residents showed me the cot used by the interns, I grimaced. It was in the middle of the conference room. There was no lock on the door, and the male adolescent ward was only a few yards away. Directly over the bare, stained mattress was a hole in the ceiling. I could see the roaches crawling along the exposed pipes. This would be my home for thirty-six hours at a stretch.

"But there's one civilized amenity here that we didn't have at Major Medical Center," Denise said. "We get to leave the building for lunch. No guilt. And here's the good news: the food is free. Ready for the catch? It's provided by the hospital. We eat what the patients eat."

That afternoon at lunch, Jonathan, Denise and I tried to guess what animal the tuna fish was made of.

"It's got gristle in it—actual gristle!" I said, pushing my plate across the table.

"Learn to love it, kid," Jonathan said. "You can have seconds and thirds, and it may be *all* you get to eat until tomorrow night."

Jonathan was right. I picked at the tuna fish, trying to ignore the strange, greasy lumps that turned up on the end of my fork.

"Let me tell you what Daniel did yesterday," Jonathan said. Daniel was his two-year-old son. "He actually put together a four-word sentence and identified objects in his picture book. This is the brightest child I've ever seen, and I'm not prejudiced just because I'm his father." Then Jonathan stroked his beard and winked.

"Matt said 'Ma Ma' the other day," I added. "I was amazed. Evie's first words were 'Da Da,' and at the time I was home with her twenty-four hours a day. With this kid I'm gone thirty-six hours at a stretch, and he says 'Ma Ma.' I must be doing something right."

Jonathan and I continued talking about our children. It was obvious that Denise was growing increasingly uncomfortable. When Jonathan's beeper went off, Denise and I were left to finish our lunch alone.

"God! Those children stories you and Jonathan tell really get to me," Denise said.

I cupped my hand under my chin. Denise was single and never talked about her private life. This was the first indication I had had that she had any feeling about mine, and the feelings weren't supportive.

"Medicine and motherhood don't mix. Especially not when you're just an intern," she said with authority.

"I don't know," I countered. "I'm doing it. I can't say it's easy, but it's not impossible. I had Matthew my last year of medical school. I planned it that way."

"My career *is* my child," Denise said. "I don't have time for anything else."

"Maybe you'll find the cure for cancer then," I said as I swallowed my coffee.

My sarcasm wasn't lost on Denise, but our conversation was cut short when Jonathan rejoined us.

"Prepare for a long night," he said. "They're piling up in the ER now, and it looks as if this will be the last chance any of us will get to eat until we go home."

"I hope Eddie has dinner ready tonight," I sighed.

"Now, don't tell me you have a husband who cooks! This is a little too good to be true. Where did you find a guy who would put up with your schedule, take care of the kids, work full-time *and* cook dinner?"

There was a familiar edge to Denise's voice. I hadn't had to defend Eddie or my life-style for a long time, but I hadn't forgotten how.

"First of all," I began, "I think my husband *is* terrific, but it's not like you think. My parents live upstairs, and they help out with the kids. Eddie usually makes dinner for himself and the children, and he puts something aside for me."

"What—a little roast beef and potatoes?" Denise laughed. "I'm lucky if I get a chance to boil spaghetti!"

"My dinner is usually something like hard-boiled eggs and cottage cheese—if I'm lucky," I answered.

"Dorothy, anyone can do that. I hardly think it's worth being married to have to come home to a dinner of cottage cheese and hard-boiled eggs and to have a husband and two kids clawing at you. You'd be better off single. Medicine is a full-time commitment. You could have your cold dinner and read up on your journals without any distractions. The way I see it, marriage is a prison, especially for a doctor."

I thought for a few seconds. I remembered all the admissions counselors when I had applied to medical school. But this time the line that marriage, motherhood and medicine didn't mix couldn't intimidate me. I had come this far, and I knew, even with all my "distractions," that I was just as good a doctor as Denise.

"Well, Denise," I said, "I think I read somewhere: 'Two men look out through the same bars: One sees the mud, and one the stars.'"

Denise looked up from her coffee just long enough to excuse herself. Her beeper had gone off.

I turned to Jonathan.

"Don't let her get to you," he said. "She has a very empty life."

"I just don't understand," I said. "After Billy's death, if I had had to go home to a lonely apartment, if I hadn't had Eddie and the children, I would have quit right then and there. They make it all worthwhile. I hate it when someone infers that Eddie is some kind of superman or oddball. He's doing what he wants to do. He's supported me every step of the way. It's something I'd do for him."

Jonathan put his hand over mine. "I know. I know. There are lots of doctors, lots of people, who think like Denise. We'll never change their minds, and they'll never change ours. We're just different."

I nodded as Jonathan scraped his chair against the floor.

"Well, Doctor," he said, "enough of this chitchat. I believe we have work to do."

I slipped my arm in his and we walked bravely toward the ER.

Miss Tills was waiting for me. Her nurse's uniform was neatly pressed and immaculate. She showed no signs of the usual ER wear and tear.

"We're plenty backed up, Dr. Greenbrown," she said, and she placed one hand authoritatively on her broad hip.

I detected a slight Jamaican accent in her voice.

"That's *Greenbaum*," I corrected her as she handed me a pile of charts.

"Ready for your first patient?" she challenged, her eyes flashing.

I could tell that there was no love lost between Miss Tills and interns. She was an experienced nurse with twenty years in pediatrics. Our relationship would be strictly business.

The children streamed through the examining room. I couldn't move fast enough. For every cut I treated, every throat I looked down and every ear I peered into, ten more patients stood outside clamoring for attention.

At one point, an angry mother, intolerant of the long wait, burst into the examining room. I was trying to look down the throat of a squirming four-year-old.

"My kid's got a one-hundred-four-degree fever! What the hell's going on in here?" she shouted.

The four-year-old began to cry. Miss Tills looked at me and waved her hand in the air. "Don't you mind," she said. "I'll take care of *this!*" Then, through gritted teeth, she threatened the irate parent: "Just who the hell do you think you're shouting at?" she asked. "Don't you dare talk to the doctor like that. Now go out and wait your goddam turn like everyone else!"

The mother backed down. "When will my child get treated?" she asked meekly.

"When Dr. Greenbrown gets to her—that's when," Miss Tills said bluntly.

"That's *Greenbaum*," I whispered as I patted my tearful patient on the head.

By two A.M., my eyes were blurry. I had seen hundreds of runny noses, split lips and infected eyes. Most of the patients were treated and released. A few were referred to the clinic. There were no life-and-death situations.

"Bread and butter," I repeated to myself as Miss Tills led in the next patient.

By two forty-five A.M., only five charts remained. I was definitely picking up speed. "Five more kids to go. How's that for efficiency?" I said, smiling.

"Don't let it go to your head," Miss Tills said as she checked her watch.

By three-fifteen A.M., I was ready to sign out. Then the phone rang. I recognized Jonathan's voice on the other end.

"I hope you're not signing out," he said.

"I'm finished, and I'm exhausted," I answered. "You bet I'm signing out."

"Nobody leaves," Jonathan said. "There's a bus load of hemophiliacs who were on their way to Camp Proplex when they got into an accident. Kids are bleeding all over." Strangely, Jonathan's voice did not seem alarmed.

"Oh, no!" I shouted. "Oh, my God! Who would have believed anything like this could happen? And past three o'clock in the morning!"

Miss Tills was unruffled. "What did Dr. Stein say?" she asked.

"A bus load of hemophiliacs on their way to Camp—Proplex?" I never finished my sentence.

Miss Tills was holding her stomach and laughing so hard, the tears were streaming down her face.

"Gimme that phone," she said as she grabbed it from my hand.

"Dr. Stein, you old dog. I can't believe you're still playing that hemophiliac joke." Then she turned to me.

"Greenbrown, I thought you'd be too smart to fall for that one. It's a classic. Why don't you just go lie down?"

I put my arm on Miss Tills's shoulder. "Tills, you don't know how happy I am to hear that. And by the way, it's *Greenbaum!*"

As the days passed, I got more comfortable at City Hospital. I learned to wolf down second helpings at lunch and to make it through long, exhausting nights in the ER or on the wards. Denise and I never spoke of my life or hers again. We were coolly professional with one another, and since we both liked Jonathan, we continued to share lunch with him whenever it was possible.

Most of my patients were not seriously ill, and Eddie, relieved that there were no more Billys or Elizabeths, rarely complained about my hours. "At least when you're here, you're really here," he said.

Gradually, even Miss Tills began to call me by my correct name. It was never "Dorothy." That would have been too informal for her. But "Dr. Greenbaum" was a definite improvement.

It was during one of my thirty-six-hour shifts that Mrs. Morales brought in her year-old baby girl. Juanita was in her arms, and three other children, all under five years old, clung to her skirt. I noticed that Mrs. Morales was pregnant with her fifth child.

"No habla Ingles," Mrs. Morales answered when Miss Tills began to question her about her little girl. Within a few minutes, a Spanish-speaking nurse was called down to the examining room.

I began to examine the baby. "What's the problem?" the nurse asked the mother.

Mrs. Morales lowered her daughter's diaper. Miss Tills looked away. I clenched my teeth. The baby's bottom was marked by an oddly shaped black eschar (a scab produced by a burn), the likes of which I hadn't seen since my days as a clerk in County Hospital. This scab was as bad as the horrible bedsores old Mr. Blum had had.

"What the hell is this?" I asked as I quickly looked the child over for any other signs of abuse. My memory of the child-abuse lectures in med school was crystal clear. The head of the foundling hospital had brought in photographs of burn marks in the shape of an iron, and bruises that perfectly matched a father's belt buckle. I remember how I had wanted to look away.

"The first time they're abused. The second time they're DOA. You are responsible. You can make the difference," he had warned us.

This wound was oddly shaped. Whitish pus seeped out the sides of the black flesh. I knew Juanita had to be admitted. I asked the nurse to continue questioning the mother.

"Looks like a case of child abuse," I whispered. Miss Tills looked at me and nodded her head knowingly. All the signs were there. A young mother, no father in sight, four young children and one on the way. It was the type of situation we had been told to be on the lookout for.

The Spanish-speaking nurse was talking to the nervous mother. I recognized a few words, but I couldn't really follow their conversation.

"Wait till you hear *this* one," the nurse said. "Mrs. Morales says she never hit or burned her child. She said there were 'little animals' in the backyard that did it."

I looked at the wound a second time. It was obviously not a rat bite, or a bite from any animal.

"I think we should call the Bureau of Child Welfare," Miss Tills said impatiently.

"And while you're at it, call plastic surgery, I'd like them to have a look at this, too," I said.

"Let's get this kid upstairs right away," Miss Tills said as soon as she had made the call.

When the distraught mother and her children had left the examining room, both nurses began to talk.

"Isn't it disgusting?" the Spanish-speaking nurse said. "What do you think she burned the kid with?"

"Who knows?" Miss Tills said. "We had a case in here a few weeks ago. The orthopedic surgeon said the kid could only have broken his bones that way if the parent had grabbed him by the legs and smacked him repeatedly against a brick wall. It was the most sorry sight I'd seen in a long time. I just don't understand how a parent can harm an innocent little baby."

"Did you see how many kids she had?" I asked.

"And another on the way," added the Spanish-speaking nurse. "And when I asked where the father was, she didn't even know."

"What do you think she meant by 'little animals'?" I asked Miss Tills.

"They never tell the truth. They'll say anything. Sometimes these parents are so ashamed and so guilty, they don't even bring the kids in for treatment."

Something bothered me about the Morales case. True, it seemed like a classic case of child abuse, but the mother's words, her reference to "little animals," kept nagging away at me. I knew that the eschar was not caused by a bite, yet there was something I had read once, something I remembered . . .

Later that night I went up to the wards to see Mrs. Morales. In my broken Spanish, I questioned her about the animals. "How big?" I asked, holding up my hands to indicate size.

"Muy poquito," she said. She held up her thumb and second finger until they practically touched.

An insect. She was talking about an insect. An alarm went off in my head.

"You're wasting your time," Denise said when I stopped her in the hall. "I've seen that Morales kid. She's been burned with an iron or something. I hope you called the Bureau of Child Welfare. Little animals, my foot."

"I know I read it somewhere," I said to myself as I walked toward the telephone. It was almost eleven-thirty P.M. I dialed Eddie. There was a good chance he hadn't gone to sleep yet.

"Hi, honey," he said. "Is everything all right?"

"I'd like you to look something up for me, Eddie. It will only take a few minutes. It's important. You know my blue entomology book? Look up *eschar*. I think there's a brown spider that leaves a bite. Tell me what it says. I'll hold on."

"It's so nice to hear from you, Dorothy," Eddie said sarcastically as he went to look for the book.

In a few minutes he was back. "Okay. There's something here about a brown recluse spider found in the United States but rarely in the Northeast. Is that what you wanted to know?"

"Thanks, Eddie," I said. "Right now I'm not sure about anything."

I knew that if I made a mistake in my diagnosis, a child's life, possibly the lives of four children, could be in jeopardy. I decided to wait until the morning. Juanita was safe. The Bureau of Child Welfare was going to meet with the mother tomorrow.

"There's a child here I want you to see," Miss Tills said when I got back down to the ER. "I've put her ahead of all the rest. She's in a lot of pain."

Sharon was doubled over. Miss Tills helped her onto the table. The girl was sixteen years old. She was all alone.

"Tell me where it hurts," I said as Sharon pointed to her belly. I immediately ticked off the most likely possibilities: appendicitis, ruptured ectopic pregnancy, pelvic inflammatory disease. I felt Sharon's belly, ran a urine test and gave her a vaginal examination. I eliminated the first two possibilities. It seemed pretty clear. She had a serious case of PID. Pelvic inflammatory disease is an infection in the fallopian tubes that can occur in sexually active women, and that causes pain and fever, and in some cases leads to a scarring of the tubes that can result in sterility.

"Have you had any vaginal infections or VD?" I asked Sharon. Sharon, fighting against the intense pain, managed to tell me that she hadn't had sex since her abortion three weeks ago.

I explained that she had an infection and would need to take medication through an IV to cure it.

"You'll have to stay here in the hospital for a while," I said, and then, touching her arm, I added, "But you'll be fine."

Sharon asked for painkillers, which I told her would be administered as soon as she was settled in. She turned her face to the wall when Miss Tills asked if she wanted her family notified.

"She's a tough one," Miss Tills said as Sharon was wheeled upstairs. "I bet she hasn't got a friend in the world."

"She's going to need one," I added. "That infection looks pretty severe."

That evening, when I got home, I was still thinking about Juanita Morales. I reread what Eddie had read to me over the telephone. It was all there. Everything fit except for one thing: these spiders were not found in the Northeast. And then there was the evidence of the Morales family itself. "I'll sleep on it," I said to myself. "By tomorrow morning I'll have a clear head."

The next day, as I walked toward the hospital, there was none of the old dread, the sinking feelings I had had so often at Major Medical Center. Here, I was treating patients. I was helping them, and if my latest hunch was right, I might even solve a mystery and cure a little girl.

The dermatologist and plastic surgeon were in Juanita's room when I arrived.

"Do you think it's possible that this isn't a burn?" I asked. Both residents listened while I explained my theory.

"But all the signs of child abuse are evident," the surgeon said. The dermatologist agreed.

"On the other hand, if Dr. Greenbaum is right and I debride the whole scab, it will leave an even bigger scar," he said.

I convinced both residents to give me a little more time to get to the bottom of this. Instead of lunch, I went upstairs and called the Bureau of Infectious Diseases. The man on the other end said it sounded like it could be a spider bite.

"Give me the exact address, and we'll go to the house and inspect it," he said.

"Please, hurry," I urged. "A little girl's life may depend on it."

When I walked downstairs I was feeling the thrill of being a doctor.

Then I saw Mrs. Morales. She was being questioned by a social worker from the Bureau of Child Welfare. Tears were streaming down the woman's face. She was wringing her hands in frustration.

"Oh, my God, she's confessing to everything," I thought. "Now everyone is going to think I'm a complete fool."

I approached the mother and the social worker. In an instant, I understood why Mrs. Morales was crying. The social worker did not speak a word of Spanish. The mother, frustrated and worried, was trying desperately to communicate with a person who she thought might be able to help her in some way.

Before the day was over, I stole a few minutes to call the Bureau of Infectious Diseases. They had news.

"Dr. Greenbaum," the man on the other end said, "I sent two of my men right over to that address. We got into the backyard. It was overgrown with weeds. My men saw the little chair the kid must have been sitting on. We've recovered and identified at least three different types of rare and stinging insects. The brown recluse spider isn't one of them, but I would say from our sample that it wouldn't surprise me at all if we went back and found that one as well. I'd assume that the child was suffering from a spider bite and proceed accordingly."

When I hung up the phone, I was floating. I had solved my first medical puzzle.

Mrs. Morales was standing by her daughter's bed, singing a lullaby. In my high school Spanish I explained about the "little animals." I told her that some men would come and clean up the backyard. I hoped she understood. She grasped my hand. *"Gracias,"* she said. Somehow I had managed to communicate to her that I had believed her story.

"This deserves a real pat on the back," Jonathan said when he heard about the Morales case. "If you had been a more jaded doctor, the mother would have been branded an abusive parent, and all the kids would have been put in foster homes. Good work, Doc."

Coming from Jonathan, those words meant a lot.

This is what I had been waiting for, what I had dreamed about when I first decided to become a doctor.

I was smiling from ear to ear when I got home.

"So how did it go today?" Eddie asked.

"This you won't believe," I said. "Remember the spider?"

"The spider. You mean the one you called me about at eleven-thirty P.M.? How could I forget that spider?" Eddie joked.

"Well, I was right. I was really right. The mother hadn't abused her baby. The backyard was all overgrown with weeds, and the child had actually been bitten by a rare type of spider."

"No kidding?" Eddie said. "I'm proud of you. My wife the doctor—my wife the detective."

"What spider?" Evie said as she walked into the kitchen. "I hope there are no spiders like that where we live."

"Absolutely not." I smiled. "They're not allowed here."

By four A.M. the next morning, all I could remember from the night before was my triumph over solving the Morales mystery and the sweet smell of my baby's skin.

The ER was jammed. The harsh lights of the treatment room seared my eyes. In the last twelve hours I had eaten only a candy bar and a package of cookies from the vending machine. The shouts, cries and angry voices from the waiting room didn't abate for a minute. Even the stoic Miss Tills seemed to be drooping. When I closed my eyes for a second, I saw Evie and Matthew. I remembered the "hold" button, pressed it and told Miss Tills to send in the next child.

Charles Reed was eleven months old. He had a fever of 104°. I examined him and saw at once that he had a red throat. He was irritable and fidgety. His worried mother told me he hadn't been eating well and couldn't seem to stop crying. He was alternately lethargic and irritable. When I questioned Mrs. Reed further, she said that Charles became increasingly irritable when she tried to move his head. Something told me that this baby had more than a high fever and a sore throat. I suspected the worst and called the resident on duty.

While I waited for him to arrive, I noticed the child's father hovering outside the treatment room. He peeked inside, looked at me and then seemed to drift back into the noisy corridor. Whenever I looked up from the baby, I'd see Mr. Reed nervously pacing outside the door.

"It's only natural," I thought to myself. "I'd be worried and frightened, too."

The resident appeared within minutes.

"This kid doesn't look right to me," I explained. "I think it might be meningitis."

The resident shook his head. "Dorothy, you're overreacting. It's been a bad night. My feeling is it's just a sore throat."

I thought for a few moments. Dr. Fisher was a good pediatrician. But I had seen several cases of meningitis, and what I had was a feeling—an intuition. There was only one way to find out. Spinal tap.

"Remember the rule?" I asked. "If you're thinking tap, do a tap."

"I won't hold you back," Dr. Fisher answered, "but I just don't agree. The kid's got a sore throat. Plain and simple."

"If Jonathan were here, he'd agree with me. I'm sure of it," I said.

Dr. Fisher shook his head. "Don't use Jonathan as a crutch. If you want to do a tap, you'll have to take responsibility for the decision. Jonathan has nothing to do with this."

I nodded. "Okay," I said. "I'm going ahead."

"We're backed up pretty badly in there," Dr. Fisher said as he gestured toward the waiting room. "Why don't you just begin? I'll talk to the parents."

The room was very bright. The baby looked especially vulnerable curled up in a fetal position on the tiny examining table. I washed his back with an iodine solution and laid him on the sterile sheets Miss Tills had prepared. As I slipped on my gloves, my eyes met hers. I would have to trust her completely to hold the child perfectly still as I inserted the needle and withdrew a few drops of spinal fluid. Then we would watch as the fluid dripped into the waiting tubes. If it was clear, it would mean Charles had only a sore throat and a high fever. If the fluid was cloudy, we would know that he had meningitis.

Outside in the waiting room I could hear people shouting, babies crying, and the hurried footsteps of nurses and orderlies. The closed door did not protect me from the sounds and the smells of City Hospital at four-thirty A.M. I thought of Matthew as I began to insert the needle in the child's spine.

I was concentrating so intently that I didn't see it happening until it was too late.

The door burst open, and the gun was pointing directly at me. "You do that tap and I'll blow your head off!"

It was a vision. A scene from a movie. A nightmare.

I looked up for a split second and saw Mr. Reed standing directly in front of me, beads of perspiration glistening on his pale skin. He held a revolver in his right hand.

I had never seen a gun before.

Everything seemed to be happening through a veil of gauze. Despite my exhaustion, a numbness set in, protecting me. My movements were precise, automatic. Miss Tills continued to hold the child. Dr. Fisher stood behind Mr. Reed, making desperate motions. He was trying to tell me he had called security. A shard of bright light shone on the little boy. I heard my own voice, steady and calm.

"Please put that gun down. Your child is very sick."

I could see the revolver clearly now. It poked through the gauze, filling the small room with its presence.

My hands continued to move. Somewhere far in the distance I thought I could hear music playing. Strains of it floated over my head and disappeared through the closed window.

Everything was very still. We all stood like statues, afraid to speak, watching the gun, watching the fluid drip from the child's spine into the waiting vials. "Freeze frame," I thought to myself. The spinal fluid had filled the first tube. It was grayish and cloudy.

I turned to Mr. Reed. I stared at the revolver.

"Your son has meningitis," I said.

The gauze began to melt. Everything speeded up. A child's life was at stake. Miss Tills said something stern and authoritative to the father. Two security guards appeared and when I looked up, the gun had vanished. Still moving automatically, I prepared an IV and began giving the child antibiotics. Mr. Reed was escorted from the hospital.

As soon as the patient was rushed up to the ICU, the numbness began to wear off. My greens were drenched with sweat. Dr. Fisher sat slumped on a folding chair. Only Miss Tills remained unruffled.

"He didn't scare me for a minute," she said. "I don't take that kind of nonsense from anybody."

I got up and looked into the corridor. Patients were lined up against the walls. They were sitting on the floors and resting on waiting stretchers.

"I don't believe any of this," I said. "A guy just stood right here and held a gun on me, and now I'm supposed to go on like nothing happened."

Dr. Fisher put his hand on my shoulder. "It's not always like this," he said. "Every now and then things just go a little haywire."

Miss Tills sniffed, smoothed her uniform and led in the next patient.

It was six-thirty A.M. From a dusty window I could see the sun just beginning to emerge over the treeless horizon. A bluish light spilled through the wards. I was looking for Charles Reed. My feet padded soundlessly down the corridor. There were cribs everywhere, infants crying softly in their sleep, young children calling for their parents. It was never quiet on the wards. I tiptoed past Sharon's room and saw that she was sleeping soundly, her IV still in place. I was concerned about her PID infection and made a note to talk to her as soon as possible.

The ICU was lit only by a bare ceiling bulb and the green light of the cardiac monitors. Charles was asleep in a small cubicle. I reached down and made sure his IV had not accidentally pulled out.

A shadow emerged from behind the glow of the monitor. The shadow moved closer until I could feel the warmth of its breath against my cheek. It was Mr. Reed. The smell of my perspiration mingled with his. We were alone. Somehow he had gotten back in, past security.

"If my son can't walk because of that tap, I'll be waiting for you," he growled. Then he opened his jacket. The revolver was tucked into his belt. I watched as his thick fingers rested on the handle.

"Your child could have died," I said.

The fingers did not move. I could hear the rasping sounds of his breathing. Looking past the shadow into the tiny crib, I could see that the baby's IV was in place. There was nothing more to do. I was tired and ready to go home. Mr. Reed did not move. We stood face-to-face in the glow of the monitor.

"This is the thanks I get," I thought to myself. I felt the familiar numbness envelop me. I turned my back and slowly walked from the room.

In the days that followed, the crowds streaming into the ER became more manageable. There were no more dramas like the one with Mr. Reed, and I was back to treating sore throats and ear infections.

When I was on duty on the ward, I stopped by to visit Sharon. She was always alone. The nurses told me that since she had been admitted, she had had only one visitor, a girl friend who had stayed for less than thirty minutes. The painkillers had made Sharon more comfortable, but her infection was far from cured.

"I wanna get out of here," Sharon said as I looked at her IV. It had come loose again, and there was a chance her vein would get inflamed if this continued.

"You've got a while to go before you can get off the antibiotics," I said. "Just give it time."

I watched as the anger welled up inside her. Sharon narrowed her eyes. "I ain't got no time," she said. "My boyfriend said if I'm not out of here in three days he won't hang around and wait."

"Sharon, where will you go when you get out? What will you do?"

"Oh, come on, you don't really want to know," she said. "You don't really care about me."

I was about to answer Sharon when my beeper went off.

"I've got to go," I said, "but don't even think of leaving yet. You need time to heal." I reached out to touch her.

Sharon pulled away. She turned her face to the wall and pretended to go to sleep.

Later that day I spoke with several of the nurses about Sharon. They told me that she refused to mix with any of the other teenagers.

"She's a street kid," Miss Tills said. "They sleep in doorways, eat garbage, do anything for money or dope. You can't change them. Take it from me. I know."

"I guess you've seen it all," I said as I got ready to leave.

Miss Tills didn't even look up.

"Working here as long as I have, you *do* get to see it all. I've seen hundreds of Sharons. They come and go. All we can do is patch them up until the next time."

I pushed Miss Tills's words from my mind when Eddie pulled up in front of the hospital. I had Saturday off and had convinced him to go with me to a party Dr. Fisher was giving in his new house. He had invited all the residents, interns and nurses who had the day off. It would be a rare opportunity for Eddie to meet my colleagues.

"Now these people will be more than just names to you," I said.

Surprisingly, Eddie had not been completely unenthusiastic. He had met Jonathan Stein once and had been impressed.

"At least I'll have one friend there," he said.

Mark Fisher's house was small and unfurnished. The party took place in the basement, which he had decorated with balloons and streamers. Jonathan was there with his wife, Ellen, and his son, Daniel. I had never met Ellen before. She was a small, fragile-looking woman who quickly sought me out and introduced herself.

"So you're Dorothy," she said, smiling. "I've heard so much about you and about your two children. It must be hard, being a mother and an intern. I know how unhappy Jonathan gets when he's away from Daniel for thirty-six hours at a stretch."

"Well, I think I'll make it." I laughed.

Then my eyes met Ellen's. For a split second I saw the sadness, the worry, the dread she lived with every day. Her husband had cancer. It was something she could never laugh away.

When I looked for Jonathan, I found him playing with all the children in a corner of the basement. He had Matthew on his lap and one of the nurses' little girls on his knee. Evie and Daniel played on the floor beside him. He was grinning from ear to ear.

"I like that guy," Eddie said to me as we got into the car and drove home.

"He's amazing," I said as I looked out at the bare trees. "You'd never know he had lymphoma. I don't know how his wife does it."

The next morning, the sun was shining and the air was tingling with the first cold snap of the season.

"I don't want to go to the hospital," I said, sighing. "It's Sunday, the whole world is off. It's a beautiful day."

"Come on, I'll drive you," Eddie said as he threw off the covers. "We'll have some 'big time' with the kids on the way there."

The familiar ride ended all too quickly. When we pulled up in front of the gray stone building, I kissed Evie and Matthew. Then I looked at Eddie.

"Oh boy, I don't want to go in there," I sighed.

At precisely that moment Eddie broke out in a huge grin and began singing: "Put on a happy face."

I hit him with my purse and ran laughing into the hospital.

"What are you smiling about?" Miss Tills asked when she saw me. "We've got a whole bunch of problems. Sharon's IV pulled out again, she's threatening everyone who gets near her, and we've got an infant here with some postsurgical complications."

There was no doubt about it—I was definitely back at work. I studied the patients' charts. They were waiting to see the doctor. I was needed here. My work meant something. I arranged my stethoscope around my neck and walked toward the room where the infant with the postsurgical complications was resting.

Juan Sanchez lay motionless in his tiny crib. He was two months old and weighed less than his birth weight. He barely opened his eyes when I looked down at him. I could see the scars from his recent surgery. Crisscrossing his pale skin, they contrasted sharply with the softness of his abdomen.

Juan had been born with his stomach and part of his intestines on the outside of his body. This condition, known as gastroschisis, required emergency surgery immediately after he was born. Cosmetically, the surgery had been successful, but a second operation was required to close the wound. Now, after two major operations, Juan, who should have been able to digest food, was vomiting and not passing a stool after he was fed. Part of his intestine had closed. The staff had called a conference and decided that since Juan was so malnourished, he would have to be fed high-caloric, high-protein food through an IV. In an infant as small as Juan, it was necessary to thread the IV through the largest vein in the body, in this case the jugular in the neck. But now Juan was beginning to squirm. Repeatedly, he pulled out the IV.

Miss Tills stood beside me as I examined Juan.

She shook her head. "Whenever we try to feed him, he vomits. When we use the IV, he pulls it out. I don't know what to do with this child."

I looked at the infant whose dark curly hair twisted into thin black corkscrews all over his head.

"He's a cute little thing," I said as I reached down to look at his stomach. A sign, NPO (*non per os,* Latin for nothing through mouth), was posted over his crib.

"He isn't cute when he pukes up all over the sheets," Miss Tills said as she adjusted her cap.

"Why don't you go check on Sharon? I think I'll spend a little time with this baby," I said.

Juan rested comfortably in my arms. His long black eyelashes flittered like delicate butterflies. His little pink hand curled instinctively around my finger.

"Listen, kid," I whispered. "If you keep vomiting like this, you'll never get well. If I could feed you, I'd do it a tiny bit at a time. I'd wait for it to pass through your gut until you got used to it." I cradled the baby closer.

"Come on, Juan, what do you say we give it a try?"

I asked the nurse on the floor for a sterile eyedropper and a solution of glucose and water. Then, very gently, I fed Juan two ccs (about half a teaspoon), drop by drop. I rocked him in my arms, talked to him, then burped him gently. For a few moments I forgot that I was here in a gloomy ward holding a sick child in my arms. It was easy to drift, to imagine I was home in my bedroom, holding my own baby.

"What are you doing feeding that child?" Miss Tills's voice sliced through my pleasant reverie. "He'll ruin the sheets. I'm telling you he can't keep anything down."

I turned to Miss Tills.

"I miss my baby. So I'm going to try to feed this little guy. Let's see if he can hold two ccs at a time."

Reluctantly, I placed Juan back in his crib.

"Come on, let's show 'em!" I whispered into his tiny ear before I left the room.

When I reached Sharon's room, she was sitting up, staring into space. Her IV was disconnected. She rubbed her arm where it had become inflamed.

"I'm better, and I want to get out of here," she said before I had a chance to look at her arm.

"You're not well. You feel better because of the painkillers," I explained, "but you're not healed yet."

"You don't understand," Sharon said. "My boyfriend won't wait."

"Where are you going? What plans do you have that can't be delayed a few more days?" I asked.

Sharon gazed past me like I wasn't there. There was an impenetrable wall between us. I looked at the sixteen-year-old girl who was an outsider to my world. Sharon lived on the boundaries. My white coat and stethoscope were symbols of a place that existed for her only on televisions viewed through store windows or watched on cold nights in Laundromats. Sharon and I sat side-by-side on the bed, but we were a universe apart.

We exchanged a few words. I sat calmly, hoping I wouldn't say anything that would release the rage. She allowed me to reinsert the IV. She breathed deeply as I threaded it through her vein. This was a painful procedure, but Sharon barely flinched.

"See you later, Sharon," I said after I checked to make sure everything was in place.

She nodded in return. This was an improvement. Before, she had merely pretended I didn't exist.

"Maybe I'm making some progress after all," I thought as I moved quickly on to my next patient.

An hour after I had fed him through the eyedropper, I checked on Juan. I questioned the nurse on duty.

"Has the Sanchez baby spit up?" I asked. The nurse shook her head and pointed to his crib.

Juan was rolled in a contented ball. His sheets were clean and dry, his black curls twisted into flat spirals across his head. I fed him another teaspoon of glucose and water and asked the nurse to beep me in two hours.

"If he can hold this, we may be able to stretch that intestine," I told her.

By lunchtime I was completely exhausted. I had been "on" for so many hours, I was no longer sure what day it was. I decided to walk over to the cafeteria and get some air.

The afternoon was unseasonably warm. I lowered myself slowly onto a park bench. I sat mesmerized as a ray of afternoon sunlight glinted off a few granite chips in the sidewalk. The reflection flashed back at me. Swirls of yellow light seemed to leap from the tiny chips of granite.

An image of my son floated on the yellow light. He appeared as a vision, crawling in his blue overalls, looking up at me with his wide smile. I yearned to hold him.

A pool of light spilled across the scrubby lawn. I leaned forward on the bench, catching the last fleeting image of Matthew in the fading glow.

I looked down at my hands. A few moments ago they had held a tiny infant, had threaded an IV into a vein of a teenager. I had comforted so many children. Now I missed my own.

I gazed at a passing cloud. "Only a few more hours to go," I whispered. Once again I reached into the back of my mind, searching for my imaginary "hold" button. I pressed it and walked reluctantly back to the hospital.

Two days later Juan was able to digest five ccs of the glucose-and-water solution. I was feeling confident and pleased with his progress.

"You can take the mother out of the house, but you can't take the mother out of the mother," Jonathan joked when he saw me feeding my two-month-old patient with an eyedropper. Juan was still very thin, but he was beginning to gain a few precious ounces. The NPO sign over his bed had been replaced with my feeding instructions.

I was leaving Juan's room when Miss Tills came rushing toward me. Perspiration dotted her forehead.

"Sharon's pulled out her IV. She's trying to leave the hospital!" Miss Tills gushed.

"She can't leave, she's still very sick," I said.

"You talk to that girl. She's so belligerent, she won't listen to anyone."

"Call security!" I shouted. "We've got to stop her." Then I began running toward the adolescent ward.

Sharon's bed was empty.

As I ran down the corridor, I caught a glimpse of the teenager heading toward the stairway. I was determined to head her off at the stairwell.

Sharon was moving more slowly than I had anticipated. "She's still very sick," I reminded myself as I called her name. Knowing I was behind her, she quickened her pace. I ran until I was alongside her. Desperately, I grabbed at her sleeve.

We stood alone in the deserted stairwell, our voices echoing against the gray cinder-block walls.

"Let go of me!" she shouted. Her face was twisted with rage and hate.

"You can't go," I said. "You'll burn out your tubes. You might not be able to have children. Please, you only need a few more days!"

Sharon pushed at me. I held tightly to her arm, but she was determined. She threw me against the wall. I lost my footing and fell against the steps, sliding down until I was lying on the floor. Sharon looked down at me with disgust.

I felt an anger well up inside me. I was tired. I missed my family. I didn't want to be here anymore, and I didn't deserve this.

I heard my own voice echo down the staircase after Sharon.

"I have my tubes and my kids!" I shouted. "It's nothing to me!" But Sharon was gone.

I picked myself up and found Miss Tills.

"Did you call security?" I asked. "Did they stop her?" Miss Tills brushed an imaginary fleck of dust from her shoulder.

"Security!" She laughed. "An elephant could slip past those guys!"

Remembering Mr. Reed, I nodded and walked toward the residents' lounge. I needed to pull myself together. I needed to talk to Jonathan.

He was reviewing charts, but when he saw me, he put them aside. I told him about Sharon.

"I wanted to help her, I really did," I explained. "But then I got so angry, so tired of it all. Maybe I'm all wrong for this, maybe pediatrics just isn't for me."

Jonathan put an arm around my shoulder.

"Dorothy, just move on. Some people are determined to self-destruct. There's nothing we can do. Just put it behind you," he said.

I walked dejectedly back to the ward.

"At least I still have Juan," I thought. "At least I'm making progress with someone."

An hour before I was scheduled to sign out, Miss Tills stopped me in the hall.

"You know that baby you're so crazy about?" she asked.

"Juan Sanchez?"

"Yep, that's the one. The nurse fed him ten ccs and he threw up."

When I got to Juan's room his sheets had been changed and he lay squirming in his crib. He still looked like a dehydrated toothpick. The nurse on duty explained what had happened.

"I followed your instructions, Dr. Greenbaum. I increased his feedings from five ccs to ten. But it must have been too much for him. He threw it all up."

Miss Tills stood in the doorway, her hands resting knowingly on her hips.

"I told you that kid can't digest. You're knocking yourself out for nothing."

The day had been discouraging, but I wasn't ready to give up.

When both nurses left the room, I sat beside Juan and began to think.

Despite my exhaustion, it didn't take me long to figure out a possible answer. Juan should be returned to the five-cc feedings for another day. When the solution was increased to ten ccs, I would wait two hours and suction out what was still left in his stomach. Feeding Juan this way meant that we could gradually stretch his intestines. Before I left the hospital for the night, I consulted with a neonatologist. I wanted to begin feeding Juan formula instead of his glucose-and-water solution. Together, the neonatologist and I came up with a combination we were sure would work. We would dilute one part formula with three parts water.

"You're going to be chubby and dimpled if I have to spend hours suctioning and adjusting your feedings," I whispered in Juan's ear before I signed out and went home.

That evening, Eddie listened sympathetically as I told him what had happened with Sharon. He put his arm around me when I confessed I was reconsidering the whole idea of pediatrics.

"Why don't you call Fern," he suggested. "Maybe she's off tonight. Talking to her might help."

I immediately agreed to Eddie's suggestion. Fern was doing her internship in surgery. That meant she was on every other night, seven days a week. Her little boy was only a few months younger than Matt. As I dialed her number, I remembered the fun we had had sharing our work and our pregnancies.

"Dorothy, is that *really* you?" Fern's voice was strained from exhaustion.

"I can't believe you called," she said. "I was going to call you myself. I've made a decision."

I had no idea what was coming next. Fern didn't mince words. She was tired and fed up.

"I've given them notice that I'm leaving surgery. I love the OR, but it's not my life. Surgery demands all my time. I can't see the point of killing myself. I've decided to go for dermatology."

"I'm shocked. When did you decide this?"

"Look, Dorothy," she explained, "this whole system is nuts. I read a Columbia University study that compared the performance of interns and residents in the ER when they were in their thirty-sixth hour of duty with interns and residents in their eighth hour. The EKG readings done by the doctors on their eighth hour were a lot more accurate than what resulted after thirty-six gruelling hours on call. It's an archaic system. It's not good for the patients, and the hospital gets three days of work for one day's pay."

"You're right about that," I answered. "It kills me when I get a paycheck for a 'forty-hour' week. It's illegal to force people to work overtime without paying them for it."

"Someday it will all change," Fern said. "This system is too macho. It's not meant for people who want full lives. I swear, it's made for compulsive workers. I overestimated the glamour of the OR. It has less appeal when I see how high a price I have to pay. Dermatology makes a lot of sense. After all, how many emergency pimples are there?"

Fern and I shared a laugh and caught up on our families. Then I told her I was thinking of switching from pediatrics to obstetrics.

"You've got to be kidding!" she shouted. "That's going from bad to worse. Why don't you consider something less demanding, like psychiatry?"

I smiled. "If I went for psychiatry, I'd be a patient before I finished my training!"

Before I hung up, Fern and I promised to get together with our children.

"Let's do it soon," she said, "before they're too old to remember who we are."

That night I talked with Eddie about leaving pediatrics.

"As long as you don't let your work overwhelm your life, and as long as you aren't bringing all the suffering home, it's okay with me," Eddie said. But then he added, "Why don't you just think about it for a while?"

As the days passed, I concentrated on my work and tried not to think about my conversation with Fern. But deep down I agreed with her—maybe the price was too high to pay. Maybe pediatrics just wasn't right for me after all.

Juan continued to be the bright spot of my days. He was growing and thriving. Even the nurses on the ward knew he was "my" baby. I held him close as often as I could. Now he was drinking a steady diet of formula, and his intestines seemed to be holding everything he took in.

"I never thought I'd see chubby thighs on him!" Jonathan joked when he came into Juan's room to take a peek.

By the end of the month, Juan had creases in his thighs. His scars had healed, and he was ready to take his first bottle. He was a completely different baby.

"We showed 'em, kid," I said. He gurgled and cooed as I gave him his bottle.

Miss Tills stood in the doorway. "I see you finally got to feed that kid," she said. Then she smiled.

I threw my head back and laughed. "Tills," I said, "it's a good thing I didn't get to take him home, otherwise he'd be on chicken soup by now!"

17

Preemie Land

This is a magical place. There are no windows here, no loud sounds. There can be no distractions. This is where human beings weighing less than one pound fight to survive.

Some of those children have been born after only twenty-five weeks *in utero;* others have had almost seven months before they were delivered. Most of these infants are too weak to breathe, to digest or even to suck. They lie in Isolettes and open warmers, some of which are decorated with cards, drawings, mobiles and little music boxes that play "It's a Small World." Anxious parents peer at their miniature children and bring them doll clothes to wear.

A cacophony of barely audible sounds never abates. The monitors beep and cast a greenish glow. Each has an alarm to tell us when a child can no longer breathe.

I have a profound respect for the delicate balance that must be maintained here. I am afraid to close my eyes, even for a second. In that second, something irreversible may happen to a life that is only moments old.

Everything here is small and frail, but it is not unimportant. If they are lucky, many of these miniature bodies will grow and thrive. They will become robust and healthy children. Everything depends upon my vigilance, and upon their determination to survive, because here medicine isn't enough. There is a mysterious equilibrium that no one fully understands, something that enables some children to make it against all odds. Nothing is ordinary or predictable here. Nothing is without wonder.

This is preemie land.

After my rotation at City Hospital, I had returned to Major Medical Center, to the basement ward known as "preemie land." Jonathan was there with me. Denise was in the adolescent unit on the fifth floor. I knew the first day I came to preemie land that it was going to be very different from the other wards.

The long corridors contained rooms that housed three or four babies. One nurse was assigned to two or three of these tiny patients, who demanded constant care and vigilant attention. The hub of preemie land was the neonatal ICU with its ten incubators. Most of the children in the ICU were on respirators, and all were fed through IVs, since their intestines were not mature enough to digest formula. Some of these preemies had congenital defects. Others were perfectly formed but not yet ready to function on their own. Parents were encouraged to visit and to make contact with their children.

As a baby began to grow and thrive, he or she was moved from the ICU at the back of the corridor to a room closer to the exit. When the child was well enough to go home, the nurses joked that the infant had been "pushed out the door."

The nurses in this unit were dedicated and devoted to the patients. I knew from my first day that in many ways they were "surrogate mothers" to these newborns. They often knit little hats for the babies and helped to decorate their Isolettes.

Children who were close to death were kept in open warmers so they could be resuscitated at a moment's notice. When their survival became doubtful, they were often switched to another nurse's care, so as to make their death less painful for the "surrogate mother."

During the first few days of my internship in the preemie ward, I sat on a desk in the center of the ICU and stared at the monitors. Twice during the night I would look at all the cribs and do a head count. If I had forty babies in my care when I signed in at the beginning of my shift, I was determined that there would be forty babies when I signed out. I didn't want to lose one child. "Forty in, forty out" became an expression I whispered to myself every time I left the hospital.

On the fourth night I was on duty, the ward was short-staffed, and it was difficult for the nurses to feed all the babies. After I finished my notes, I approached a young nurse named Heather. I had watched her for several days, and I appreciated how involved, caring and competent she was.

"Let me feed this little guy," I said to Heather.

Surprised by my request, she watched as I held a squirming infant.

"You're very good with him," she remarked.

I looked up from my patient. "I have an advantage," I confessed. "I have two children of my own."

Heather looked even more surprised. Her face relaxed into a warm smile. We began to talk.

She had two children almost the same ages as Evie and Matthew.

"I purposely requested the night shift," Heather explained, "so I can be with them during the day. How do you do it? How can you bear being away for thirty-six hours at a time?"

I placed the infant back in his crib. "It's painful," I said. "But what's the alternative if I want to be a doctor?"

Heather laughed a knowing laugh. Instantly, I was accepted as a mother, not "merely" a doctor.

"I thought there was something different about you the first time I saw you wrap a baby up in a blanket after you examined him," Heather explained. "So many of the interns we get here are young unmarried men who have never even diapered a baby. They treat these kids like they aren't really human beings. You know how we feel about them. We watch them every second. We root for them. In a way, they're our babies."

I nodded as Heather spoke. On my first day, an intern who was rotating out of the ward had told me that the nurses here were "a bunch of bitches," and were "impossible to get along with." I remembered being unnerved by his statement. So far, in my short medical career, I had always had a good rapport with nurses. It was a relationship I had always counted on both personally and professionally. I knew as Heather and I spoke about our children and our lives that in preemie land I would come to depend upon the knowledge and compassion of these women even more than I had in the past. These nurses knew a great deal about their charges. They watched for little changes, subtle indications that a particular baby was improving or worsening.

During that long night, Heather told me how only a few weeks ago an intern had dismissed her when she questioned an order he had written up. "You're the nurse. *I'm* the doctor," he had scoffed.

Alarmed that the baby he was treating was in real danger, she called the director of the unit. Dr. Miller asked to speak to the intern.

"Until you know as much as these nurses, keep your mouth shut and your ears open," he had shouted.

"It's going to be a relief working with someone who understands what having a baby is all about," Heather said as she cradled a now healthy two-week-old in her arms.

I looked down at a baby who had been born after only twenty-seven weeks of gestation. My babies had both been twice her size when they were born. Observing this infant was like seeing through my own womb. "That's what Evie looked like after almost seven months," I thought. And so, like the nurses, I began to develop an emotional bond with these children. But it was a bond that did not hamper my functioning as a physician. For the first time I felt a comfortable merging of my identities. Being a mother was making me a better doctor.

In this quiet place where children balanced precariously between birth and death, a solution to my own personal dilemma was beginning to emerge.

It was an uneventful evening on the ward. I had just finished reviewing the day's notes and was about to check on a patient when I heard a strange sound come from one of the monitors. A four-pound baby girl was "alarming"; her heart rate was dropping rapidly. Nurses and doctors went into high gear—everyone knew exactly what to do. A blood gas was taken. This is a report that analyzes the amounts of oxygen, carbon dioxide and acid in the child's blood. With this information, it is possible to decide how to adjust the pressure, force and rate of vent (how many breaths per minute) of the respirator.

I was relieved that Jonathan was on duty that night. Heather handed him a shungun, a large tube with a rubber rim on the outside and a light on the end that presses against the chest. If the light shines easily through the chest, it means that the patient has blown a hole in his lung. If not immediately treated, the patient will be unable to breathe. After Jonathan used the shungun, we immediately knew that the child had a collapsed lung.

Dr. Miller, the director of the unit, watched as Jonathan showed me how to insert a needle in the child's chest and withdraw the excess air that was filling the baby's chest cavity and squashing her lung closed.

We were all expecting to see the baby's color return and her heart rate pick up. I kept withdrawing air from her chest cavity, but she did not seem to improve.

"Check her respirator tube. Maybe there's a plug in it," Dr. Miller shouted. He knew from past experience that babies often produce mucus that can clog the bottom of the respirator tube.

"I don't see anything," Jonathan said, "but I'm pulling the tube and I'm going to reintubate her."

Intubation is a dramatic, delicate and difficult lifesaving procedure. A fiber-optic device called a laryngoscope—a long tube with a light on one end—goes down the baby's throat, illuminates the back of the throat to the opening of the windpipe and pushes the tongue forward. This allows the doctor to thread a soft plastic tube through the baby's nose and down the back of its throat. Then, using a forceps device, the physician inserts the edge of the tube into the trachea, so that direct access to the lung is achieved through the patient's nose. The respirator tube can then be attached and can breathe for the baby.

All of this must be done in seconds.

When Dr. Miller saw Jonathan beginning to intubate the child, he stopped him and said, "Let Dorothy do it."

Jonathan handed me the laryngoscope. In a moment, when the baby was still close to death, I found myself attempting, for the first time, to perform this delicate procedure. It sounded so simple and looked so easy. I tried to thread the tube down the baby's nose. It buckled. "I can't get it into the trachea," I said. Perspiration was running down my sleeves. The tiny child lay helpless and gray while doctors and nurses milled about.

"Her heart rate is dropping," Heather said. I could hear the urgency in her voice.

"Jonathan, *you* do it," I insisted. "We don't have much time."

Jonathan tried to insert the tube. It buckled.

Realizing the severity of the situation, Dr. Miller, who had performed this procedure thousands of times, took over. It buckled on his first try, too. The second time he was successful, but the patient was still not responding. Everyone was working frantically now. The child was pumped with drugs. Dr. Miller took over. As I watched him, I memorized every order he gave, every action he took. The next time I might be on my own.

The scene was organized and precise. Dr. Miller rolled up his shirt sleeves. His tie was askew. Everyone was sweating. Not a word was spoken. Then Heather broke the silence by announcing that the baby's pressure was dropping. X rays showed that one of the child's lungs had collapsed and that the other was filled with fluid. In the hubbub of activity, I barely noticed the time. It seemed like only a few minutes since Jonathan and I had attempted to intubate the child. When I looked up at the large clock, I saw that a little over forty-five minutes had passed.

Despite everyone's best effort, by the end of the hour the baby had died.

No one spoke. Dr. Miller rolled down his shirt sleeves, adjusted his tie and threw his jacket over his shoulder. "Goddam it!" he whispered.

Within minutes, the IV poles, monitor lines and ventilator tubes were disassembled. Everything was coming back to life— everything but the tiny body on the white sheet.

Dr. Miller motioned for Jonathan. They spoke briefly in a corner of the room, then Jonathan walked toward me. His face was expressionless. His voice was steady.

"Dorothy, take the baby to the lab and practice intubating until you're sure you've got it right."

Heather handed me the lifeless body wrapped in a clean towel. She pointed to a corner of the lab. Then she handed me a laryngoscope and a tube. She left without saying a word.

Alone in the lab with the body of a four-pound baby girl, I was surrounded by slides, bottles of chemicals, stains and smears. High up on a shelf I saw a Bunsen burner, a microscope and a tube of spinal fluid. In a corner of the room a paper towel lay crumpled beside a garbage can.

The last time I had worked on a dead body had been years ago in anatomy class. I expected to feel the same prickly anticipation and horror I had felt then. But things were different now. I was different.

I looked at the small, slightly purple body. There was nothing to be afraid of. There would be no bad dreams this time.

"In death there is nothing," I whispered to the empty room.

I unwrapped the blanket. The baby's eyelids were half-closed. Her eyes were blank. Knowing I wasn't hurting her, knowing that she was beyond pain now, I pushed her head back and opened her mouth. In less than a fraction of a second I intubated her. There was no resistance. No fear. No panic. The patient was dead.

I repeated the intubation four more times. I did not leave a single mark on the infant's body. No one would ever know. Then I thought of her mother. I prayed that if she ever found out, she'd forgive me. What I had just learned from her child might help me to save another little girl or boy. I didn't cry. It wasn't because I had stopped feeling, it was just that I had begun to understand what had always been so difficult to grasp before.

I rewrapped the baby and placed her gently on the sheets.

I felt older, wiser. "Thank you," I whispered.

As I left the lab, I handed Heather the laryngoscope and the tube. She looked at me and nodded.

"How did you do?" Jonathan asked.

"No problem," I said.

Jonathan nodded his head grimly. "Good. Now you'll be prepared for the next time."

The rest of the night was punctuated only by the gentle beeps of the ever-vigilant monitors. There were no more alarms, and in preemie land everyone slept peacefully in his tiny crib.

When I got home, I told Eddie about the intubation. He was horrified that I had practiced on a dead child.

"Before I might have thought it was ghoulish," I explained,

"but now I think it would have been a sin not to have learned on that infant."

Eddie seemed shocked. Our eyes met, and for a split second, I was sure I saw a flash of disillusionment.

There wasn't much time for me to think about Eddie's reaction to the intubation. The next morning I was on call. Jonathan was out sick.

"What's wrong?" I asked, feeling a sense of foreboding. His replacement, Dr. Sid Weiss, knew why I was so concerned. "Don't worry. It's just a flu. He'll be back tomorrow," he reassured me. Dr. Weiss and I had just begun to review the charts when we got a call to go on an emergency transport to an outlying hospital that did not have a preemie unit.

Sid talked and I listened.

"A hypertensive mother in her eighth month is having seizures. They're going to give her an emergency C-section. Are you ready for this?" he asked. "They've got *three* heartbeats!"

"Triplets? Preemie triplets? How are we going to do this?"

"Very carefully and very quickly," Sid said as he began to assemble the equipment and the personnel we would need.

"We have only two free respirators," he explained. "If it's necessary, one of us will have to bag one of the babies by hand on the way back here. But we do have three warmers and three IV poles."

I pictured three tiny blue babies unable to breathe. It was hard enough saving one preemie. I wasn't sure we could manage with three at the same time.

The mother was in her last stages of labor when we arrived, but the delivery room was too small to hold us and all our equipment. Sid, the two nurses and I arranged the warmers, respirators and IV poles in the corridor outside the delivery room. We stood waiting outside the closed door. We were gowned and gloved and ready for anything. I was nervous and worried about the condition of the infants. Just as I began to imagine the worst, the door to the OR opened. A nurse peeked out and handed us a small bundle.

"One's out!" she said.

The baby boy was pink and kicking. He was small, but he was absolutely fine. Sid checked him out. "He's terrific," he said, smiling. "No respiratory problems. I'll baby-sit for this one. The next guy is yours."

The door opened for a second time.

"Here's number two," the nurse said.

I held another baby boy in my arms. "Look at him!" I said. "He's a fighter, all pink and strong!"

Sid looked over my shoulder. "I'll baby-sit for him, too," he joked. "Let's keep our fingers crossed for number three."

But there wasn't time for finger crossing. The last triplet had already been born.

"This is it!" the nurse sighed as she passed him to me.

He was a little gray, and I administered oxygen. In minutes he had a good cry and turned a healthy shade of pink.

The obstetrician opened the door to examine the triplets. He was giddy with delight.

"I can't believe it," he said. "Three good ones!"

Although the babies weighed only three pounds apiece, they were alert and vigorous.

We rushed them into the ambulance and watched as they rested in their Isolettes.

"The mother's water broke two days before she went into labor," Sid explained. "The stress of being without amniotic fluid seems to have matured the infants' lungs. I'd say we're lucky. Very lucky."

Sid, the two nurses, and I laughed and congratulated ourselves, the triplets and their parents, all the way back to the hospital.

It was a terrific feeling to march triumphantly into the preemie unit with three Isolettes filled with three pink babies.

I was just beginning to bask in the glow of our success when a nurse rushed up to me and shouted: "Upstairs! Quick! Preemie twins!"

In an instant I was back in my gown and gloves. We all ran up to intensive care. The twins were not in as good shape as the triplets had been. A boy and a girl, they weighed about three and a half pounds each. The boy was a bit smaller than his sister. His color was bad, and his pressure was dropping rapidly. I threaded an IV through his umbilical cord and began giving him fluid to bring his pressure up. By the time we brought the twins downstairs to preemie land, their prognosis was good.

After everyone was "suited down" and calm, I peeked at my triplets and my twins.

"I feel like I should hand out cigars!" I laughed.

Just then Dr. Miller arrived for his rounds.

"Any new admissions?" he asked routinely.

I pointed with maternal pride to our new additions.

"Five," I said with a grin. "We had quints today, and everyone's doing just fine!"

It was the sort of day doctors dream about. I had worked hard, but the result was more than worth it. Five premature infants in one day, five new and healthy lives. I was smiling when I left the hospital after thirty-six hours on call.

"Mommy's home!" Evie shouted as I dragged myself through the door. She grabbed me around the waist and began to tell me about her day at school. I listened attentively, although I longed for sleep.

As I fought to keep my eyes open, I sat down beside her on the couch and I told her about my day.

"I had so much fun today," I said, smiling. "We had quintuplets!"

"Are you kidding?" Eddie asked as he walked into the living room.

While Eddie and Evie sat in rapt attention, and Matthew gurgled in his crib, I told my family about the wonder of holding the three-pound triplets in my arms, and about saving the twins.

"Are you still thinking of leaving pediatrics?" Eddie asked as I headed toward the bed and a night I knew would be rich with sweet dreams.

I was aware that the day I had had with the triplets and twins was unusual, but it seemed to carry me on a tide of optimistic well-being. I spent my next evening on call watching monitors, examining infants and chatting with Heather when I had a spare moment.

Jonathan was still conspicuously "out sick." Despite Dr. Weiss's reassurance, I called him from the hospital. His wife, Ellen, answered the phone.

"How's Jonathan?" I inquired.

"He's down with the flu," she answered. "Here, let him tell you himself."

For the next few minutes I talked casually with my friend. I brought him up to date on the five new preemies, and we joked about the recent "population explosion."

Although he sounded exhausted, I could tell from the timbre of his voice that he wasn't seriously ill.

"Thank God," I said as I hung up the phone and pressed my sweating forehead against the cool receiver.

As I walked thoughtfully back toward the ICU, Heather caught up to me. She was almost out of breath.

"Dorothy, get up to the delivery room—*stat!*"

I got upstairs just in time. There wasn't a second to spare. A woman had just had an emergency cesarean. The obstetrician handed me a limp, blue six-and-a-half-pound baby.

I pressed my stethoscope against the infant's chest, but I could barely hear a heartbeat. Immediately, I intubated the child, connected a central IV through the navel and began pumping glucose water and epinephrine into the child's system. As I forced oxygen into the infant's lungs, I shouted orders to the nurses.

"Breathe. Please breathe," I prayed as I glanced up at the clock. Less than five minutes had passed since the obstetrician had handed me the moribund child. In a few more minutes, the newborn was pink, breathing and squirming normally.

The obstetrician left the mother for a minute.

"That was fast," he said. "Good work. Is it a boy or a girl?"

We had both been working with such urgency, we hadn't taken the time to check.

I looked down at the infant. Goose bumps rippled up and down my arms.

The child had a scrotum but no penis.

On closer inspection, I noticed that the baby had unusually low-set ears and rocker-bottom feet.

"Chromosomal defects," I whispered to the obstetrician.

Our eyes met. I saw the perspiration behind his glasses.

"Take the baby downstairs to the preemie unit," he said quietly as he glanced at the mother. "She's been through enough already."

Heather met me as I came off the elevator. She stared at the baby I carried in my arms. I felt betrayed by my own skill. I had worked on automatic pilot, never taking the time to make what would have been an impossible choice.

"Why the hell did you have to be so vigorous?" Dr. Miller asked when he saw the child.

I swallowed hard. "I'm grateful I didn't have the opportunity to think. I honestly don't know what I would have done."

Dr. Miller stared straight ahead. "Well, it can't be undone now." Then, seeing how disturbed I was, he put a comforting hand on my shoulder.

"I understand. I've been there myself."

I walked back to the ward. I had always fought to save every patient. Life was precious. This was the first time I had ever experienced such a confusing ambivalence. I had felt so powerful, performed so well. The irony was that I was no longer sure if what I had done was "right."

There was little time to contemplate my actions. When I got

down to the residents' lounge, Eddie was there waiting for me. He had Matthew in his arms. I felt a lurching in my chest.

"What's wrong?" I asked.

"Your mom noticed he had diarrhea all day today. When I got home, he still had it. I think you ought to check him out."

I had been my children's doctor since my last two years in medical school. The feeling I was experiencing now was a familiar one. There was no one I wanted to take care of more than Matthew.

I looked down at my baby. I began to move automatically. He was pale, but he was active and alert. He was eagerly drinking his bottle. His diaper was wet.

"He's not dehydrated," I said. "That's good. Do you know how many bowel movements he's had today?"

"Your mother and I figure it must have been around fourteen," Eddie said.

I knew that Matt was not seriously ill, but the guilt I felt at not being able to stay with him was unbearable.

"What am I going to do?" I said. "I can't leave here. There's no one to cover for me."

Eddie stood up very straight and spoke sharply. "You've got to trust me to take care of our children. I'm *not* a baby-sitter. I'm their father. After all we've been through, how can you talk this way to me? Just talk to me like a doctor would. Tell me what I have to do and I'll do it. If he gets worse, I'll call you."

Eddie's words struck a chord. We had decided a long time ago that although both of us could not be with them one hundred percent of the time, between the two of us, and with some help from my parents, our children would get one hundred percent parenting. In this instance, I was providing the doctoring while Eddie provided the nurturing. I knew I owed him an apology.

"I'm sorry," I said. "Of course I trust you, but it's so hard for me to be a mother and not be there when my child needs me. It's my guilt that I'm dealing with. I know the children couldn't be in better hands. Here's all you have to do: avoid giving him milk and orange juice. Stick to tea and sugar. Watch to make sure his diapers remain wet and his mouth doesn't get dry. These are all signs that he isn't becoming dehydrated by the diarrhea. If he stops urinating, bring him in and we'll put him on an IV."

Eddie listened carefully. "Don't worry, Doc, he'll be fine. I'll call you if anything changes."

I reached down and held my baby in my arms. He was sick, but there was a ward filled with other babies who were much sicker and who needed me much more.

When Eddie left, I scrubbed like mad before I returned to the ward. I had always been careful to scrub before I returned to my own family. It was easy to transmit germs and viruses from the hospital to the home. But this time things were reversed. The virus Matt had was not serious, but if one of the preemies was exposed to it, it could be lethal.

Heather stopped me as I walked into the ICU.

"What's wrong with you?" she asked. "If it's that baby you intubated—"

"No, it's not that," I interrupted, then remembering that Heather had two children of her own, I opened up and told her about Matt and about how guilty and conflicted I felt.

"Are you reacting now as a doctor or as a mother?" Heather asked.

"I don't know anymore where one identity ends and the other begins," I answered. "Throughout my training, I worried that I bonded too closely with my patients. I was always a mixture of doctor and mother with them. I could never establish that cool, clinical, professional demeanor. Now things are a little reversed. I can examine my own children as a physician. I can utilize my medical knowledge and judgment. But when it's my own child, there's an added dimension of anxiety and guilt."

"Dorothy, you're not alone. I feel the same way with my kids at home and with my babies here. Maybe it's not so bad to be a maternal doctor and a doctorly mother. Maybe that way the patients get the best parts of who you are and your kids get the medical expertise along with the kisses."

I put my arm around my friend's shoulder. I wasn't sure if she was trying to make me feel better or if she was trying to work out some of her own conflicts or both. It didn't matter. Her words were soothing. No one had ever put it quite that way before.

As I watched Heather reach down and adjust an infant's IV, another piece of my own personal puzzle slipped quietly into place.

When I got home that evening, I quickly examined Matthew. He still had diarrhea, but he wasn't dehydrated. But now there was a new twist. Evie had come down with a milder version of the same virus. I sat on her bed, examined her and brushed her long blonde hair.

"Mommy," she said, "can you stay home with me?" My heart ached. I knew she wasn't very sick, but I knew she wanted me to be there for her. She wanted to know that she was as important as my work. Jonathan was still out sick. I wracked my brains, but I couldn't think of anyone who could cover for me. I also knew I had to save my absences for real emergencies.

I gathered Evie in my arms. "If I were anything else but a doctor, I would stay home, but in medicine you just can't *not* show up. There are too many sick people who need me. You're going to be just fine."

I could tell Evie was disappointed. She didn't cry, but for a few minutes she didn't say anything at all.

"I think I want to go to sleep now," she said.

I tiptoed sadly out of her room. I was crestfallen.

Eddie was waiting for me in the kitchen. We had a cup of coffee and discussed our day. I listened as he told me about his students and the new unit he had created on the Kennedy assassination. Then I looked up and saw Evie standing by the kitchen door in her pajamas and robe. She walked toward me and sat down.

"Mommy, I've been thinking," she said. "In a way, I'm glad

you're a doctor. If you were anything else and I got sick, you'd be *taking* me to a doctor. That would be scary."

I smiled. Evie crawled in my lap and fell asleep. Eddie's eyes met mine.

"She's something else," he whispered. Blinking back the tears, I nodded in agreement.

The next day at the hospital I pressed my "hold" button and forced myself not to worry about my children too much. My parents were both home, and Eddie would be there with them from four o'clock on. Still, I called home every chance I could.

I had to perform a long and tedious exchange transfusion in which I replaced two times the volume of a baby's blood with fresh whole blood. The procedure took more than two hours, and for that entire time I had to stand and carefully watch the monitors, the baby and my own actions. By the time I finished I was exhausted. My sneakers were stained with Betadine and blood, my ankles were swollen and my feet ached. I was on my way to the bathroom when Dr. Miller caught up with me.

"Just who I wanted to see," he bellowed.

I wiped the sweat from my brow. "Not another emergency, I hope."

"No, nothing like that. You're going to like this, Dorothy. Instead of going on rounds, I'd like you to lead a tour of influential women who are important benefactors to this unit. It won't take long. Show them around. Show them the triplets and the twins. Your team is doing well. Make sure they walk away with a good impression of the work we're doing here."

Dr. Miller had given me no time to prepare and no time to refuse. I stumbled toward the interns' lounge, hoping to change out of my sweaty greens, comb my hair and brush my teeth before I was transformed into an enthusiastic tour guide. But I was too late. As I walked down the corridor, I bumped into a group of powdered, perfumed, immaculately groomed women "civilians." They wore beautiful gabardine suits, silk blouses and elegant jewelry. One woman sported beige lizard shoes that showed off her delicate anklebones. Another wore soft brown leather pumps. Everyone's feet looked incredibly dainty.

I stood before them in my stained sneakers with my swollen ankles, sweaty greens, greasy hair and what was left of my mascara smeared across one cheek.

"Are you Doctor Greenbaum?" the leader of the group asked as she waved a perfectly manicured hand in the air. I stepped back, hoping they wouldn't notice how much I was perspiring.

"Yes," I answered. "Yes, I am."

"Dr. Miller told us you'd be showing us around. Well, here we are." She smiled graciously. I casually crossed my arms in front of my chest, making sure I didn't expose the damp stains that were spreading beneath my armpits.

"Follow me," I said, forcing a smile. "We've got a set of triplets I think you'd like to see."

For almost an hour I led the women on a tour of the ward. I explained how the monitors worked and why the tiniest babies were kept in open warmers. I pointed with pride to the babies who were thriving and explained that the nurses knit little caps so that the largest body surface of the child, the head, could remain warm. The women were fascinated and thanked me for answering their many questions.

"How did it go?" Heather asked as she saw me wave good-bye to the group. She was on duty in the afternoon for the first time in months.

I leaned over an empty Isolette. "God! I felt like the Jolly Green Giant," I said, sighing. "Did you *see* them? Every hair in place. Makeup perfectly applied. And those tiny feet! I look like such a slob. I didn't even get a chance to comb my hair or brush my teeth. I'm a mess."

"But look what you're doing with your life," Heather coun-

tered. "In two more years, when you're through with your training, you'll look like that, too."

Two years seemed like an eternity.

I stared down at my feet. "Let's face it, even when the swelling
goes down, they'll never look petite. Sometimes I feel like there's
no happy medium. I have no time for myself. Today it didn't
matter that I was a doctor. I wanted to feel pretty. I wanted to feel
like a woman."

Heather nodded sympathetically.

"On my next day off, I'm going to buy some makeup and do
something with my hair. I hate feeling like this. I don't even want
to look in the mirror."

"That sounds like a nice idea," Heather said. "But right now
you've got to concentrate on being an M.D. They need you in the
ICU."

Despite my busy day, I was determined not to forget my promise to myself. It was Friday, and I had the weekend off.

Eddie was waiting for me when I walked out of the hospital.
Not realizing that I had called home during the day, he reported
in minute detail Matthew's and Evie's progress.

"I think they're both well enough to go to my cousin's birthday
party on Sunday," he said. "And I'm really looking forward to it, I
can tell you that."

I leaned back in the seat and watched as the world moved outside the car windows. Then I thought about the tour group and
how unattractive I had felt. Catching a glimpse of myself in the car
mirror, I averted my eyes.

"I've got to get myself together," I explained to Eddie. "I can't
believe how I've let myself go. I'm a wreck. I never looked this
bad."

Eddie seemed surprised. Usually I talked about my day at the
hospital and asked about the kids. But when I told him about the
women who had visited the hospital and how messy and sloppy I
had felt, he seemed to understand.

"Okay," Eddie said. "Listen, why don't you take some time tomorrow and buy a little makeup and whatever you need?"

"Enough with being a doctor twenty-four hours a day," I thought as I stared at the traffic on the highway. "For the next two days I'm going to feel feminine and attractive. I'm going to feel good about myself."

And it was a perfect weekend. I stopped by a local department store and bought new lipstick, blush and mascara. The children, who were restless from having been confined to bed, were brimming with excitement about getting dressed up and going to a birthday party.

Evie perched on my bed while I brushed and braided her hair. She turned around to look at me.

"Mommy, you look so pretty," she said.

I glowed. It was the first time I had worn a dress, high heels, perfume and lipstick in months.

"I *feel* pretty," I answered. Evie and I smiled at our reflections in my bedroom mirror.

"You're gorgeous!" Eddie proclaimed when I put the final touches on my hair and makeup.

"I feel like a new woman," I said, winking, as I wrapped my arms around him.

Our spirits were high as we drove to Eddie's cousin's house. Both my parents and my in-laws were at the birthday party. Everyone fussed over Matthew, who was decked out in a blue-and-white sailor suit, and Evie, who wore a dress decorated with tiny red hearts.

"That schedule must be exhausting," my mother-in-law said as she put a sympathetic hand on my arm. The makeup helped, but I knew it couldn't entirely hide the fatigue of an intern's life.

"It sure is," I said. "But it's good to be here with all of you today."

She smiled as she handed me a plate piled with food.

"Eat. Eat. You need your energy!"

I made myself comfortable on the living room couch and watched the children play games and the adults catch up on family news. For a few hours I was free from the intensity of the hospital. My relatives no longer made a fuss about my medical career.

"I guess they're accustomed to having a doctor in the family. The novelty has finally worn off," I mused. Deep down I was pleased. Today I was feeling like a "civilian"—like a woman, a wife, a mother. I glanced down at my shoes. My ankles were still swollen, but somehow, by wearing stockings and heels, they didn't look nearly as bad as they had yesterday.

"I wish this feeling could last forever," I whispered to Eddie as he sat down beside me. "I wish I didn't have to go back to the hospital."

Eddie slung his arm around my shoulders. "Let's enjoy *today*," he said as he offered me a piece of birthday cake.

Returning to the hospital on Monday morning was like seeing the same movie for the hundredth time, like sitting in a soft comfortable chair in a darkened theater, knowing exactly what to expect. The yellow walls were marked with scrapes and scratches. The linoleum was chipped and worn. Windowless and almost silent, the preemie ward was still magical. Monitors hummed, nurses scurried back and forth, miniature newborns stared at the mobiles and pictures their worried parents had hung over their cribs. I sighed as I slipped into my jacket and slung my stethoscope around my neck.

Dr. Weiss was the first person I spoke with. "Boy, it's hard coming back here after a weekend off," I said.

Then something strange happened. Dr. Weiss began talking. He said it was hard for him, too. Then he said something else, but I couldn't hear. There was a rushing in my ears as he finished his sentence.

I was on the bottom of the ocean. I was down where nothing could touch me. I was suspended in deep water, gazing up at the surface. I could see the light spreading itself on the water. I could hear voices, but the ocean wrapped around me. It muffled the sounds, making them indistinct ripples in the waves.

As Dr. Weiss put his hand on my arm, I felt a strange burning sensation. His voice seemed to be echoing through the depths.

"I'm sorry you had to hear it this way," he was saying.

I shook my head as if to clear my ears of the sea.

"What?" I asked.

Now Dr. Weiss's voice was penetrating, echoing through the space around me. But I didn't want to hear. I fought to submerge myself.

This time his voice was strong. It reached down. Tentacles grasped for me as I groped and hid in the darkness.

The ocean receded. I was thrown brutally against a wall of words.

"Jonathan died this weekend."

I was sitting in a chair as Dr. Weiss leaned forward and spoke to me. I concentrated on the movement of his lips, catching each sound as it bobbed to the surface.

"His flu turned into pneumonia. They rushed him to the hospital where he was put on a vent and intubated. He died quickly and didn't suffer. At the end he slipped into a coma. The chemotherapy had weakened him, and he didn't have the strength to fight it off."

I waited for the world to stop. I waited to hear the sobs and wails twist down the silent corridor. I expected to see the residents' lounge draped in black. Nothing changed. I wanted to shout: "It isn't fair! He was so beautiful, only thirty-one years old. What was the point of all his chemotherapy, all his suffering and sacrifice if he was going to die?"

The water washed me onshore. I was out now, fully emerged, aware of what was happening.

"When is the funeral?" I asked.

"It was this morning," Sid answered.

"I can't believe no one called me. This is unreal. I can't accept this."

"Pull yourself together. We have a long hard day ahead of us. Maybe you need a few minutes. A staff psychiatrist is going to meet with those of us who knew him in the conference room this morning, so we can sort out our feelings. I think you should be there."

My body seemed welded to the chair. I longed for sleep, for the protection of my ocean floor. Instead, I floated listlessly toward the conference room.

The room was full. Nurses, interns, residents and orderlies sat in chairs and leaned against the walls. My eyes scanned the faces for Heather. Then I remembered that today was her day off. But I saw another familiar face: Denise. We hadn't been friendly for a while, but we both loved Jonathan. I drifted until I stood beside her. She reached down and gripped my hand. My fingers warmed in her palm.

As the psychiatrist spoke and members of the hospital staff expressed their shock and grief, I closed my eyes and ran a series of photographs back in my mind. Still lifes. I saw Jonathan as he had been on that first day in Major Medical Center when he smiled at me and helped me administer Elizabeth's chemotherapy through a tiny vein in her foot. I recalled how he had taught me and comforted me, how he had spoken to me after Sharon fled the hospital. Then I saw the last photograph, the portrait I would always remember. Jonathan at the party. Jonathan holding Matthew on his lap. Jonathan glowing as he watched his son, Daniel, play with Evie.

The sadness was heavy and black and different from any other I had ever experienced. Jonathan had been my friend and my teacher. He was not supposed to die. He was the one who had always believed in happy endings.

I followed the crowd into the hallway. The meeting had been

brief. There was no more time to mourn. Everyone was needed elsewhere. Death had never stopped us before.

Denise was still holding my hand. She was crying and talking at the same time. It was difficult to hear, but I strained to catch her words.

"Dorothy, when you got so involved with Billy I looked on from the sidelines. I never felt what you felt. But now it's different. Jonathan was one *of us*. This doctor thing, it's so much sacrifice. What's the reward? I've given up everything in my life to do this. Now I'm not so sure. I'm going to take a six-month leave of absence. I've been thinking about doing it for a while. After today, nothing makes sense anymore."

I agreed with Denise by nodding my head. The words didn't come.

"What about you? Are you still thinking of switching out of pediatrics?"

My throat felt dry, my chest heavy, as I answered her. "I'm not sure," I said.

"Good luck," Denise whispered. Her cheek was moist as she leaned over to kiss me good-bye.

An unfamiliar, dreamy feeling washed over me as I made rounds and visited with my patients. All day long I rode the tides of my own grief and rage.

At four o'clock I called Eddie. I don't remember saying it, or exactly how the words arranged themselves, but somehow I let him know that Jonathan had died. Eddie was quiet for what seemed like a long time. Then he asked if he could come and be with me at the hospital. He said he was leaving the children with my parents, packing dinner up in a paper bag and driving right over.

When Eddie arrived, we sat down in the interns' lounge and unwrapped our sandwiches. The sadness was overwhelming. Neither of us could eat.

"I can't believe it really happened," Eddie said.

I moved over so we could both sit on the narrow cot and hold each other.

"Just when I thought I was beginning to understand the mystery, just when I believed I could really *do* something, really change things, this happens."

A nurse knocked at the door. Her white nylon uniform made rustling sounds as she spoke.

"Dr. Greenbaum, there's a six-day-old male who's wheezing and pulling to get air. I think you'd better come."

I rose from the cot.

"It never ends," I whispered. "Eddie, please wait for me. This shouldn't take long." He nodded as I followed the nurse to the ICU.

I took one look at the infant and immediately asked for a blood gas report. The results were not good. The child was having great difficulty breathing. While I was examining the child, Dr. Miller called to check in. The nurse handed me the phone.

"There's nothing wrong with that baby," Dr. Miller stated emphatically. "He just has croup. There must have been a mistake in the blood gas report. Just give him racemic epinephrine. He'll respond immediately."

Following Dr. Miller's instructions, I administered the drug, an adrenaline in saltwater that was sprayed as a fine mist in front of the child's face to help open his airways.

Then I waited.

The seven-pound body began wheezing, and the skin between the child's ribs was sucked in in desperate attempts to breathe. His belly rocked back and forth. His eyes froze in panic. I stood horrified as the color drained out of his body.

I could feel the power of the undertow, pulling him—drawing him in. I thought of Jonathan. A spark ignited. Circuits connected, electricity flowed through my hands. I was ready to fight.

"You're not going to get *this* one," I whispered to the undertow.

I called for a vent, a tube and a laryngoscope.

"I'm on my own," I thought. "I'm the doctor now."

Without a moment's hesitation, I intubated the baby. There was so much constriction in his lungs I could no longer hear breath sounds in his chest. I double-checked the position of the tube and increased the ventilator pressure beyond anything I had ever used before. I adjusted the rate of oxygen flow.

My eyes remained fixed on the baby. I prayed that what I had done was right.

The room became a cube of space in which I floated alone with the dying child. Then the space began to open up. The sounds returned. The infant's color turned from gray to pink. The ocean receded. The darkness healed over. The undertow had been defeated.

The nurse was patting me on the back. The respiratory therapist was pumping my hand. I walked over and reassured the baby's parents. Then I turned and saw Eddie framed by the doorway. I walked toward him.

"How long have you been here?" I asked.

We were standing in the corridor. The fluorescent light sprayed our distorted shadows across the yellow walls.

"I saw what you just did," Eddie said. "I've never seen you in action before. I had no idea."

I slipped into the circle of his arms.

"This is really what it's all about," I whispered. "Pediatrics is where I belong."

Eddie smiled as he took my hand in his.

"You know something, Doc? We really did it!"